IMAGINATION AND CHANCE

INTERSECTIONS:
Philosophy and Critical Theory
Rodolphe Gasche and Mark C. Taylor, Editors

IMAGINATION
and CHANCE

◆ ――――――――――――――――――――――――――――

The Difference Between the Thought
of Ricoeur and Derrida

―――――――――――――――――――――――――――― ◆

LEONARD LAWLOR

STATE UNIVERSITY OF NEW YORK PRESS

Published by
State University of New York Press, Albany

For information, address State University of New York
Press, State University Plaza, Albany, NY 12246

Production by Bernadine Dawes
Marketing by Dana Yanulavich

Library of Congress Cataloging-in-Publication Data

Lawlor, Leonard, 1954–
      Imagination and chance : the difference between the thought of
   Ricoeur and Derrida / Leonard Lawlor.
         p.   cm. — (Intersections)
      Includes bibliographical references and index.
      ISBN 0–7914–1217–2 (hard : alk. paper) : $44.50. — ISBN
   0–7914–1218–0 (pbk. : alk. paper) : $14.95
      1. Ricoeur, Paul. 2. Derrida, Jacques. I. Title. II. Series:
   Intersections (Albany, N.Y.)
   B2430.R554L39   1992
   194—dc20
                                                                92–13359
                                                                    CIP

10 9 8 7 6 5 4 3 2 1

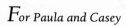

For Paula and Casey

CONTENTS ◆

ACKNOWLEDGMENTS ◆

I would like to thank the following people. Of course, Rodolphe Gasché who has supported this project from its inception; Hugh J. Silverman, Edward S. Casey, and David B. Allison at State University of New York at Stony Brook, who inspired this project and helped me complete its initial phase; Dennis J. Schmidt, for his encouragement and friendship during my one-year visit at State University of New York at Binghamton; and John Protevi, for his encouragement and friendship during his one-year visit at Memphis State. I would like to thank Robert Bernasconi and Thomas Nenon, also here at Memphis State, for their support. The following graduate students who participated in my seminars at State University of New York at Binghamton and at Memphis State helped me clarify what I was doing: Amy Morgan, Victoria Burke, Diane Burkhead, Steve Pemberton, and Amit Sen; in particular, Kevin Thompson forced me towards a higher level of complexity. Lastly, certain enduring friends have been invaluable: Daniel L. Tate, Gary Aylesworth, Deborah Chaffin, Richard White, Tina Chanter, Mario Moussa, and Kevin MacDonald. Out of these, I must single out Fred Evans who has been my most diligent interlocutor. The writing of this book was made possible by two Memphis State University Faculty Research Grants (Summer 1990 and 1991). My "A Little Daylight: A Reading of Derrida's 'White Mythology'" is being reprinted as part I, chapter 1 with the permission of Kluwer Academic Publishers; it first appeared in *Man and World*, volume 24 (1991), pp. 285–300.

LIST OF ABBREVIATIONS ◆

The following abbreviations are shown in the text between parentheses, with page numbers to the English translation first, then to the French edition. Translations have sometimes been modified to be consistent with the commentary.

Works by Derrida

DIS   *Dissemination*, tr., Barbara Johnson (Chicago: University of Chicago Press. 1981); *La dissémination* (Paris: Seuil, 1972).

INF   *Edmund Husserl's Origin of Geometry: An Introduction*, tr., John P. Leavey Jr. (Lincoln, Nebr.: University of Nebraska Press, 1989); *L'origine de la géométrie, traduction et intro-duction par Jacques Derrida* (Paris: PUF, 1974 [1962]).

MAR   *Margins of Philosophy*, tr., Alan Bass (Chicago: University of Chicago Press, 1982); *Marges de la philosophie* (Paris: Minuit, 1972).

RM   "The *Retrait* of Metaphor," trs., Frieda Gardner, Biodun Iginla, Richard Madden, and William West, in *Enclitic* (1978), 4–33; "*Le retrait de la métaphore*," in *Psyché: Inventions de l'autre* (Paris: Galilée, 1987), 63–94.

Works by Ricoeur

HHS   *Hermeneutics and the Human Sciences*, tr., John B. Thompson (New York: Cambridge University Press, 1981); the French version of some essays collected in HHS can be found in *Du texte à l'action: Essais d'hermeneutique, II* (Paris: Seuil, 1986).

INT   *Interpretation Theory* (Fort Worth, Tex.: The Texas Chris-
        tian University Press, 1976); INT's third chapter is rough-
        ly based on *"Parole et symbole"* in *Revue des sciences
        religieuses*, 49, 1–2 (Strasbourg), 142–61.

MV   *The Rule of Metaphor*, tr., Robert Czerny (with Kathleen
        McLaughlin and John Costello, SJ) (Toronto: University
        of Toronto Press, 1978); *La métaphore vive* (Paris: Seuil,
        1975).

TNIII   *Time and Narrative*, volume III, trs., Kathleen Blamey and
        David Pellauer (Chicago: University of Chicago Press,
        1988); *Temps et récit*, tome III (Paris: Seuil, 1985).

INTRODUCTION ◆
A Barely Visible Difference

It is easy to see overwhelming similarities between the works of Paul Ricoeur and Jacques Derrida. For instance, virtually the same philosophers have influenced them, Hegel, Husserl, and Heidegger, and the same topics have focused their interest: time, history, writing, metaphor. The most striking similarity, however, can be seen in their respective projects, the project of Ricoeur's hermeneutics and that of Derrida's deconstruction. Both Ricoeur and Derrida attempt to describe *mediation*, that is, the relation between two beings or the movement between an origin and an end.[1] Even the names each gives to mediation—Derrida calls mediation, *différance,* iterability, dissemination, writing, *mimesis*, traditionality, traces; Ricoeur calls mediation, distanciation, discourse, dialectic, writing, mimesis, traditionality, traces—reinforce the similarities.

Ricoeur's and Derrida's similar attempts at conceiving mediation are based on three insights. First, it is absolutely impossible for thought to achieve complete self-knowledge or self-understanding by means of intuitive self-reflection. In other words, subjective idealism in the strictest sense is impossible. Both Ricoeur and Derrida have noted not only the critiques of consciousness arising from Freud, Nietzsche, and Marx, but also and especially the incompleteness implied by Heidegger's descriptions of Dasein. Second (and this insight is implied by the first), it is absolutely necessary for thought to externalize itself in what both Ricoeur and Derrida have called signs. Thought must mediate itself in repeatable structures (of which language is the primary example) in order to gain determinations, objectivity, and universality. In other words, externalization brings about the truth of the original structures of thought. Third and most importantly, while mediation in signs

1

makes truth possible, it also makes truth impossible. Linguistic mediation postpones the end of "complete mediation" in which the origin would be recovered in all of its determinations. As metaphor indicates for both Ricoeur and Derrida, linguistic mediation is open to indefinite deviation, even while mediation maintains some sort of continuity.

On the basis of the three insights, both Ricoeur and Derrida oppose the hubris epitomized by Hegelianism: the *hubris* of the completed circle in which difference and alterity are mastered. Both affirm, to borrow Ricoeur's phrase, "the fullness of language," or, to borrow that of Derrida, "the play of difference." Thus, the respective projects of Ricoeur's hermeneutics and Derrida's deconstruction consist in the articulation of the plurality, the openness, the plus and the surplus, that arise from linguistic mediation. On the basis of these three insights, both Ricoeur and Derrida attempt to conceive the absolute inseparability of identity and difference, universality and singularity, continuity and discontinuity, repetition and event, the absolute inseparability which is mediation itself.

Within these similarities, however, a barely visible difference exists between the ways each conceives mediation. With *différance* (to chose one of the many names Derrida gives to mediation), Derrida attempts to articulate mediation as such. This means, on the one hand for Derrida, that mediation is prior to thought or perception. Nonpresence, discontinuity, and difference, then, are prior to presence, continuity, and identity. On the other, it implies for Derrida that when mediation adopts its traditional position in the middle, it does not function merely as a passage from thought back to thought, from the present back to the present. What turns mediation away from its destination is the aleatory, *chance*. Différance accounts for the unforeseeable accident and not the novel production of imagination. Différance implies not only the reuse of signs (repetition and differentiation), but also their mis-use (an alterity beyond sameness). The "mis" of misuse is not a contingency infecting the sign from the outside, but is internal to the sign's structure. Disclosing something totally unexpected in the sign, every accident sends us indefinitely back and forth to rethink the origin and transform the end. Différance can, therefore, be conceived only as a zigzag movement. There is no circularity or linearity, no regulative horizon of totalization.

Conceived as such, mediation, for Derrida, is no longer mediation. Dissemination, as Derrida has said repeatedly, is not a dialectical concept.

For Ricoeur, however, distanciation (one of the many names he gives to mediation) is a dialectical concept; it attempts to articulate mediation *in terms of its origin and end*. This means on the one hand for Ricoeur that the immediate, the present, identity, and continuity are prior to mediation, absence, difference, and discontinuity. On the other, the dialectical character of distanciation implies that mediation functions as a passage from and back to the present. For Ricoeur, our singular experiences of the world always distance or transcend themselves into repeatable structures such as discourse. As Ricoeur points out repeatedly, because discourse originates in the world, all expressions are about or refer back to the world. They return to our belonging-to-the-world, to thought, to spirit, to being. Even novel constructions such as symbols and metaphors refer because they are *imaginative* expressions of new experiences of the world. While new imaginative expressions prevent complete understanding, incompleteness makes us, as Ricoeur says, "think more." While the surplus produced by distanciation always makes mediation incomplete, surplus is nevertheless intelligible. The interpretation of discourse then, according to Ricoeur, should lead to some idea of the diverse ways being is said. Reflection and self-understanding can be maintained as a task. Consequently, distanciation is regulated by the always receding horizon of complete identity. Even as it spirals, the circle, for Ricoeur, should close.

The barely visible difference between distanciation and *différance* unfolds into the difference between hermeneutics and deconstruction. Hermeneutics, for Ricoeur, attempts to construct a system out of the diverse ways being is said. This would not be a closed system which would reduce the multiple meanings of being down to strict univocity, but an open system that places diversity, novelty, and surplus within an analogical unity. It would be a "regulated polysemy of being." Hermeneutics then—at least as Ricoeur conceives it—must be seen as a philosophical project. While hermeneutics opposes the most confining type of metaphysical mastery, it nevertheless attempts to recover Western metaphysics' original project: Aristotle's, Aquinas's, Husserl's, and (in certain respects) even Hegel's thought of reality as an indefinitely altering identity organized by a postponed *telos*. As Ricoeur says in *The Rule of Metaphor*:

> When the philosopher fights on two fronts, against the seduction of the ineffable and against the power of "ordinary speech"..., in order to arrive at a "saying"...that would be the triumph neither of the unintelligible nor of manipulatable signs—is he not in a situation comparable to that of the thinker of Antiquity or the Middle Ages, seeking his path between the powerlessness of a discourse given over to the *dissemination* of meanings and the mastery of univocity through the logic of genera. (MV, 310/393-94; my emphasis)

By his allusion to Derrida here, Ricoeur himself recognizes that the hermeneutical project differs from that of deconstruction.[2] Indeed, Derrida also has noted this difference:

> polysemia, as such, is organized within the implicit horizon of a unitary resumption of meaning, that is, within the horizon of a dialectics—...Ricoeur...in his essay on Freud (and [in his]...hermeneutics, his theory of polysemia...) [speaks of a dialectic]—a teleological and totalizing dialectics.... Dissemination on the contrary, although producing a nonfinite number of semantic effects, can be led back neither to a present of simple origin...nor to an eschatological presence.[3]

Deconstruction then—at least as Derrida conceives it—must be seen as something like a perversion of philosophy. If Ricoeur's hermeneutics must be seen as the recovery of the most generous instances of metaphysics, then deconstruction must be conceived as an attempt to be more generous. Deconstruction gives not for the sake of a purpose (of some postponed *telos*), but merely for the sake of the giving. In other words, lacking a horizon, it lets an impossible accident happen. By means of such donations, deconstruction attempts to break a path beyond any analogy of being, any regulated polysemy. It cannot, therefore, be seen as the recovery, return, or repetition of an original project, of some possibility forgotten by the metaphysical tradition.

The difference, therefore, between Ricoeur and Derrida, between hermeneutics and deconstruction, between distanciation and différance, is a difference between imagination and chance, between presence and absence, between zigzag circulation and spiraling circularity, and finally between revived philosophy and perverted philosophy.[4] Because the similarities, however, are striking, the difference becomes almost invisible. The similarities between Ricoeur and Derrida, the similarities between hermeneutics and deconstruction in general and not simply limited to the works of Ricoeur and Derrida, could inspire a hybrid, an assimilation of hermeneutics to deconstruction (or vice versa). Such assimilations, of course, are always possible, perhaps even necessary in particular situations. Nevertheless, if we do not first clarify the difference, an assimilation risks dissipating the powers that hermeneutics and deconstruction separately present, singular powers that ultimately affect how we conceive ethics and politics. Thus, the similarities demand a clarification, perhaps a deepening and a broadening, of the difference. This book responds to that demand; it aims to make the difference as visible as possible.

In order to do this, we shall begin where the difference can be most easily seen. During the 1970s Ricoeur and Derrida participated in a "polemic" (this is Ricoeur's word) over metaphor. Part I, then, consists of readings of the three texts that constitute the polemic: Derrida's "White Mythology" (1971), Ricoeur's "Eighth Study" in *The Rule of Metaphor* (1975), and Derrida's "The *Retrait* of Metaphor" (1978). While the polemic focuses on metaphor, the issue is not that of metaphor's correct theory. Rather, as we shall see, Ricoeur and Derrida focus on the relationship between metaphor and concept, between poetry and philosophy. What Derrida in "White Mythology" calls "the law of supplementarity" (a notion intimately connected to différance) threatens linguistic univocity, the identity and unity of thought and being, and, therefore, threatens the autonomy of philosophical discourse. Ricoeur's "Eighth Study," then, attempts to preserve the autonomy of philosophical discourse by showing how philosophical discourse distances itself from metaphor. On the basis of his defense of philosophical discourse, Ricoeur criticizes Derrida's "White Mythology." Finally, Derrida's response in "The *Retrait* of Metaphor" does not extend the polemic, but merely shows that Ricoeur misreads certain passages in "White Mythology." Because of its extreme complexity, I shall not analyze Derrida's reading of Heidegger in "The *Retrait*." Nevertheless, it should be kept in mind that Heidegger's shadow casts itself across this entire book.

While the polemic establishes a clear difference between Ricoeur and Derrida, between hermeneutics as revived philosophy and deconstruction as perverted philosophy, it never brings to light the basis of this difference. Ricoeur's defense and polemic depend upon his notion of distanciation; Derrida's claims in "White Mythology" and his response in "*Retrait*" depend upon what he calls "the law of supplementarity," différance. Ricoeur, however, does not address Derrida's notion of différance; Derrida does not address Ricoeur's notion of distanciation. Thus, Parts II and III examine respectively distanciation in Ricoeur and différance in Derrida.

Part II's discussion of distanciation starts from Ricoeur's descriptions of discourse (chapter 1). In these descriptions distanciation's basic characteristics come to light, all of which can be summarized under the heading of "the dialectic of event and meaning." Chapter 2 then turns to Ricoeur's descriptions of live metaphor and symbol. As we shall see, the descriptions of discourse and of live metaphor and symbol characterize distanciation as productive imagination, as a finite production guided by a regulative idea. Chapter 3 then turns to Ricoeur's descriptions of the historical present, a notion which recapitulates all of distanciation's basic characteristics. What becomes apparent in this recapitulation is dialectic itself, that is, distanciation's idea of totality. Chapter 4 finally makes the transition to Derrida. By examining Ricoeur's *Time and Narrative* (III) interpretation of Husserlian temporalization we shall see the exact difference between Ricoeur and Derrida for the first time. For Ricoeur, immediacy precedes mediation; for Derrida, mediation precedes immediacy.

Following the examination of Ricoeur's interpretation of Husserlian temporalization, part III's discussion of différance begins with a reading of Derrida's first major published work, his introduction to his French translation of Husserl's *The Origin of Geometry*.[5] In this early work, we shall see Derrida define Husserlian temporalization—the precursor to différance—precisely in terms of fact (event) and essence (meaning), precisely in terms of dialectic, precisely in terms of an idea of totality, precisely in terms of unity (or identity). Yet, Derrida's descriptions of the living present in terms of a relation, in terms of space, in terms of a "zigzag" movement, finally even in terms of chance, will be seen to imply a break with dialectic and imagination (a break which perhaps Derrida himself did not recognize in 1962). In chapter 2, we shall see, then, by reading Derrida's essay on Mallarmé, "The Double Session," that différance cannot be conceived as immediacy or time, as dialectic, as imagination; it cannot be totalized. Instead, we shall see that différance must be conceived as the *milieu*, as structural inexhaustibility, as dissemination, which means that its structure is always divided by spaces and that the force of its production is chance. Dissemination does not engender novelty but surprises.

Thus *Imagination and Chance: The Difference between the Thought of Ricoeur and Derrida* can be seen as a response to a demand. Its goal is to place the similarities within the context of difference, to clarify what takes place between Ricoeur and Derrida, to bring "a minimum of lucidity" to hermeneutics and deconstruction.[6] Then, perhaps, we can let these texts be read in unforeseen and diverse ways, in ways that are novel and surprising. Then, perhaps, we can respond to the following two comments. Ricoeur in the "Eighth Study": "The critical remarks I offer here cannot of course encompass the entire project of deconstruction..." (MV, 289/368). Derrida in "The *Retrait* of Metaphor": "[I] leave aside, intact in reserve, the possibility of a quite different reading of these two texts, *La mythologie blanche* and *La métaphore vive*..." (RM, 16/74).

PART I

The Polemic Between Ricoeur and Derrida

1 ◆
The Law of Supplementarity:
A Reading of Derrida's "White Mythology"

In the "Eighth Study" of *The Rule of Metaphor*, Ricoeur provides a reading of "White Mythology," on the basis of which he initiates his polemic with Derrida. In order to evaluate Ricoeur's reading and subsequent criticism we must attempt (as much as this is possible) an independent reading of "White Mythology."[1] The reading will be guided by earlier Derridean texts, in particular, "The Pit and the Pyramid" and "Ousia and Grammé" (both in *Margins* like "White Mythology"), and *Speech and Phenomena*. It will proceed in three steps. By examining the first two sections in "White Mythology" ("Exergue" and "Plus de métaphore"), we shall see that metaphoricity, what Derrida calls "the law of supplementarity," targets not only any metadiscourse (such as philosophy or rhetoric) that claims univocity and domination over its subject matter, but also Hegelian reflection and the *Aufhebung* (a word Derrida renders as *relève*). Then the examination of the third and fourth sections in "White Mythology" ("L'ellipse du soleil: L'énigme, l'incompréhensible, l'imprenable" and "Les fleurs du rhétorique: L'héliotrope"), will show that the law targets not only linguistic univocity in Aristotle's "exemplary" discourse on metaphor, but also the Aristotelian notion of the analogy of being. In the concluding section of "White Mythology," "La métaphysique—Relève de la métaphore," the third step's focus, Derrida generalizes metaphor beyond the philosophical concept of it, indeed, beyond the philosophical concept.[2] Thus most generally, I hope to show that "White Mythology" can be reconstructed according to deconstruction's two phases.[3] The first two steps reconstruct "White Mythology" according to the critical phase; the third reconstructs according to the reinscriptive phase. Finally, a fourth step will reconnect this "independent" reading with the concerns of Ricoeur's reading.

11

1

In the opening section of "White Mythology," "Exergue," Derrida recalls the obvious fact that metaphysical concepts consist of worn out (*usée*) metaphors; *logos* consists of "bleached out" *mythos*. The Greek word, *eidos,* for instance, means not only a supersensible idea, but also outward appearance. Because of this fact, Derrida envisions (as Nietzsche did [cf. MAR, 217/258]), a metadiscursive project (a rhetoric or a metaphilosophy) that would decipher philosophical discourse as a system of figures of speech. Instead of taking up such a metadiscursive project, Derrida wants to demonstrate its structural impossibility (cf. MAR, 219/261). In order to do this, Derrida presents in "Plus de métaphore" a sort of "argument," that I am now going to reconstruct.[4]

The argument's first premise is based in a Heideggerian insight (cf. MAR, 226n29/269n19): "...metaphor remains (*reste*), in all its essential characteristics, a classical philosopheme, a metaphysical concept" (MAR, 219/261). For Derrida, this connection does not mean that metaphor is a metaphysical concept in itself. Rather, any use of the signifier metaphor imports with it a system of terms which belongs to or is derived from the philosophical tradition. How could metaphor be articulated without appealing to this series of oppositions: *physis/techne*, *physis/nomos*, sensible/intelligible, space/time, signifier/signified, sensory/sense, sensual/spiritual? Or, without this system of concepts or concepts derived from them: *theoria, eidos, logos*, etc.? *Metaphor* is not a tool designed singularly for this project (MAR, 224/266-67); it is not an arbitrary X (MAR, 254/304).[5] Rather, it is a remainder (*reste*) from metaphysical discourse, a discourse from which it cannot be entirely separated.[6]

The second is: "Metaphor has been issued from a network of philosophemes which themselves correspond to tropes or to figures, and these philosophemes are contemporaneous to or in systematic solidarity with these tropes or figures" (MAR, 219/261). This means that the words that constitute philosophy's system of operative terms (*eidos, theoria, logos, metaphora*, etc., and their cognates) themselves bear a metaphorical charge. These words are always already circulated in common or nonspecialized parlance. In circulation they have always already acquired some sort of relatively literal sense. When they enter philosophical discourse, they acquire a metaphorical sense, which is eventually reduced in favor of a new conceptual determination. Although the concept prevails, the metaphor can still be read beneath it.

To recapitulate, the first premise consists in that metaphor remains a classical *philosopheme*, a metaphysical concept; the second in that the network of *philosophemes*, to which metaphor belongs, itself bears a metaphorical charge. The conclusion consists in that "[if] one wished to conceive and to class all the metaphorical possibilities of philosophy," one must define philosophical metaphor with philosophical metaphors. In order to identify philosophical metaphors and, thereby, decide what belongs to this field or set and what does not, a characteristic (*trait*) must be determined. In other words, a way of circumscribing the field of philosophical metaphor is needed. This definition, however, would necessarily contain characteristics or signifiers whose sense would import the whole system of philosophical conceptuality because one is using *metaphor*, a *philosopheme*; and, the characteristics which constitute this definition would themselves be metaphorical because the philosophical terms derive from common parlance. Thus, the definition of philosophical metaphor would be a philosophical metaphor, but one not included in the field.

And, if one wants "to conceive and to class *all* the metaphorical possibilities of philosophy," one must construct another definition which would conceive and class the first definition. The second definition, however, would also fall prey to the same problem. It, too, could not not be a philosophical metaphor. The process, therefore, would necessarily continue *ad infinitum*. Every definition would *participate in without belonging to* the field of philosophical metaphors.[7] As Derrida says, "The field is never saturated" (MAR, 220/261); the analysis is interminable; it cannot be counted.

It is impossible then to dominate philosophical metaphor. A rhetoric, which would take up a position *outside* philosophical discourse, would still have to make use of certain terms which would derive from the discourse it attempts to dominate. A metaphilosophy (a more general but still philosophical discourse), which would take up a position *inside* philosophical discourse, would be able to "perceive its metaphorics only around a blind spot or central deafness" (MAR, 228/272). A metaphilosophy would still have to use the resources of its own discourse, philosophy. Thus, a metaphilosophy would be able to construct a metaphorology only by ignoring (by not seeing or hearing) the tropological charges of its own terms (MAR, 228–29/273). In short, any definition of metaphor, especially of philosophical metaphor, includes the defined (MAR, 230/274, 252/301); it begs the question.

Derrida calls the essential impossibility of dominating philosophical metaphor "the law of supplementarity" (MAR, 229/273).[8] The law implies that the definition of philosophical metaphor possesses *too much* metaphor and the field, *too little*. Because the field of philosophical metaphor *lacks* the metaphor that makes the definition of philosophical metaphor possible, the field always needs a supplement. Because the definition participates in the field, it always possesses *too much* metaphor. As Derrida says,

> This extra (*en plus*) metaphor, remaining (*restant*) outside the field that it allows to be circumscribed, extracts (*ex-trait*) or abstracts itself (*s'abs-trait*) from the field, thus substracting itself (*s'y sous-trait*) as a metaphor less. (MAR, 220/261, my hyphenations)

Thus, the extra turn of speech (*le tour de plus*) is the missing turn of speech. As the title of "White Mythology's" second section, "Plus de métaphore," suggests, there is always too much metaphor and not enough.

"White Mythology's" first two sections, therefore, define an irresolvable problem: how can one speak about metaphor nonmetaphorically? "Hegel...," as Derrida points out, "determines the [same] problem with an answer indistinguishable from the proposition of his own speculative and dialectical logic" (MAR, 225/267). In the *Lectures on Aesthetics*, which Derrida cites (MAR, 225–26/268–69), Hegel says that concepts come about through the metaphorization of terms circulating in ordinary speech. Through usage (*Abnutzung*: Derrida connects this word with the French *usure*), through usage, terms with a sensuous sense have been internalized and elevated (*aufgehobene hatte*) into a spiritual sense. Thus, words like *begreifen* (to grasp and to conceive), according to Hegel, are worn out or inactive metaphors.

In "The Pit and the Pyramid," an essay parallel to and somewhat earlier than "White Mythology," Derrida connects the issue of metaphor in Hegel to thought itself, to the self-relation or reflection (MAR, 91/105).[9] Metaphor in Hegel, according to Derrida, refers not only to linguistic change, but also to the interiorization (*Erinnerung*) and temporalization which elevates (*aufhebt*) sensuous intuition into thinking (into the concept). In short, for Derrida, metaphor refers to all forms of Hegelian idealization. Because of "The Pit and the Pyramid" analysis, in "White Mythology" Derrida can describe Hegelian metaphorization as

> a movement of idealization. Which is included under the master category of dialectical idealism, to wit, the *relève* (*Aufhebung*), that is, the recollection (*Erinnerung*) that produces signs, interiorizes them in elevating, suppressing, and conserving the sensory exterior. (MAR, 226/269)

Understood as idealization, metaphorization (in either thought or language) presupposes for Hegel a continuous unity underlying the transformations (MAR, 215/256). Metaphorization is only the becoming conscious of truth. The "tropic system" is nothing more than a figural passage or transition through which the Idea circulates and returns to itself completely (MAR, 303/254). Hegelian metaphor, therefore, implies no rupture and no need for a supplement.

Keeping in mind the rough similarities between Hegelian and Husserlian reflection (idealization and temporalization), *Speech and Phenomena* can help us see how "White Mythology's" discursive law of supplementarity applies to Hegelian thought.[10] In *Speech and Phenomena's* fifth chapter, as is well-known, Derrida shows that Husserlian temporalization implies an irreducible division of the now from the past (retention), which the future always tries to synthesize. This insight guides chapter 6's analysis. Chapter 6 explicitly concerns reflection or auto-affection, which is the basis of Husserl's attempt (like Hegel's) to disclose universal cognitive structures. What follows reconstructs chapter 6's "argument." Or, to put this in Derridean terms, it describes *différance*.

Most fundamentally, when I reflect upon my self, I must turn away from things (the "natural" object of perception) and turn my self into an object for me. This turn, however, implies that the self which views does not see its self. Returning as opposed, I do not return as identical, but as different. The self which I am *now* cannot be found in the returning self which I *was*; there is an interval, a *space*, between the "now" self and the past self. Because the returning self lacks the *now* self, I must try again to add my self on. I have to supplement what is not present: myself. Thus, the returning self is *less* than me; yet, the now self is *more* than me. Every attempt to add my now self on only turns out an other self, a self which I am now but was not, and so on. Exhausting *my* efforts at complete self-understanding, the infinity of the relation calls for a infinite supplement: language.

The irreducible "intertwining" of language with visual (and thus silent) auto-affection, which Derrida stresses at the close of chapter 6, makes the transition to chapter 7, which is devoted to language. Because language, for Husserl, is iterable (meanings as well as phonemes and graphemes), language, too, is infinite or indefinite. Language transcends any singular use of it; after my death language remains. Thus, each attempt (by me or by any finite subject) to understand the totality of language will be incomplete. Language is always *more* than itself; language, however, is always *less* than itself. Each *time* I hear or speak, read, or write, I produce a *new* language which the *past* linguistic system lacks. This other language needs to be understood as well, and so on. Thus, the conclusions of *Speech and Phenomena*'s sixth and seventh chapters respectively are: the self is always more and less than itself; language is always more and less than itself. A certain indecision (more and/or less) always remains. The relation can never saturate itself; it *metaphorizes* the self and language without end.[11]

Stressing the *inadequacy* of the every self and linguistic relation, *Speech and Phenomena*'s argument forms the basis of that of "White Mythology" (and that of "The Pit and the Pyramid"). Thought and language are simultaneously similar to and different from that upon which they reflect. Simultaneity implies that thought and language are constituted by traces, minimal unities that are always more and/or less than themselves. A trace is a universal transforming itself through singular instantiations. The trace's "operation" (*différance*) is even, according to Derrida, better understood on the basis of the trope, catachresis, the forced extension of a term (MAR, 255–57/304–07).

2

"White Mythology's" third and fourth sections attempt "to verify" the law of supplementarity "in several 'examples'" (MAR, 229/273). In the verification, Derrida focuses on two types of examples: examples of discourses on metaphor and examples of metaphor within each discourse. The first, primary, and primordial discourse on metaphor, however, is that of Aristotle, within which the entire history of rhetoric unfolds. The first, primary and primordial example of a metaphor is that of the sun, a metaphor that looks back to Plato and ahead to Hegel. Instead of following the exact division between "White Mythology's" third and fourth sections, "The Ellipsis of the Sun" and "The Flowers of Rhetoric," I am first going to reconstruct from them Derrida's analysis of Aristotle's discourse on metaphor. Then I am going to assemble Derrida's two analyses—one from each section—of Aristotle's solar examples.

At the opening of "The Ellipsis of the Sun," Derrida says that "There is a code or a program—a rhetoric if you will—for every discourse on metaphor" (MAR, 231/275). Obeying this code, Derrida recalls Aristotle's famous definition of metaphor and focuses on its location within Aristotle's *Poetics*. The definition arises within a discussion of *lexis*. *Lexis* is defined by the name (*onoma*), which has the purpose of signifying something. This placement, according to Derrida, links Aristotelian metaphor to the disclosure of meaning and reference, to the disclosure of "an independent being identical to itself, intended as such." As Derrida says, "It is at this point that the theory of the name, such as it is implied by the concept of metaphor, is articulated with ontology" (MAR, 237/282).

To demonstrate the connection between Aristotelian metaphor and ontology, Derrida expands the definition's context again. The discussion of *lexis* takes place within a discourse on mimesis, which "is never without the *theoretical* perception of resemblance or similarity (*homoio-sis*)." Because of the link to mimesis, metaphor belongs to *logos* as "the possibility of meaning and truth in discourse" (MAR, 237/282-83). Expanding the context yet again, Derrida points out that the *Poetics* opens with a discussion of poetry's and thus mimesis' origin: nature. Being a special science, the study of nature (*physis*) is determined by the study of being *qua* being; nature's basic principle, *dynamis* and *energeia*, is one of the multiple ways being is said. Thus bound to nature, metaphor belongs "to the great immobile chain of Aristotelian ontology, with its theory of the analogy of being, its logic, its epistemology..." (MAR, 236/281, 244/291).

In "White Mythology" Derrida does not interpret Aristotle's ontology; concerning the analogy of being, Derrida merely refers to Aubenque (MAR, 244n45/291n31). Nevertheless, it is well-known from *Metaphysics* book IV that the so-called analogical unity describes a relation of reference to "one thing" (*pros hen*). The multiplicity of ontological principles refer to the presence, unity, and identity of *ousia* (substance).[12] The diversity of being's appearance are based in *ousia* (as *hypokeimenon*); nature's movement must actualize it (as *energeia*). Everything, for Aristotle begins and ends in unity. As he says in book IV, "it is impossible to think of anything if we do not think of one thing (*me noounta hen*)." Because Aristotle's ontology is based in *ousia* and because his ontology determines his metaphorology, Aristotle must, according to Derrida, privilege the proper over the metaphorical (MAR, 244/291).

Most of the discussion in "The Flowers of Rhetoric" concerns the Aristotelian notion of propriety. For Aristotle, according to Derrida, both metaphor and the proper (*idion* or *kurion*) concern what can be said about a being, an individual or concrete subject (MAR, 249/297, cf. 237/282–83). The *Topics* implies, according to Derrida, that both propriety and metaphor are possible because a concrete subject or individual is capable of several predicates or properties which can be extracted and exchanged (MAR, 247/295, 249/297). The proper is an exchange regulated by the identity of the essence. Any predicate that can be attributed to the subject without contradicting its essence is proper and true. While humanity, for example, is the essence of Socrates, it is proper to say that

Socrates has *logos*. The essence (or essential predicate) and the proper predicates exist in a "an element of quasi-synonymy" (MAR, 249/297). In other words, while saying something different from essence, the proper does not destroy the unity of the essence. By saying something different, in a way it says identity, the one, the unique or singular essence (the genus or species) and thing. The proper says essence immediately.

In contrast, metaphor extracts a property belonging to one essence in order to attribute it to a subject of another essence (or genus or species). Metaphor does not attribute predicates to a subject in a quasi-synonymous way; it predicates equivocally. It is improper or metaphorical to say that Socrates is a plant (*phutos*) (cf. MAR, 249/296). Metaphor then, in a way, destroys the unity of the subject's essence by not saying the same. Metaphor says essence twice. Therefore, metaphor does not "directly, fully, and properly [state] essence itself"; it does not immediately bring "to light the truth of the thing itself" (MAR, 249/297). Nevertheless, metaphor makes manifest, for Aristotle, a thing's properties by means of resemblance.

Because of metaphor's mediate capacity to reveal a thing, "analogy is metaphor par excellence" for Aristotle (MAR, 242/289). Analogy makes explicit the mediating exchanges that produce metaphors. In an analogy, according to Derrida, "all the terms...are present or presentable. One can always convene four members, two by two, a kind of family whose relationships are evident and whose names are known" (MAR, 242/289). If all the terms can be presented, then the substitutions can be reversed, and propriety reestablished. If all metaphors are elliptical analogies, then metaphors can always be converted back to analogy and thus to propriety's immediacy. Derrida points to the necessity of this conversion when he cites Aristotle's famous criticism of Plato's use of metaphors (MAR, 238/284). Even if metaphors provide knowledge through resemblance, Aristotle always prefers the proper and univocal discourse of philosophy (MAR, 247–48/295–96).

Aristotle's privilege of analogical metaphor brings us to Derrida's analysis of the first solar example (in "The Ellipsis of the Sun"). In the *Poetics*, Aristotle recognizes that analogies are sometime inventive; a term in an analogy might be missing. If a term is anonymous, then it must, as Derrida says, "be supplemented" (MAR, 242/289). Aristotle provides the example of the sun's generating power, for which no word exists. By comparing the sun's power to the casting forth of seeds, the poet, however, can say "sowing around a god-created flame." Although the terms present (the sun, the rays, the act of sowing, the seed) seem to be proper names with fixed meanings and referents, the metaphor implies otherwise. Because the sun's power lacks a proper name, the sun's essence has never been disclosed without mediation, in complete presence. The disseminating sun metaphor, which Derrida calls "an ellipsis of an ellipsis," implies absence. The sun—the "original, unique, and irreplaceable" referent—seems to have been already elided.

Through the second solar example (discussed in "The Flowers of Rhetoric") we can explicate exactly why the sun needs supplementation. In the *Topics* (V, 3, 131b20–30), Aristotle states that a debating opponent can be defeated by "seeing whether he has rendered a property of the kind whose presence is not obvious except by sensation." He goes on to say that when a sensory attribute passes outside the range of sensation, it becomes obscure. It is impossible to know whether it still exists because we know about it only by sensation. Due to the thing's always possible absence, the predication of any attribute to it is incorrect. Anyone who says that the sun is "the brightest star that moves about the earth" has spoken incorrectly or improperly, "for," Aristotle says, "it will not be manifest, when the sun sets, whether it is still moving above the earth, because sensation then fails." Derrida makes the following comment on the passage from the *Topics*:

> The sensory in general does not limit knowledge for reasons that are intrinsic to the *form of presence* of the sensory thing; but first of all because the *aistheton* can always not present itself, can hide itself, absent itself. It does not yield upon command, and its presence is not to be mastered. Now, from this point of view, the sun is the sensory object par excellence. It is the paradigm of the sensory *and* of metaphor: it regularly turns (itself) and hides (itself). (MAR, 250/299)

In order to clarify this passage, we need to extract a series of points from Derrida's analysis of Aristotelian temporality.[13]

"Ousia and Grammé's" analysis (MAR, 58/67, 61/71) begins with Aristotle's well-known "enigma of the now" (*Physics* IV, 10–13). The "now," as Aristotle says, seems to be always "other and other" and yet remains one and the same (218a10). If the now is like this, can we really say that time *is*? Aristotle solves this *aporia* by interpreting the now as an accident that supervenes upon the essence of time (MAR 61/70–1). Time's division into parts, the "before" and the "after," is an affectation. Its division into numbers is foreign (*allothi*) to time.[14] For Aristotle, there is no essential pause or gap disrupting time's continuity. The "other and other" of time never destroys the "same and same" of time. The now or the present as continuous substratum is; the now as division or limit is not. The now possesses "points," for Aristotle, only insofar as these points always turn into what has no divisions, no beginning and end. The line must turn into a circle. Thus, the *physis* of time, which is *physis* itself, is *dynamis* directed towards *energeia*, potentiality actualizing itself in the present, in the one (MAR, 52/59).

As Derrida points out, however, Aristotle's descriptions of the *physis* of time are descriptions of *aisthesis*, of sensation or experience. Because Aristotle separates temporal movement fron local motion or exterior movement, *aisthesis* here means inner experience (a sort of proto-reflection or auto-affection) (MAR, 48–9/54–5, cf. 43/47). By turning inward, time is discovered to be psychical "movement" (cf. 218b21–219a). Psychical "movement" is not strictly movement because it cannot consist of coexisting places or points in space. In temporal "movement," nows cannot coexist. If past nows would coexist with the same present now—like points in a line—then "things which happened ten thousand years ago would be simultaneous with what has happened today." Lack of coexistence or simultaneity implies that the now is always different, "other and other." Temporal succession always and absolutely implies this lack.

Derrida stresses, however, a "correspondence" between time and space. Time must be like space because the sameness of the "now" would make no sense without coexistence (MAR, 54–5/62–3). The "now" could not *remain* the same unless it returned in an other now. No present could exist without a certain simultaneity or without something like spatial coexistence. Thus, the now demands the supplement of a "between" *two* nows.[15] According to Derrida, Aristotle's use of the adverb *hama* (simultaneous), a locution which is neither temporal nor spatial, indicates this "synthesis" of same and other. *"Hama,"* according to Derrida, "says the dyad as the minimum" (MAR, 56/65). Thus, "Ousia and Grammé's" analysis shows that a sensory or aesthetic object is always divided and "synthesized" by time. Simultaneous temporalization and spatialization—différance—put the two before the one.[16]

To return from "Ousia and Grammé" to the passage cited from "White Mythology," we can see now that the sun as "the paradigm of the sensory" indicates that nature is a sort of trace (*gramma*). The turning and hiding of the sun implies that the sensory thing is always differentiating itself as and in the now, dividing and duplicating itself as other than itself. Like Hegelian reflection, the "aesthetic synthesis" generates the sensory thing as a nonadequate self-relation. The sensory thing "is" always more than itself and/or less than itself: less than itself because the catalogue of properties lacks the properties it possesses now; more than itself because now the sensory thing possesses properties that it did not have. Because of the sensory thing's indecision, it is not a unique, unified, and identical referent; it lacks substantial continuity. Lacking substantial continuity, being is not analogical, but metaphorical, or better, homonymic.[17]

The phrase, "the sun is the paradigm of metaphor," implies one of "Plus de métaphore's" claims: the metaphoricity of all discourse, including philosophical discourse. Because every metaphor must include a sensory element (its vehicle), every metaphor can be understood only by consulting "the Idea, paradigm, or parabola of the sensory," the sun. Every metaphor then must be in some way a heliotrope (some sort of sunflower)—but also must every concept. Philosophical discourse is constituted by terms and oppositions with sensuous referents, terms such as *phainesthai, aletheia,* etc., oppositions such as the visible and the invisible, appearing and disappearing, presence and absence. All these basic terms' and oppositions' senses derive from the sun, its light and movement. Thus, as Derrida says, philosophy's "natural" language "should always lead back to *physis* as a solar system, or, more precisely, to a certain story of the relationship earth/sun in the system of perception" (MAR, 251/299). Yet, this most natural, normal, literal story must be metaphorical because "...each time there is sun, metaphor has begun" (MAR, 251/300).

3

The first two steps of this reading have brought us to two different con-clusions by means of two routes. The first conclusion, which we see in Derrida's discussion of both Hegel and Aristotle, is critical. At the spe-cific level of language, the law of supplementarity demonstrates that there is no nonmetaphorical place from which to designate metaphor. The relation by which one moves from metaphorical discourse to a rhetorical or philosophical discourse is itself tropical. The movement produces another metaphor for which the metadiscourse did not and cannot account. Philosophical domination of metaphor (univocity) is a pretense. Similarly, because the term *metaphor* is a philosopheme, rhetorical domination of philosophy (rhetoric as non- or anti-philoso-phy) is a pretense.

At the most general level (again in both Hegel and Aristotle), the law of supplementarity implies that thought and being are constituted by an inadequate relation. Because of reflection's irreducible temporal character, auto-affection produces another instance of the concept, for which the concept did not and cannot account. Because of its irre-ducible temporal character, sensation produces another property which the sensory thing did not possess. The self and the sensory thing are divided and duplicated; the self and sensory thing are always more and less than themselves. Thus, thought and being are always marked by indecision.

If we focus on the most general level, we can see the second conse-quence based in the first two steps. Derrida has generalized metaphor beyond its traditional limits. Derrida states this generalization explicitly at the close of "White Mythology's" last section where he speaks of two self-destructions of metaphor. The first self-destruction is based in the metaphysical determination of metaphor. Exemplified by Aristotle and Hegel, metaphysics defines metaphor as continuity. So defined, metaphor can always be elevated into a concept or into the proper. As

the last section's title, "La métaphysique—relève de la métaphore," indicates, the elevation (relève) of metaphor is metaphysics. The second
self-destruction destroys the metaphysical determination of metaphor.
Metaphor, for Derrida, happens everywhere; thus, the "reassuring"
opposition between the metaphorical and the proper is "exploded"
(MAR, 270/323). Not opposed to the proper or the conceptual,
metaphor must be understood as supplementarity, thanks to which
thought and being themselves are discontinuous from themselves. The
discontinuity of the relation implies that Derrida has reinscribed
metaphor as catachresis or homonymy.[18]

<hr/>

4

Because we have attempted to provide a relatively independent reading
of "White Mythology," certain points related to Ricoeur's "Eighth
Study" were only noted in passing. These points must now be stressed
in order to anticipate the polemic. First, Derrida's premise that
metaphor remains a metaphysical concept arises out of Heidegger.[19] In a
footnote appended to the Hegel discussion (MAR, 226n29/269n19),
Derrida mentions Heidegger's connection of metaphor with metaphysics in Der Satz vom Grund. Heidegger "distrusts" the concept of
metaphor because the sensory/nonsensory opposition determines it.
Derrida agrees that this metaphysical opposition is "important" for
understanding the concept of metaphor, but he goes on to say that it is
"neither the only, nor the first, nor the most determining characteristic
of the value of metaphor." Indeed unlike Heidegger who rejects the concept of metaphor, Derrida reinscribes it otherwise, as catachresis and
homonymy.

What does Derrida mean by metaphysics in the first premise? In
"White Mythology," Derrida not only connects Aristotle's definition of
metaphor to his metaphysics, but also, by means of the solar examples,
connects Aristotle's metaphysics to that of Plato (cf. MAR, 242/289).
Then, in "White Mythology's" final section, the sun metaphor is connected to Descartes, Hegel, and Husserl (MAR, 266/318). Because of
these solar connections, the entire history of metaphysics, according to

Derrida, forms a system. The same system, however, organizes the entire history of rhetoric as well. Because DuMarsais and Fontanier (the leading figures in traditional French rhetoric) virtually repeat Aristotle's definition of metaphor, rhetoric, for Derrida, unfolds within the history of metaphysics. As Derrida says, all metaphor theory belongs "to a more general syntax, to a more extended system that equally constrains Platonism; everything is illuminated by this system's sun, the sun of absence and of presence, blinding and luminous, dazzling" (MAR, 267/319). Thus, as is well-known, for Derrida, the tradition, "as much philosophical as rhetorical" (MAR, 229/273), defines being as presence (MAR, 266/317–18). Derrida's definition, of course, derives from Heidegger's *Being and Time* notion of *Vorhandenheit*.[20]

Derrida's contention that the tradition forms a general syntax must be read, however, in conjunction with the style Derrida adopts in "White Mythology." Although "White Mythology" can be reconstructed according to Derrida's almost classical formulation of deconstruction, "White Mythology" is not written in the style of Derrida's 1967 texts. Instead of possessing a developmental, argumentative structure (like *Speech and Phenomena* or *Of Grammatology*), "White Mythology" is convoluted. This is the case because here Derrida first attempts to elaborate "a new delimitation of bodies of work and of a new problematic of the signature" (MAR, 231/275, cf. 216–15/257, 254–55/304, 265–68/317–20). This new delimitation is based on Derrida's earlier insight into the notion of tradition. In his 1962 *Introduction to Husserl's The Origin of Geometry*, Derrida discovered that tradition consists of an irreducible unity of fact and essence.[21] This unity, from which supplementarity, différance, and dissemination will spring, implies that tradition is neither linear nor circular, but zigzag. Thus, Derrida's style in "White Mythology," especially in the last three sections, attempts to "write" the zigzag. In fact, if Derrida is "writing" the zigzags of tradition, then all the French structuralist oppositions Derrida uses in "White Mythology," *langue* (or system) and *parole*, substitution and combination, code and message, paradigm and syntagm, synchrony and diachrony, syntax and semantics, have been reinterpreted according to the unity of essence and fact.

In connection with Derrida's "zigzagging"—*zigzagging* defines the way Derrida reinscribes and perverts certain terms against the tradition's system—we must now stress Derrida's recognition that the philosophical tradition defines metaphorization as *usure* (wearing away, as in the wearing away of a coin's exergue). Derrida's discussion of *usure* takes place mainly in the "Exergue," but he also recalls this notion in his Hegel discussion in "Plus de métaphore." Within the tradition, *usure* presupposes, according to Derrida, that a continuous kernel of sense underlies the transition from literal to figurative to concept (cf. MAR, 215/256). According to the tradition then, metaphorization is simply concept formation. Concepts overcome the difference or eliminate the relation between the literal and the figurative. Connected to metaphysics, *usure's* continuist presupposition implies, for Derrida, that concepts elevate and absorb metaphor just as the intelligible elevates and absorbs the sensible (cf. MAR, 226/269).

In the *Aesthetics*, Hegel connects *usure* (*Abnutzung*) to the traditional distinction between live and dead metaphors (MAR, 225–26/269). The live/dead distinction, according to Derrida, implies that metaphoricity resides in the consciousness of it. In order for a term to function metaphorically, to be alive, one must recognize a relation between the literal and figurative senses. As Hegel stresses, after the literal sense has been erased, it occurs to no one to take *begreifen* as to grasp by the hand. *Begreifen* contains no recognizable tension. Concepts are dead (used up) metaphors and not true (live) metaphors.

The continuist interpretation of *usure* also implies, for Derrida, etymologism. Through usage, metaphors "abstract" terms from their "native soil" without "extraction" (cf. MAR, 215/256). Lacking division from (or possessing resemblance with) their original meanings, terms then can always be traced back to their *etymon*. In the "Exergue" Derrida cites passages from Anatole France's dialogue *In the Garden of Epicurus* where the interlocutors decipher the original meanings of metaphysical terms. Later (in "The Flowers of Rhetoric") Derrida himself notes that "metaphora" and "epiphora" in Aristotle's definition of metaphor signify not only linguistic transportation but also "a movement of spatial translation." "Genos" signifies not only a classificatory category, but also "an affiliation, the base of a birth, of an origin, of a family" (MAR, 252–53/301–02).

As we saw, in "White Mythology" Derrida opposes the metaphysical domination of the phenomena of metaphor and reinscribes metaphor; he does the same with *usure*. The domination of the phenomena of *usure* takes place through its continuist interpretation, and through the notions connected to this interpretation, the location of metaphoricity only in the conscious recognition of it and etymologism (cf. MAR, 253/302). Derrida opposes *usure*'s domination with the law of supplementarity, which implies, as we have seen, an irreducible difference or discontinuity within the same linguistic element and within the same sensible thing (and within the self). It implies an irreducible, divided relation. Being irreducible, division takes place even when we are unaware of it; the live/dead distinction is irrelevant. Defined by division, difference, and discontinuity, metaphorization and *usure* are reinscribed as catachresis or homonymy, neither of which relate etymologically (or by resemblance) to their bases (cf. MAR, 253/302). Because catachresis, homonymy, and the law of supplementarity imply discontinuity, metaphorization and *usure* are, for Derrida, equal to "a displacement with breaks,... reinscriptions in a heterogeneous system, mutations, doublings (*écarts*) without origin" (MAR, 215/256).

Intersection: A Reading of Ricoeur's "Eighth Study" in *The Rule of Metaphor*

In *The Symbolism of Evil* (1960), Ricoeur says that speculative thought can be instructed by symbols (or, more generally, equivocal expressions) and yet remain fully rational.[22] On the basis of the interpretation of symbols, there is "positing" not more symbolism.[23] In *Freud and Philosophy* (1965), Ricoeur argues that the interpretation of symbols must fight on two fronts: against sophistic equivocity and against Eleatic univocity.[24] Appropriating Aristotle's philosophy, Ricoeur argues that the multiple meanings of being are neither reducible to one signification nor indicative of "a pure disorder of words." Thus, Ricoeur sees early on that a generalization of equivocity, symbolism, or metaphoricity threatens his project of a "philosophical hermeneutics": a hermeneutics animated by reflection or speculation; a philosophy instructed by equivocal expressions.[25]

The "Eighth Study" in *The Rule of Metaphor* (1975) echoes these earlier works; it (and the first) constitute an extended "polemic" with "White Mythology" (cf. MV, 290/368). To Derridean generalized metaphoricity Ricoeur opposes a discursive pluralism that implies neither a radical heterogeneity of discursive types nor a radical homogeneity (MV, 257/323). Throughout the "Eighth Study" he constantly tries to steer between a discontinuity which would eliminate the intersection of discourses, and especially the intersection between poetical and philosophical discourses, and a continuity which would collapse the difference between discourses. Above all, Ricoeur's discursive pluralism does not imply that philosophy is merely one discourse among many. Rather, as Ricoeur says, "it is important to recognize in principle the *discontinuity* that assures the autonomy of speculative discourse" (MV, 258/324). Thus, the reading of the "Eighth Study" that follows must focus on the Ricoeurean view of continuity/discontinuity. The notion of intersection is the basis from which Ricoeur criticizes Derrida.

1

Ricoeur's working hypothesis in the "Eighth Study," therefore, is that philosophical discourse *differs* from metaphorical or poetic discourse even as it intersects with poetry. The difference lies in the specific type of "philosophical act," in philosophy's "stated intentions," in its "aim" (*visée*). As Ricoeur says, this terminology is borrowed from Husserlian phenomenology (MV, 280/357). Thus, Ricoeur attempts to establish the difference between philosophic or speculative and poetic discourse by means of "a phenomenology of semantic aims." Due to the Husserlian influence, we might even say that Ricoeur articulates philosophy's essential noesis-noema correlation.

According to Ricoeur, the intention which animates ordinary discourse (and for Ricoeur scientific discourses derive from ordinary[26]) is twofold: the determination of the conceptual features of reality, and the discovery of new referents (MV, 297/377). In other words, in ordinary discourse we determine the abstract sense of predicates and present the things to which the appropriate predicates apply. According to Ricoeur, the abstract sense of a predicate is mastered only by applying it in the context of a sentence to a variety of referents. Conversely, we investigate new referents only by describing them as precisely as possible. Such a use of description, however, means that reference investigation can proceed only because the predicate's established senses have already been mastered. Thus, the need to master a predicate's established senses turns us away from sense to reference; the desire to discover new referents turns us away from reference to sense. Ordinary discourse's aim, therefore, exhibits a circular dynamism, which Ricoeur calls the historicity of signification, in which reference and predication lend support to each other (MV, 298/377–78). The distinguishing characteristic of ordinary discourse's circular dynamism lies in its restriction to *one* referential field, the one that we naturally, ordinarily, or immediately see.

That referents can be described implies, for Ricoeur, that the referential field can extend beyond things which are directly accessible. In other words, we can describe what we cannot normally see. Metaphorical discourse exploits this possibility by working in *two* fields. In metaphorical discourse, ordinary discourse's same twofold aim fulfils itself by transferring predicates already functioning in one familiar field to a new referential field which it then tries to describe. In other words, metaphor uses sedimented predicates to describe new experiences, experiences of new "things."

Transfer, for Ricoeur, consists of two "energies," both of which are activated by resemblance (MV, 296–97/376, 299/379). First, the new field, "already in some way present," exerts an attraction or "gravitational pull" on the already constituted senses of the predicate (MV, 299/379). Gravitational pull is possible, according to Ricoeur, because meaning or sense is itself dynamic (MV, 299/379). If sense was a stable form, it could never migrate to a new field, it could never transform itself. The second energy then lies in the dynamism of sense already exhibited in the predicates' polysemy. Polysemy "pushes" the predicate in a certain direction or on a certain vector into the new field. Ricoeur, in fact, describes the predicate's already constituted senses as an "inductive principle" for the production of the predicate's new sense and the new meaning of the metaphorical sentence as a whole (MV, 298/378). The new meaning of a metaphor, therefore, bases itself on the predicate's polysemy and yet terminates it. The new meaning erupts out of the past, but its newness lies in its being cut off from the past in the present (cf. MV, 298/378). This event of meaning—Ricoeur refers at this point, as always, to Benveniste's "instance of discourse" (MV, 298/378)—is a "live metaphor."[27]

According to Ricoeur, a live metaphor constitutes only a "semantic sketch without any conceptual determination" (MV, 299/379). The metaphorical aim does not provide a concept for the predicate which now exceeds the familiar referential field where its sense was constituted; it provides only an image or a trajectory of sense beyond the familiar field. The metaphorical intention brings to language an unknown referential field, but without clarifying it. This sketch or *schema* must reconcile (*mettre en rapport*) itself with the requirements of the concept.

At this passage from schema to concept, Ricoeur appeals to Kant's and Hegel's terminology. As he notes, Hegel's description of the *Aufhebung* is "not fundamentally distinct from what Kant conceives as the production of the concept from its schema" (MV, 292/371). Thus, the passage is made by something like Kantian notion of productive imagination (cf. MV, 296–97/376). Ricoeur, however, also calls this mediating passage interpretation or hermeneutics (MV, 303/383). Because interpretation is mediate, Ricoeur says,

> Interpretation is a mode of discourse that operates at the intersection of two impulses (*mouvances*), that of metaphor and that of speculation. It is therefore a mixed discourse, which, as such, cannot not suffer the pull of two rival demands. (MV, 303/383)

Interpretation then struggles to respect poetical discourse's multiplicity and to achieve the univocity of a concept. Productive imagination for Ricoeur, we might say, explicates the implicit conceptual meaning of a metaphor.

For Ricoeur, imaginative explication of the concept from the schema does not mean, however, that metaphorical discourse somehow induces philosophical discourse. While it is possible to discern in a metaphorical signification (or schematization, or assimilation) a meaning that is "one and the same," and, therefore, speak of the metaphorical genesis of concepts, according to Ricoeur this discernment is only part of concept formation. In order to "work free" of all schematizing interpretations, the nascent concept must be connected to a "network of significations of the same order, according to the constitutive laws of logical space itself" (MV, 301/381). A horizon of "speculative *logos*," a metalanguage, must be prepared in advance, into which the new "concept" is placed (MV, 302/382). Not generated by metaphor, speculative discourse "offers" its already constituted systematizing resources to metaphor.

Thus, for Ricoeur, we can pass from metaphorical to speculative discourse only by means of an *epoché*. Here Ricoeur directly appeals to Husserl's critique of the image (MV, 301/381). Metaphorical discourse only achieves the similar, while philosophical discourse achieves the same:

> The speculative is the very principle of the disparity (*inadéqua-tion*) between illustration and intellection, between exemplifi-cation and conceptual apprehension. If the *imaginatio* is the kingdom (*règne*) of "the similar," the *intellectio* is that of "the same." In the horizon opened up by the speculative, "same" grounds "similar" and not the inverse. In fact "wherever there is 'similitude,' there is also an identity in the strict and true sense." (MV, 301/381)

Having its own special *noesis*, the thought of the same, speculative discourse begins from itself and finds within itself its own principles of articulation (MV, 300/380). Its *necessity* proceeds, as Ricoeur says, "from the very structures of spirit" (MV, 300/380). Philosophical discourse's aim or task lies in articulating the very structure or "configurational properties" of the "logical space" in which meanings or concepts are inscribed (MV, 300/380). For Ricoeur, the speculative articulates the conceptual's condition of possibility; it aims at forming a system of categories.

Aristotle's metaphysical discourse forms Ricoeur's primary speculative example.[28] At first, Aristotle's analogical unity of the multiple meanings of being appears as a counterexample to Ricoeur's distance between speculative and poetical discourse. Because Aristotle attempts to introduce analogy into philosophical discourse as an intermediate modality between strict univocity and equivocity, it seems philosophical discourse reproduces the semantic functioning of poetic discourse. The word *analogy* belongs to both discourses; therefore, it looks as though poetic discourse in some way induces or causes philosophical discourse. Concepts would seem to be hidden metaphors. Philosophical discourse would lack the univocal precision that Aristotle claims for it.

In opposition to this view, Ricoeur argues that Aristotle's "work of thought," applied to (but not caused by) the linguistic paradox "being is said in many ways," produces a type of discourse which deviates from both poetic and ordinary discourse. The philosophical act produces a self-sufficient interconnection (*enchaînement*), a structure that draws its support from nowhere other than itself (MV, 261/327). When confronted with the multiple meanings of being, Aristotle, according to Ricoeur, in order to rescue these meanings from dissemination (*dissémination*), orders them *pros hen*. Ricoeur says, "The first term—*ousia*—places all the other terms in the space of meaning (*l'espace de sens*) outlined by the question 'What is being?'" (MV, 260/326–27). This question in the *Metaphysics*, according to Ricoeur, breaks with all "language games"; it opens the space, in the *Categories*, within which the categories of thought or of the predicative function as such arrange themselves (MV, 260/326–27). *Pros hen* orders the predicative function, not in the manner of a genus' univocity nor in the manner of a simple word's chance equivocity, but in the manner of a "regulated polysemy of being" (MV, 261/327). For Ricoeur, the *Categories*, therefore, exhibits a nonpoetic model of equivocity and suggests a nonmetaphorical theory of analogy.

Ultimately, Ricoeur agrees with "modern logicians" that Aristotle's extension of analogy to the categories' organization fails (MV, 270/340). Aristotle's analogical unity does not form a system but rather, as Kant says, only a "rhapsody." According to Ricoeur, Aristotle's failure leaves the question of being's unity unanswered but not asked in vain (MV, 272/343). "[This]...project must be taken up again" he says, "on some basis other than analogy and yet still remain faithful to the semantic aim that presided over the search for a *non-generic unity* for the meanings of being" (MV, 272/343, Ricoeur's italics). In fact, for Ricoeur, the very disproportion between Aristotle's analysis and its ideal attests to this project's radical semantic intention. The work of thought crystallized in Aristotle's text aims to form a system or a self-sufficient structure of the meanings of being, a nongeneric unity. This aim is, for Ricoeur, *the* philosophical project (cf. MV, 260/326). Thus, because philosophical discourse's aim lies in forming a system, a unity, "...the conceptual order is able to break free (*s'affranchir*) from the play of double meaning and hence from the semantic dynamism characteristic of the metaphorical order" (MV, 302/382).

2

We see now that Ricoeur's articulation of the intersection between metaphorical and speculative discourse consists of three propositions. First, the continuous movement leading from *schema* to concept abstracts the same from the similar; it aims to overcome the relation between image and concept. Second, the discontinuity (or distance) between metaphor and speculation lies in the specific noetic-noematic correlation of each. Metaphor "thinks" the similar; speculation "thinks" the same. Third, the noematic structure (*enchaînement*) functions like a context restricting the transferred terms' senses. Like a theme, *pros hen* determines the categories as nonpoetically equivocal or relatively univocal. On the basis of these three propositions Ricoeur turns to Derrida.

In the "Eighth Study's" critical section, Ricoeur begins by posing a filial relation between Heidegger and Derrida. Ricoeur himself has maintained an ambivalent relation to Heidegger. While Ricoeur recognizes the insights achieved in the Dasein analytic, for example, he is always suspicious of Heidegger's attempt to overcome metaphysics (cf. MV, 311–13/395–98).[29] As we saw in the last chapter, Derrida's relation to Heidegger is based in a footnote in "White Mythology's" second section where Derrida quotes Heidegger's claims about metaphor. As far as Ricoeur is concerned, Derrida's "assertions" (that is, the two premises) in "White Mythology" exaggerate Heidegger's "celebrated adage" from *Der Satz vom Grund*: "the metaphorical exists only within the metaphysical." Ricoeur then examines this "adage."

In *Der Satz vom Grund*, Heidegger wants to rearticulate one of Western metaphysics' basic principles, the principle of sufficient reason. In order to do this, Heidegger uses certain words in unusual ways (*Denken, Einklang, Sehen,* and *Hören,* for example). He makes his pronouncements on metaphor to prevent his words from being interpreted according to the traditional poetic or artistic concept of metaphor (MV, 282/359). Such an interpretation would assume that the terms were being used figuratively, transferred from the literal or proper. Correlatively, the linguistic transfer would be seen to correspond to a transfer from the sensible to the nonsensible. Because of this correlation, for Heidegger, metaphor belongs to metaphysics as "representational thought," the very metaphysics Heidegger is trying to overcome here (MV, 283/360). For Heidegger, therefore, metaphor is in "collusion" (this is Ricoeur's word) with metaphysics.

According to Ricoeur, three conclusions seem to follow from Heidegger's adage (MV, 280/357). First, the entire Western rhetorical tradition implies a Platonic ontology centering around the transference from the visible to the invisible or from the sensible to the nonsensible. Second, metaphor means transfer from a proper sense to a figurative sense. Third, transfer from proper to metaphorical is the same as that of the visible to the invisible. Ricoeur counters these conclusions by asserting that Heidegger's criticism can be understood only by examining the adage's context.

First, according to Ricoeur, Heidegger is making a digression. He is not analyzing metaphor as such or even poetical discourse as such (MV, 280/357). Second, Heidegger's adage arises as a warning against a particular interpretation of his words. This particular interpretation is just that, *particular*. Metaphor, for Ricoeur, cannot be reduced to this "allegorizing interpretation" which equates proper and figurative to sensible and nonsensible. Thus, on the basis of Ricoeur's contextual reconstruction, Heidegger's criticism appears limited and not directed at metaphor in general. This means, for Ricoeur, that Heidegger's constant use of metaphor, live metaphor, and Heidegger's interpretations of poets is "infinitely more important" than what he says in passing and polemically against a particular manner of casting metaphor (MV, 280/357, 282/359).

In contrast to Heidegger's "restrained" criticism, Derrida's "White Mythology" deconstruction appears to Ricoeur "unbounded" (MV, 284/362). This is because Derrida unearths, as we saw, the unavowed and unstated metaphoricity in philosophical discourse and the unavowed and unstated metaphysics in rhetorical discourse. Without repeating the detailed analysis of the last chapter, what follows is an abbreviated presentation of "the two assertions" that Ricoeur ascribes to Derrida based on his reading of "White Mythology" (cf. MV, 285/362). These two assertions parallel the law of supplementarity's two premises.

1. that the movement of metaphorization, that is, the movement by which a word becomes a metaphor, then becomes worn down, and then a concept, is that of idealization, a movement from sensible being to intelligible being. In other words, the metaphorical movement from proper to figurative is the same as that of the ascension from the sensible to the intelligible (MV, 285–87/362–65). Here Ricoeur focuses on

Derrida's treatment of Hegel and Aristotle. He especially focuses on Derrida's discussion of the role of the sun in philosophical discourse. Two subassertions follow:

   a. that the metaphysical tradition possesses certain dominant metaphors (in particular, the sun) due to their ability to express the sensible-intelligible movement (MV, 288–89/366–68).

   b. that these dominant metaphors indicate that metaphysics possesses an "epochal unity," Platonism (MV, 288–89/366–68, 294/373–74).

   2. that philosophical concepts, the primary philosophemes, are worn out (*usée*) metaphors (MV, 285–87/363–65). Here Ricoeur focuses on Derrida's use of the word *usure* and his appropriation of the "particularly eloquent text" from Hegel's *Aesthetics*. Two subassertions also follow:

   a. that worn-out metaphors are dead metaphors (MV, 287/365, 291–92/369–71).

   b. that metaphors are single-word substitutions that undergo a change from literal or proper sense to figurative (MV, 290/368–69).

These two assertions result in this conclusion (C1), which Ricoeur calls the "paradox of the auto-implication of metaphor." The paradox is this: metaphor is always said or defined metaphorically and metaphysically (MV, 286–87/364–65, 289/367). The paradox implies two subconclusions (C2 and C3). All discourses on metaphor commit themselves unwittingly to a metaphysics, that is, to Platonism (MV, 288/366), and philosophical or speculative discourse is "ruined," that is, metaphorical (MV, 287/365).

The first assertion and its subassertions form what Ricoeur calls "the theoretical core common to Heidegger and Derrida" (MV, 294/373). Although Ricoeur contextually restrains Heidegger's adage, he still wants to eliminate what seems to follow from it (MV, 282–83/359–60, 294–95/373–74, 311/395–96). Ricoeur believes that when Heidegger and Derrida speak of *the* metaphysics, they do not respect the specificity of each philosopher's system or text. Can it be that every philosopher prior to Heidegger is a Platonist? As Ricoeur says, "I am afraid that only a reading forced beyond any justification can make Western philosophy lie on this Procrustian bed" (MV, 282/360). According to Ricoeur, each philosopher's use of the sun metaphor, for example, must be interpreted as an innovation and, therefore, according to his specific text's intention and structure (MV, 311/395). In Heidegger's case in particular, Ricoeur sees in this so-called unity of metaphysics "an expression of vengefulness" and "an after-the-fact construction...intended to vindicate [Heidegger's] own labor of thought and to justify the renunciation of any kind of thinking that is not a genuine overcoming of metaphysics" (MV, 311/395–96).

In Derrida's case, Ricoeur thinks the literal-figurative and sensible-intelligible collusion results from a stress on denomination and, thus, on the substitution theory of metaphor (MV, 294/373). Denomination reduces language to its paradigmatic aspect and overlooks the syntagmatic aspect. Language seems to be merely one-to-one correspondences between words and meanings (classes of things). In such a view it is quite easy to associate a word's metaphorical meaning with an intelligible object. When the misplaced stress on denomination is removed, then language can be seen essentially as a sentential and not nominal phenomenon (MV, 294/373). The refocus on sentences clears the way for Ricoeur's own metaphor theory, a tension or interaction theory. Metaphor can now be seen, according to Ricoeur, to express not a static world of ideas but action (*praxis*), living experience, being-in-the-world. Thus (against C2) every metaphorical discourse does not unwittingly rest upon Platonism.

Ricoeur believes that the same misplaced stress on denomination and substitution results in Derrida's fascination with worn out or dead metaphors (MV, 290–91/368–70). In fact, Ricoeur believes that the dead metaphor fascination ultimately arises from a particular metaphysics, "a metaphysics of the proper." This metaphysics asserts that "words possess a proper, that is, primitive, natural, original (*etumon*) meaning in themselves" (MV, 290/369). In this view words are like Platonic ideas, possessing meanings apart from their particular, contextual instantiations. Ricoeur, in the "Third Study," for instance, describes linguistic codes in much the same way. Codes have only virtual existence, as opposed to the message's actual existence. For Ricoeur, this metaphysics seems to be the only explanation for the metaphoricity Derrida brings to light. Aristotle does not intend *epiphora* as transportation; this sense is not there in the *Poetics*. So it seems that a philosophical term's metaphoricity appears only if one follows the paradigmatic or associative link to the term's codified signification which exists somewhere "out there." Against this meaning in itself, the term's philosophical meaning contrasts and appears figurative. In effect, Ricoeur accuses Derrida of being metaphysical. Ricoeur argues (against the second assertion and its subassertions) that a more precise semantics dispels this "illusion" of meanings in themselves and that of dead metaphoricity.

For Ricoeur, the real problem of metaphoricity lies in the play of what he calls semantic pertinence and impertinence. According to Ricoeur, "the criterion of delimitation is clear" between metaphors and nonmetaphors: a word, in the predicate position in a sentence, possesses a metaphorical sense only in contrast to a literal sense. For Ricoeur, literal does not mean proper in the sense of originary, but simply the current or "usual" sense, a word's polysemy.[30] Polysemy itself, for Ricoeur, arises from the lexicalization of terms (MV, 290/368). If, in a particular language, one paraphrase of a metaphor becomes prevalent, it enters into the word's dictionary list of meanings, it becomes one of the word's literal meanings. Now, the metaphor is dead. According to Ricoeur, in ordinary discourse, however, when the word is used after lexicalization, only the word's lexicalized sense (the paraphrase) is brought into discourse. In the definite context of a sentence, only the lexicalized sense is pertinent. The word is used without deviation because its usual or literal sense has been "forgotten," and only its lexicalized, formerly metaphorical, sense is now recognized. Dead metaphors, therefore, are no longer metaphors, true metaphors. Polysemy is not metaphoricity, live metaphoricity. Ricoeur stresses that live metaphor exists only in an interpretation that recognizes a deviation in sense. A live metaphor, for Ricoeur, exists only in the awareness of it.

Although lexicalization determines the meaning of a word, it is still not, according to Ricoeur, concept formation. Ordinary discourse is not philosophical discourse. Turning to Hegel's text, Ricoeur argues that Hegel actually describes two operations or intentions (MV, 292–93/ 370–72). The first operation, as Ricoeur calls it, makes a spiritual or

transported signification out of a proper or literal meaning. Ricoeur recognizes that philosophers import words from discourses other than
their own in order to describe things which have no prior name, and
that catachresis accurately decribes this importation. This, for Ricoeur
however, is "a relatively banal case of an 'extended' use of words." These
words are defined and fixed in the discourse, lexicalized, thereby wearing down their metaphoricity. The phenomenon in philosophical discourse that Derrida calls metaphoricity, according to Ricoeur, is actually
polysemy and lexicalization, dead metaphoricity.

The second operation, however, makes this transported signification a new proper meaning. For Ricoeur, only the second operation, the
philosophical act, makes a proper sense in the spiritual order out of the
worn-down metaphor. When Aristotle, therefore, defines metaphor as
the *epiphora* of the word, the network of intersignifications formed by
physis, logos, onoma, etc. conceptually qualifies *epiphora* (MV, 293/372).
The sense of *epiphora* is encircled (*encadrée*) by these major concepts
and made rigorous or definite. The major concepts form a whole system
or structure. Differences in the strategy of *lexis* and exemplifications,
according to Ricoeur, also aid in discerning *epiphora's* proper or abstract
sense. "*Epiphora* is thus separated from its metaphorical status and constituted as a proper meaning, although 'the whole surface of [this dis-
course],' as Derrida says, 'is worked by metaphor'" (MV, 293/372).
Thus, against C1 and C3, Ricoeur says, "Speaking metaphorically of
metaphor is not at all circular, since the act of positing the concept (*la
position du concept*) precedes dialectically from the metaphor itself"
(MV, 293/372).

The phrase *precedes dialectically* is the key to Ricoeur's criticisms of
Derrida (#2). As *the* philosophical activity, the *Aufhebung* works to construct a system of being's polysemy, *the* philosophical aim. *Aufhebung* is
distinct from transfer and wearing away. *Aufhebung* is purely abstract;
usure is "purely metaphorical." These "two operations intersect—at the
point of dead metaphor—but remain distinct" (MV, 292/371). According to Ricoeur, there is no collusion between the two operations (MV,
292/371). The abstract meaning produced by the philosophical act and
surrounded by the philosophical structure is primary. Ricoeur sees
exactly what is at stake in this separation:

> If these two operations [that is, *usure* and *Aufhebung*] were not
> distinct, we could not even speak of the *concept* of *usure*, nor of
> the *concept* of metaphor; in truth, there could be no philosoph-
> ical terms.... No philosophical discourse would be possible,
> not even a discourse of deconstruction, if we ceased to assume
> what Derrida justly holds to be "the sole thesis of philosophy,"
> namely, "that the meaning aimed at through these figures is an
> essence rigorously independent of that which carries it over."
> (MV, 293/372, my emphasis)

Ricoeur never ceases to assume this "sole thesis of philosophy." Indeed
this merely restates the first proposition of Ricoeur's articulation of
speculative discourse. Reflective distance aims to produce an essence
rigorously independent of that which carries it over; it aims to overcome
the relation between image and concept, the relation which is metaphor
itself. Arising out of immediacy, mediation for Ricoeur should return to
immediacy. This is Ricoeurean intersection, indeed Ricoeurean distanciation: on the basis of the imaginative schema, intersection aims at a
whole concept; on the basis of continuity, distanciation aims at a non-
relational discontinuity.

3 ◆
Distanciation and *Différance*:
Derrida's Response to Ricoeur in
"The *Retrait* of Metaphor"

As we have just seen, Ricoeur begins his criticisms of Derrida by posing a filiation between Heidegger and Derrida. This filiation gives Derrida two purposes in "The *Retrait* of Metaphor": to respond to Ricoeur's criticisms, and to reinterpret his relationship with Heidegger. His response emphasizes reading errors Ricoeur makes in his examination of "White Mythology."[31] Derrida's reinterpretation of his relation to Heidegger extends into the complicated question of Heidegger's metaphoricity (a question I shall not examine here). By focusing on reading errors, on the one hand, and by steering away from Ricoeur into Heidegger, on the other, Derrida, however, never resolves the polemic with Ricoeur. Derrida, as we shall see, never addresses the foundation of Ricoeur's criticisms, his dialectical notion of distanciation. Similarly, Ricoeur's criticisms never address the foundation of the law of supplementarity, *différance*.

1

Ricoeur bases his claim of filiation on one footnote in "White Mythology" (MAR, 226n29/269n19). Here Derrida mentions Heidegger's distrust of the concept of metaphor due to its close association with the sensible-nonsensible opposition. Derrida's most general response in "*Retrait*" lies in pointing out Ricoeur's neglect of the note's "place and scope" (RM, 12/69). Put simply, Derrida believes that Ricoeur misreads the note and, thus, "White Mythology." Consequently, Ricoeur exhibits, according to Derrida, a "disconcerting logic" (RM, 12/69). He attributes propositions to Derrida which Derrida himself treats in a "deconstructive mode" in "White Mythology" (RM, 13/70). In what

43

amounts to an argument *pro domo* Derrida focuses, therefore, on two traits of Ricoeur's misreading.

The first takes up the scope of the note. According to Derrida, Ricoeur bases his entire reading of "White Mythology" on Heidegger's adage. We in fact saw that Ricoeur speaks of the "theoretical core common to Derrida and Heidegger," and, in contrast to Heidegger's "restrained criticism," he speaks of the "unbounded deconstruction in 'White Mythology'" (RM, 12/69–70; MV, 284/362). According to Ricoeur, Derrida's focus on the efficacy of worn-out metaphor in philosophical discourse (the second assertion and its subassertions) exagerates Heidegger's adage on the collusion between metaphor and metaphysics (the first assertion). Contesting this trait, Derrida stresses that Ricoeur overlooks the qualification which makes up part of the footnote on Heidegger. The footnote goes as follows:

> This explains the mistrust that the *concept* of metaphor inspires in Heidegger. (Derrida underlines "concept" in "*Retrait*"; it is unemphasized in "White Mythology.) In *Der Satz vom Grund*, he stresses especially the "sensible/nonsensible" opposition, an important trait but not the only, nor doubtless the first to appear, nor the most determinant for the value of metaphor. (RM, 12/70; MAR, 226n29/269n19)

The remainder of the footnote consists of a lengthy quote from *Der Satz vom Grund*. This passage from "White Mythology" shows that Derrida, unlike Heidegger, does not restrict the concept of metaphor to this sole opposition. Ricoeur too hastily equates Derrida and Heidegger.

This error results in the dramatic difference between Derrida's first premise of the law of supplementarity and Ricoeur's formulation of it in the first assertion. Derrida indeed affirms that metaphor is a metaphysical concept. This does not mean, however, that every time one articulates metaphor or uses the literal-figurative opposition one assumes a sensible-intelligible transportation, a Platonism. Rather it means that the "unity" of sense attached to the word *metaphor* inseparably participates in the traditional philosophical discourse, in some indefinite set of oppositions which constitute this tradition. In fact, metaphor cannot be understood or articulated without in some way appealing to oppositions such as name/thing, literal/figurative, usual/unusual, absence/presence, etc., all of which have a philosophical, or better a metaphysical, history. Whenever the word *metaphor* is used, certain traditional oppositions come into play.

Irreducible "participation in" does not imply, however, that one use of *metaphor* cannot be differentiated from another. This is indeed Derrida's second point about the footnote: "...the whole of 'White Mythology' constantly puts in question the current and currently philosophical interpretation (in Heidegger as well) of metaphor as transfer from the sensible to the intelligible" (RM, 13/70). Thus, Derrida does not subscribe to Heidegger's adage but agrees with Ricoeur's evaluation of it. It is overly restrictive and Derrida submits it to deconstruction. "White Mythology," like *The Rule of Metaphor*, attempts to reinscribe the word *metaphor*. Where *The Rule of Metaphor*, however, attempts to rejuvenate the entire metaphysical tradition, "White Mythology" attempts to pervert the tradition.

Ricoeur, however, is not quite correct when he accuses Derrida of characterizing the entire Western metaphysical tradition as Platonism.[32] As we saw, following Heidegger, Derrida claims that the metaphysical tradition possesses something like a unity, the meaning of being as presence. This means for Derrida that the entire philosophical tradition can be defined as idealism, of which there are two forms.[33] The first is Platonism itself (or "ancient" philosophy), in which the word *idea* refers to an object preserved in a transcendent outside (*topos ouranios*). The second is phenomenology (or "modern" philosophy), in which the word *idea* refers to an object preserved in a transcendental inside (representation). Either an exterior guards the object from all change (in which case the object is strictly objective) or an interior guards the object (in which case the object is made subjective). Change can, of course, supervene upon the object, but in both idealisms genesis should teleologically or dialectically turn into structure. Thus, the so-called constraining syntax of Western thought is based in a desire for permanent availability.

To claim, however, that the tradition unfolds logically—a claim Hegel made as well—does not equal the self-serving claim that every philosophical text prior to one's own simply repeats the first idealism, that of Plato. Rather, it attempts to account for the complex differences in the tradition, from Plato to Husserl, from Platonism to phenomenology, from transcendent idealism to transcendental idealism, from objectivism to subjectivism, from structuralism to geneticism (cf. MAR, 63–7/73–8). Perhaps Heidegger himself must ultimately be seen as a variation of idealism.[34] Finally and most importantly, Derrida's claim about the unified meaning of the tradition must be understood on the basis of Derrida's style which attempts, as we claimed in chapter 1, to "write" tradition's "zigzags." The zigzags (based in the irreducible unity of essence and fact) imply that the metaphysical tradition does not form a "homogeneous unity of a whole," or a circle enclosing a homogeneous field or a straight line of a development (cf. RM, 14/72; MAR, 230–31/ 275). If the tradition did not consist of zigzags, deconstruction itself would not be possible; the possibility of reinscription would be closed.

The second trait deals with the footnote's placement. The footnote arises out of a discussion of *usure* (*Abnutzung* in Hegel). The discussion emphasizes that by means of a particular interpretation *usure* belongs to the metaphysical concept of metaphor. In "White Mythology" Derrida stresses that this interpretation, the continuist presupposition of etymologism, does not, however, exhaust *usure*'s sense. In fact, Derrida attacks this very presupposition by reinscribing *usure*. In this reinscription *usure* signifies not the continuous erosion of a sense, but mutations, deviations in a heterogeneous system, surplus value that does not turn into capital. In *"Retrait"* Derrida asserts that Ricoeur overlooks *usure*'s plural sense and thereby attributes to Derrida exactly what he targets in "White Mythology," *usure*'s metaphysical interpretation (RM, 13/71).

We indeed saw that Ricoeur in the "Eighth Study" restricts the sense of *usure* to wear and tear through usage. This makes *usure* an easy target for Ricoeur's notions of polysemy and lexicalization. In turn, worn-out metaphor collapses into dead metaphor, which restricts metaphor, that is, living metaphor, to that of which one is aware or conscious. Ricoeur then can assert that philosophical discourse possesses no metaphoricity because no one *notices* there a contrast between semantic pertinence and impertinence. For Derrida, *usure*, however, is not etymologism or polysemy and lexicalization. It does not describe a continuous unity of sense nor does it equal only that of which one is aware or conscious. Rather, *usure* refers to a relational discontinuity, simultaneity, which happens automatically or unconsciously, whether we like it or not.

Ricoeur's confusion over *usure* seems to lead him to claim that Derrida privileges the name or the paradigmatic. Alone, however, the emphasis of syntax should have dispelled this (MV, 290–91/369; RM, 15/73). In "*Retrait*" Derrida says, "[to] this primacy [of the name] I have regularly opposed attention to the syntactic motif in 'White Mythology'" (RM, 15/73). Dead metaphor leads Ricoeur to believe that Derrida privileges the associative or similarity link between signifiers in a system of language. Through similarity Aristotle's *metaphora* is substituted or exchanged for "transportation" and then a certain metaphoricity is identified in Aristotle's text. Such etymological metaphoricity, however, constitutes only one axis of Derrida's reading. Its role lies in exemplifying the homonymy of being which Aristotle's own descriptions indicate. In Aristotle, Derrida examines the combinational or syntagmatic placement of terms. He looks at Aristotle's system and discovers theoretical comments about sensibility and propriety which pervert Aristotle's analogy of being. Thus Ricoeur again overlooks a crucial aspect of "White Mythology" in the "Eighth Study," its systematicity (a systematicity reinterpreted again according to the unity of essence and fact).

2

Without question, Derrida shows in "The *Retrait* of Metaphor" that Ricoeur's reading does not focus on what is crucial in "White Mythology," the law of supplementarity. Supplementarity questions *usure*'s continuist presupposition; it is the basis for Derrida reinscription of *usure* or metaphorization. Supplementarity describes an irreducible discontinuous relation within a word, within a sensible thing, within the self. Through this broken relation something like an essence comes about, a generality that never entirely separates itself from sensibility. Supplementarity, therefore, describes the production of difference as the same, as *différant*. Indeed, Derridean *différance* is what Ricoeur most overlooks in his reading of "White Mythology." Ricoeur does not recognize that supplementarity targets the Hegelian *Aufhebung* and the Aristotelian analogical unity of being.

Derrida, however, in "The *Retrait* of Metaphor" is not entirely fair to Ricoeur. Although Derrida notes "the wealth" of *The Rule of Metaphor*, he never takes into account the basis of Ricoeur's criticism of "White Mythology," the intersection of poetic and speculative discourse.[35] Intersection is possible, for Ricoeur, because of distance:

> speculative discourse is possible, because language possesses the *reflective* capacity to place itself at a distance and to consider itself, as such and in its entirety, as related to the totality of what is. Language designates itself and its other. This reflexivity extends (*prolonge*) what linguists call the meta-linguistic function, but the function is articulated in speculative discourse rather than in linguistics. (MV, 304/385)

Speculative discourse, for Ricoeur, appropriates (continuity) the sense hermeneutics explicates from the metaphor. Appropriation, based in the specificity of speculative discourse's intention, breaks (discontinuity) with metaphor (cf. MV, 313/398).[36] Speculative discourse aims to make the kernel of sense implicit in the metaphor what it truly is, a concept. Distanciation is dialectical abstraction in which the metaphorical relation is elevated and absorbed (cf. MV, 295/374). Speculative discourse should be sameness without difference. Derrida, therefore, never addresses in "The *Retrait* of Metaphor" Ricoeur's dialectical notion of distanciation.

It might seem that we could resolve this failure to address each other directly by going back to Ricoeur's and Derrida's 1971 Montreal round table discussion on the problem of communication. (See Appendix below.) Here, however, Ricoeur and Derrida again speak at crosspurposes. Indicative of the whole round-table discussion is what they say about the role of difference in language. Derrida, of course, asserts its primacy; a "semiological strata," he says, is "irreducible," and a theory of discourse cannot do away with it.[37] In contrast, Ricoeur asserts that the discursive act, which is directed at the same, is primary; "difference," he says, "is a functional instrument in discourse."[38] Derrida responds to Ricoeur's assertion by stressing that the insertion of an "a" in "différence" "implies that alterity would not be the simple barrier between the different things, but that there would be an economic system of differences which in fact presupposes the intervention of the same."[39] Then, Ricoeur connects his mention of the same to the distanciation of meaning.[40] When this happens, Ricoeur and Derrida are at a point of almost absolute proximity; distanciation as well as *différance* seem to consist in identity and difference. If the concepts of distanciation and *différance* are this close, then we must ask: what is the basis of Ricoeur and Derrida's disagreements here in the round table and in the later polemic over metaphor?

This question establishes the task of the next two parts. Both *différance* and distanciation consist of continuity and discontinuity, identity and difference, specificity and generality. Both distanciation and *différance* describe a passage from literal to figurative to concept; they describe mediation. Thus, the next two parts must illuminate the difference between distanciation and *différance*. Only this difference will allow us to understand the polemic involved in the three texts just examined. The difference between distanciation and *différance* will establish the difference between the thought of Ricoeur and Derrida.

Already we have guides to the difference. As we saw from the "Eighth Study," speculative distance is discursive. Thus, we are going to have to define Ricoeurean distanciation by means of his theory of discourse. Because distanciation is dialectical, it stresses the elevation of figurative sense to concept. Thus, we are going to have to define distanciation by means of Ricoeur's metaphor theory. As we shall see, both discourse and metaphor are defined by temporalization (even though the notion of distanciation suggests space). In our examination of Ricoeur, we are then going to have to turn to his *Time and Narrative* (III) analyses of the historical present. Finally, we are going to have to turn to the *Time and Narrative* (III) interpretation of Husserlian temporalization; this will make the transition to Derrida.

We have already seen that the law of supplementarity could be explicated only by including Derrida's own analysis of Husserlian temporalization in *Speech and Phenomena*. Thus, we are going to have to return to the basis of *Speech and Phenomena* in Derrida's 1962 *Introduc-*

tion to Husserl's The Origin of Geometry. Although the *Introduction's* analysis of Husserlian temporalization will seem to overlap completely with Ricoeur's own descriptions of the historical present and with his own basic definition of distanciation as the dialectic of event and meaning, we shall come to our first clear view of the difference between Ricoeur and Derrida here. We shall see that for Ricoeur mediation derives from immediacy, while for Derrida mediation precedes immediacy (presence). Nevertheless, even with the aid of *Speech and Phenomena* again, Derrida's similarities with Ricoeur will remain. Thanks to our reading of "White Mythology," we also know that *différance* cannot be defined by Hegelian dialectic; the law of supplementarity explicitly criticizes the Hegelian notion of *Aufhebung*. Thus, we are going to have to examine the explicit term Derrida substitutes for dialectic, dissemination. When we examine the notion of dissemination, as it is developed in "The Double Session," we shall see that chance displaces imagination. This displacement is the difference between Ricoeur and Derrida.

PART II

Ricoeur's Notion of Distanciation

4 ◆
The Dialectic of Event and Meaning

Ricoeur's expressed lifelong project lies in reflective philosophy. "A reflective philosophy," according to Ricoeur, "considers the most radical philosophical problems to be those which concern the possibility of *self-understanding*."[1] Reflective philosophy, as we have seen, aims at constructing a system of categories of human existence in all its facets, a system of categories of thought and being. As is well-known, Ricoeur's divergence from traditional philosophy lies in the way its aim fulfills itself. Taking account of Heidegger's ontological critique of Husserl and the Freudian and the Frankfurt school attacks on consciousness, Ricoeur always stresses that self-understanding does not come about through intuitive reflection. Rather, for Ricoeur, self-understanding comes about only through the type of mediation he calls distanciation (HHS, 144/117).

Distanciation, for Ricoeur, is not an empirical or contingent condition, but a transcendental or essential condition; it is basic to all experience. He indicates distanciation's irreducibility by associating it with the Husserlian notion of intentionality (HHS, 112/53). Intentionality, of course, refers to the fact that consciousness always transcends itself toward a repeatable meaning or sense. Through repetition, for Ricoeur, consciousness has the ability to transform (*figure,* according to the *Time and Narrative* terminology) what is merely subjective and singular into what is objective and universal. Distanciation, therefore, establishes the relation and division between subject and object. Distanciation, as Ricoeur says, is the reflective, critical or suspicious moment within consciousness (cf. HHS, 113/54).[2]

Prior to this division, however, is belonging (*appartenance*). Unlike distanciation (which is a relation mediated through repetition), belonging is an immediate or unreflective relation. Based in Heidegger's notion of being-in-the-world, belonging implies that we always already find ourselves functioning in historical situations.[3] We are always already practically or concernedly involved with things in the world. Thus, on the one hand, belonging for Ricoeur is a positive expression of a negative condition, human finitude; we are not autonomous, self-grounding subjects, the source of the world's meanings (HHS, 106/45). On the other, because belonging is action, Ricoeur can associate it with "what Hegel called the 'substance' of moral life" (HHS, 116/58).[4]

This Hegelian formulation of belonging indicates that its relation with distanciation is dialectical.[5] For Ricoeur, the interplay between belonging and distanciation exploits *Aufhebung's* two crucial senses. Distanciation *cancels* a subjective, singular content in an objective, universal form.[6] Because, however, distanciation also *preserves* the singular, the universal is never entirely abstract or formal. Belonging "corrects" distanciation, as Ricoeur says (cf. HHS, 110/51), by concretizing the universal; it resingularizes distanciation. Following the dialectical spiral, distanciation, therefore, not only begins, but also completes itself in belonging.

As we have seen, Ricoeur never retreats from his affirmation of human finitude; there is no possible absolute knowledge. Distanciation's dialectic is an always "incomplete mediation." Nevertheless, as we shall see now in Ricoeur's theory of metaphor and in his theory of historical consciousness, distanciation's irreducible singularizations or deviations must be regulated by a Kantian idea; they must be sublated, perhaps even negated. The reason Ricoeur is always led to a regulative idea lies in his appropriation of Kantian productive imagination, a notion not unrelated to the *Aufhebung*. Ricoeur's appropriation of productive imagination we shall see most clearly in live metaphor. Although live metaphor and the historical present will expand and complete the basic description of Ricoeurean distanciation given so far, Ricoeur's theory of discourse provides its primary characteristic: the dialectical interplay between universality and singularity.[7] As Ricoeur says,

Discourse, even in its oral form, displays a primitive type of distanciation which is the condition for the possibility of all the characteristics we shall consider later. This primitive type of distanciation can be discussed under the heading of the dialectic of event and meaning. (HHS, 132/103)

The dialectic of event and meaning is distanciation.

1

As is well-known, Ricoeur's theory of discourse opposes the linguistics articulated by Saussure and appropriated in French structural semiotics. Structural semiotics attempts to reduce all linguistic phenomena (all signifying phenomena) down to synchronic systems or codes composed of differentially determined signs (INT, 2–6; MV, 66–9/88–92).[8] In contrast, Ricoeur's "semantics of discourse" takes the message as the fundamental unit of language. Ricoeur does not, however, simply identify discourse with the semiological concept of message. Rather, discourse designates the whole of what takes place between speaker and hearer.[9] Primarily then, discourse is dialogue aiming at communication (INT, 16).

Consequently, discourse begins with speaking. For Ricoeur, the distinguishing characteristic of speaking is the fact that it has "temporal existence." It is an event (*événement*). Ricoeur overtly draws upon the message-code distinction and calls the speech event the "temporal existence of the message" (INT, 9). The message exists in time and is, therefore, actual, according to Ricoeur; the codes, on the other hand, do not exist in time and, therefore, have, as Ricoeur says, "virtual existence" (that is, no existence apart from their actualization in speech) (MV, 70/92–3). Because the codes have only virtual existence, the speech event for Ricoeur has an "ontological priority" (INT, 9).

Ricoeur clarifies temporal existence or "actuality" further, and thus gives more support for the ontological priority of the event, by saying that "…discourse is realized temporally and in the *present*" (HHS, 133/104, my emphasis). In *The Rule of Metaphor* he makes even a stronger statement: "The present is the very moment at which discourse is being uttered. This is the present of discourse. By means of the present, discourse qualifies itself temporally" (MV, 75/99). Or, as he says in "Structure, Word, Event,"

> For discourse has an act as its mode of presence—the instance of discourse…, which, as such, is of the nature of an event. To speak (*Parler*) is a present event, a transitory, vanishing act.[10]

The speech event's actuality is the present. Thus, for Ricoeur, even though it suggests spatiality, distanciation is defined by temporality.[11]

While the event, being temporal, is transitory and vanishing, the meaning (*sens* or *signification*) of the speaking, according to Ricoeur, is omnitemporal, relatively permanent, ideal (INT, 20, 90; HHS, 134–35/105–06, 184: MV, 74/98).[12] Meaning is the "realization" (*effectuation*) or expression of the speaker's intention (HHS, 132–33/103–04). Without positing psychological states or entities, Ricoeur's use of *effectuation* attempts to capture the transition that takes place from experience (perhaps even inner experience) to language. This transition between an event which is present, transitory, vanishing, and a meaning which is ideal, omnitemporal, relatively permanent is made possible through repetition. In order to express and communicate, the speaker must repeat polysemy or the lexical code. Taking place in the present, however, the meaning constructed out of the codes is singular, discontinuous, distanced—and distanciable. Although singularized, the meaning is itself repeatable. As Ricoeur says in *The Rule of Metaphor*,

> Such, then, is the instance of discourse: an event which is eminently repeatable. This is why this trait [of discourse] can be mistaken for an element of language (*langue*); but what we have here is the repeatability of an event, not of an element of a system. (MV, 70/92–3)

This repeatability is not that of an abstract form (like a code), but the repeatability of the expressed content itself, the same event of meaning. Universal meaning cancels and preserves the singular content for communication; defined by this dialectic, discourse for Ricoeur must take place within a horizon of univocity.

Dialectically mixed universality and singularity, meaning itself, captured in a sentence (*phrase*) or a statement (*énoncé*), consists of two parts which Ricoeur designates in the following ways: the utterer's meaning and the utterance meaning, the speaker's intention and the intended (*l'intente*) or propositional content (MV, 70/93), and, appropriating Husserl, *noesis* and *noema* (INT, 12–13).[13] By means of shifters or indexicals, every spoken sentence, for Ricoeur, refers back to the present speaker. As he says, the speaker's intention "can be found nowhere else than in discourse itself. The utterer's meaning has its mark in the utterance meaning" (INT, 13; cf. HHS, 133/104, MV, 75/98). The utterance meaning or intended, for Ricoeur, indicates the fundamental polarity between individuals and universals. Picking an individual out and classifying it, every sentence or speech event unifies two functions: singular identification and universal predication (MV, 71/93–4). Predicates or "categories" do not refer to anything, but for Ricoeur "correspond" to referential fields (classes of individuals). Only through singular identification does discourse for Ricoeur refer to things in the world ("positivistic reality" or "basic particulars") (MV, 71/93–4, 216–19/273–76). Again shifters or demonstratives make reference (in the Fregean sense) possible (INT, 13, 20). Because shifters are occasional, they link or glue the sentence to this thing present here and now, and to me. Thus, shifters, in particular, the word *I,* specify the meaning as unique (cf. INT, 9). Although the sentence must repeat the accepted senses of the words used (cf. HHS, 133/104), the meaning of the sentence is, so to speak, "singularized" by referring to *me*, to *this* thing, right *now*, right *here* (INT, 14–9; HHS, 135/106; MV, 72–3/96).[14]

Singular meaning, however, for Ricoeur, is also a structure (INT, 11). Every time Ricoeur incorporates the French structuralist notion of structure, he always qualifies it in the following way: the structure is synthetic not analytic. Ricoeur does not use *structure* in the sense of a combination of dependent, opposed units, but in the sense of an "interlacing" (*sumploke*) of the "functions of identification and predication in one and the same sentence" (INT, 11; MV, 70/93). "The verb," he says in *Fallible Man*, "is what makes the sentence 'hold together'(*tenir ensemble*)."[16] The sentential structure then is more a substance than an interplay of relations. Thus, it seems for Ricoeur that one cannot even strictly speak of separable parts in a sentence. The sentential structure, the sentence itself, is a whole, a unit complete in itself.[17]

The importance of Ricoeur's concept of synthetic whole cannot be underestimated. It supports his assertion that the sentence and the sign (and thus semantics and semiotics) are radically discontinuous. Not determined differentially, the sentence is independent; it is not equivalent to a Saussurean sign. Thus, according to Ricoeur, a system of mutually dependent paradigmatic propositions cannot be abstracted from the variety of sentences (INT, 10). At the syntagmatic level, the contiguity of sentences is not "the same sort of contiguity as...the concatenation of phonemes in morphemes" (MV, 179/228). The individual sentences do not function according to their difference from contiguous sentences, but according to the coherent unity or whole which they form. The concatenation of sentences, as in an extended dialogue, for Ricoeur, is also a synthetic whole. Lastly, synthetic structure is equal, for Ricoeur, to context. Thus, it makes communication possible.

2

Communication is a task or a process for Ricoeur, because the spoken sentence must repeat codified forms such as lexical meanings, polysemy. As we've already seen in our examination of the "Eighth Study," polysemy for Ricoeur originates in the past use of words in sentences; it does not, therefore, include chance relations or affinities among forms. Because of this—because polysemy is semantic not syntactical, content rather than form—polysemy is context sensitive (MV, 121–25/155–61). The plural senses found in the dictionary are actually rules for usage (MV, 197–98/251–52).[18] Polysemy's sensitivity to context implies then that it can be reduced (HHS, 44/77). Listeners, therefore, adopt a contextual strategy to insure communication (MV, 124/160, 127–31/163–68).[19]

The contextual strategy is based, according to Ricoeur, in "a code of pertinence" (MV, 151–52/193–94). Ricoeur asserts that the code of pertinence is not a code of *langue* but of *parole* because the code specifies itself in the present sentence (MV, 152/194). Words used in a sentence belong to a prior categorization that dictates which predicates can combine intelligibly with which subjects. Each sentence, however, uniquely synthesizes a subject and a predicate; the hearer must return to *this* sentence to see which sense of the words make sense together. For example, "is blue" can be pertinently predicated of *water* because the signifieds, a color and a physical thing, make sense together, but not of *angelus* because a color and something spiritual are not logically coherent. Although grammatically correct, "the *angelus* is blue" (Mallarmé's "blue *angelus*" in *L'Azur*) would be received as nonsense in an ordinary conversation. Thus, in order to make sense of the sentence, the hearer, so to speak, must move back and forth from possible senses of the particular words to the sentence as a whole. Moving back and forth within the whole sentence mutually determines the pertinent senses of the words used and the meaning of the sentence as a whole.

If a sentence is unusually plural, then for Ricoeur, the dialogue itself forms a whole, a whole context circumvented by the topic or theme under discussion. The theme refers to the thing under discussion, about which the individual speaker is trying to say something. Through question and answer, the hearer can check and verify whether he has correctly understood the intended sense of the words. The speaker is present right here, right now. If the hearer has misunderstood and identified the wrong thing, the speaker can use shifters to point out *this* present thing and not *that*. The theme then progressively determines the meaning of particular sentences and the particular words.

The hearer participates in the production of meaning; therefore, communication, for Ricoeur, is the dialectic of event and meaning. The hearer must contextually interpret the speaking in order to screen unintended senses and achieve univocity (HHS, 44/77). As Ricoeur says, interpretation "consists in recognizing which relatively univocal message the speaker has constructed on the polysemic basis of the common lexicon" (HHS, 44/77). As we see in this passage however, Ricoeur qualifies the communicated meaning as "relatively univocal" (HHS, 44/77). In fact, he even admits that the contextual strategy ultimately fails: "Misunderstanding finally prevails."[20] The irreducibility of misunderstanding implies that the interpretative process is endless. Meaning's repeatability implies that more events and, thus, more meanings are possible; there is always more distance to cross, another destination.

3

Although spoken discourse provides Ricoeur's primary description of distanciation, writing or the text, Ricoeur says, "is, *par excellence*, the basis for communication in and through distance" (HHS, 111/51, 131/168). Writing fixes transitory discourse in a medium which "explodes" the inscriptive event. The material medium takes discourse beyond the particular, limited horizon of the author and his original audience to a potentially universal and infinite (or at least indefinite) audience. The text's meaning then no longer coincides with the author's intention, with the limited meaning it had for its original addressees. For Ricoeur, however, this deviation is positive. The text now acquires a more universal meaning that makes writing "more spiritual" than speaking (INT 31, 36). Thus, a text is like a letter (INT, 29). Although addressed to a determinate person, a letter can be delivered to anyone. Like a letter, a text is available to anyone who can read; it is really addressed to you (INT 31–2).

Writing's apostrophic character implies, for Ricoeur, that writing is the full manifestation of the dialectic of event and meaning, of something "...nascent and inchoate in living speech, namely the detachment of meaning from event" (INT 25). The written text, Ricoeur says,

> is a kind of atemporal object, which has, so to speak, cut its ties from all historical development. The access to writing implies the overcoming of the historical process, the transfer of discourse to a sphere of ideality that allows the indefinite widening of the sphere of communication. (INT, 91)

As ideal (or omnitemporal [INT, 93] or transhistorical), writing explicates the type of repeatability that characterizes sentential meaning for Ricoeur.[21] Writing *preserves* the singularity of the inscriptive event; the authorial content is captured in shifters; style singularizes universal literary codes, innovates sedimented genres (HHS, 137/108–09).[22] Writing, however, also cancels singularity because the intentional content remains the same even as it is distanced from its origin. The written text, as Ricoeur says, is autonomous (INT, 27–8; HHS, 139/111); it is the achievement of the universality of meaning. Its indefinite audience implies, however, that written meaning is always available for resingularization. Thus, the text, for Ricoeur, is a "dynamic identity."[23]

The dynamics of textual identity comes about through reading. As is well-known, much of Ricoeur's work in the 1970s was devoted to synthesizing the classical hermeneutical opposition of explanation and understanding. Suffice it to say that this dialectic repeats the dialectic of event and meaning. First, there is a moment of understanding; a reader "guesses" at the text's meaning based on his particular context or situation. Then in a moment of explanation, this subjective meaning is compared with other possible ways of construing it in order to arrive at the most "probable" reading. When a sort of objective meaning is achieved, then "the task of hermeneutics," for Ricoeur, lies in following this "arrow" of sense (*sens*) to a reference (HHS, 62/100, 192–93; INT, 94), in appropriating ("making one's own") the alienated meaning (INT, 89–95; HHS, 143–44/116–17, 158–62/152–56, 178, 182–93, 220/210–11).[24] When the reader applies the objective meaning to his own life, the text is rendered contemporaneous. Appropriation, therefore, for Ricoeur engenders a new event in the "present moment" (INT, 92; HHS, 142/115, 159/153).

Ricoeurean appropriation, however, does not imply a sort of textual "absolute knowledge" (HHS, 193).[25] On the one hand, we do not and cannot return to the original event; it has expired. We are neither transferred into the mental life of the author (Dilthey) nor do we reconstruct the past world which produced the text (Schleiermacher). On the other hand, the text's omnitemporality implies that the text outdistances any finite reader; its repeatability is open to an infinite number of events. Nevertheless, as we saw in our reading of the "Eighth Study," interpretation is a mixed discourse seeking the clarity of a concept and preserving textual dynamism. It is a work of concepts "and consequently a struggle for univocity" (MV, 303/383). "The Ideas of reason," Ricoeur says in the "Eighth Study" [MV, 303/383], always regulate the work of interpretation (and understanding). For Ricoeur, an Idea in the Kantian sense is defined by the interplay of openness (or infinity) and totality (or completeness). Therefore, while recognizing the impossibility of attaining it, interpretation obeys the Idea's imperative of univocity; the "arrow" of meaning points to a horizon.[26]

5 ◆
Imagination in Metaphor and Symbol

Dominated by the dialectic of event and meaning, Ricoeur's metaphor theory continues to highlight distanciation's interplay between singularity and universality. Throughout the bulk of his descriptions Ricoeur stresses live metaphor's innovation, deviation, novelty; live metaphor is an event in meaning, not a mere instantiation of polysemy. Yet, as we have seen and as we shall see again now, a live metaphor is regulated by univocity. It is an implicit concept. Even more than Ricoeur's metaphor theory, however, his theory of the symbol stresses, as is well-known, an excess of meaning. Even more than live metaphor, the symbol is open to inexhaustible; within it humans belong to what is "totally other." Although Ricoeur asserts that the symbol's alterity resists conceptualization more than innovative metaphor, the symbol, he says, is a gift to speculative thought. Symbolic excess, like metaphorical deviation, always points to conceptual identity. This is the case, it seems, because Ricoeur traces them back to Kantian productive imagination.

1

Like his discussion of discourse in general, Ricoeur's discussion of metaphor opposes certain contemporary theories of metaphor, some of which take the semiological approach. According to Ricoeur, these theories (with the notable exceptions of those proposed by Richards, Black, and Beardsley) form variations of the substitution theory. Focused on the word or name, the substitution theory states that metaphor extends a word's sense from its literal sense by substituting it for the normal or proper word. The proper word, however, could just as well have been used (INT, 49/145). In the substitution theory, metaphor is merely decorative or rhetorical (aiming at emotive effects). Thus, what disturbs Ricoeur most is that the substitution theory fails to account for innovative metaphor, for live metaphor.

Although Ricoeur opposes the substitution theory, he does not deny the word a role in metaphor. For Ricoeur, metaphor involves the deviant or improper use of a word, a use that makes the word deviate from its literal sense. Deviation, however, for Ricoeur happens only within the context of a sentence. Unlike ordinary discourse, where context screens the unintended but accepted senses of the words used *except one*, a metaphorical sentence preserves the polysemy of the words used *plus one* (MV, 130–33/167–71; HHS, 169).[27] Thus, Ricoeur sees metaphor as an interplay between the sentence and the word (MV, 125/161); his theory of metaphor is "tensional" or "interactive."[28] Only by means of a tensional theory can one account for innovation.

Ricoeur's theory first provides a semantics which describes metaphor's predicative structure (HHS, 170). Like any sentence, a metaphor combines a subject and a predicate. Unlike an ordinary sentence in which the combination obeys the code of pertinence, a metaphorical sentence, for Ricoeur, breaks the code. A metaphor is a case of impertinent predication, "a category mistake," as Ricoeur says borrowing from Ryle (INT 51/147; MV, 89/115). The recognition that categories (and their corresponding referential fields) clash is based in a literal interpretation that attempts to make the sentence conform to the code of pertinence (HHS, 174; MV, 151/194).

When the literal interpretation self-destructs, the reader or hearer must reinterpret the metaphor otherwise, metaphorically. The interpreter must search among the words' proper or literal senses in order to find a way of synthesizing the subject and predicate harmoniously. Ricoeur defines literal or proper as the word's polysemy or its set of possible contextual uses (HHS, 169; MV, 140/180–81). As we saw earlier, for Ricoeur polysemy does not include contingent associations based in graphic or phonic form. Because polysemy for Ricoeur is semantic, it is context sensitive. In fact, in his metaphor theory Ricoeur defines polysemy as "a plural identity" (MV, 130/167). Along the lines of identity, polysemy's plural senses can be enumerated, and classified by their relative proximity or distance from the central sense; a hierarchy can be established because polysemy has the outline of an order (MV, 113–15/146–48). Along the lines of plurality, polysemy appears as a semantic capital, an open texture, a potentiality of meaning which can be actualized only in a new sentence (MV, 130/167). Only because polysemy is *simultaneously* plural, can we, according to Ricoeur, construct a new meaning for the terms constituting a metaphor, a new meaning for the sentence as a whole, which recognizes deviation (novelty) and reduces it. Thus, Ricoeur's semantics of metaphor consists of two complementary interpretations: (1) deviation: predicative impertinence, (2) reduction of deviation: new predicative pertinence (MV, 152/195, 155/198). Within a metaphor, there is both destruction (or even deconstruction, as Ricoeur says in *The Rule of Metaphor*'s "First Study" [MV, 22/32]) and reconstruction (INT, 50/146).

One of Ricoeur's favorite examples (borrowed from Marcus Hester) is Shakespeare's description of time as a beggar in *Troilus and Cressida* (INT, 51/147, 51n6; MV, 211/267). If we try to read or interpret this passage (abbreviated as "Time is a beggar") literally, then its meaning is absurd. If "beggar" means a person who makes a living by asking for charity, then time is not a beggar. The words "time" and "beggar" do not make sense together, even though the sentence is grammatically correct. The predicate "is a beggar" is compatible only with individuals belonging to the referential field of humans. "Time" normally belongs to the "category" of physical or inanimate objects. In the literal interpretation, "time is a beggar" appears as a clash between the "categories" (and the corresponding referential fields) of the inanimate and the human or animate. In the metaphorical interpretation, we create a new sense for the sentence based on the way the polysemy of the words "beggar" and "time" contextually interacts. Perhaps we recall the Christian significance of poverty and the Greek significance of the planetary movements. This allows the sentence to take on a new religious significance. The new sense allows the clash between the two categories to be reconciled or synthesized. The deviation is reduced and a new predicative pertinence saves the meaning of the sentence as a whole.

2

New predicative pertinence for Ricoeur makes the metaphor live; following Fontanier, Ricoeur calls live metaphor metaphor of invention and not catachresis (MV, 62–4/84–6). Because a live metaphor "invents" something (MV, 306/387–88), Ricoeur's "semantics" alone does not solve the mystery of the transition from a predicative impertinence to a new predicative pertinence (MV, 191–93/242–45).[29] A live metaphor results from "creative work," which Ricoeur calls mimesis (RM, 39/57).[30] Reinterpreted, mimesis for Ricoeur is not rule governed imitation; it is imagination (MV, 214/272). To solve the mystery of transition, of creation, of invention, Ricoeur appropriates Kantian productive imagination, the schematization of a synthetic operation, and, therefore, the mediation between the two opposed poles of sensibility and understanding.[31] Productive imagination is both a seeing or an experience *and* a thinking or an act. Ricoeur appropriates this notion because he wants to show that imagination is immanent or intrinsic, and not superficial, to the predicative process. Imagination, being at once experience and act, mediates between metaphor's verbal predication and its nonverbal or sensible image. According to Ricoeur, we arrive at a new predicative pertinence because we construct out of a metaphor's verbal impertinence an image through which we understand the metaphor's meaning. Imagination's mediating process proceeds in three steps (HHS, 233–42; MV, 173–215/221–72).[32]

First, there is "predicative assimilation" (or approximation), which emphasizes imagination's thinking or act character. When we read a metaphor, according to Ricoeur, we first seek a similarity or a proximity between the two clashing "categories" (and between their corresponding referential fields) of the words used. Predicative assimilation is not free association. It is not "a kind of mechanical attraction between mental atoms"; rather it is a "*making* similar." Similarity has to be made because it always runs counter to a previous categorization or code of pertinence. The code of pertinence dictates that "time is a beggar" expresses a contradiction. The "categories" of the animate and the inanimate (and their corresponding fields) are distant or remote. Thus, predicative assimilation restructures these "categories." Restructuring, however, does not eliminate the previous categorization, but rather holds it in tension with a new categorization. Thus, the type of similarity or resemblance produced in the first step consists of similarity *in spite of* contradiction, proximity *in* remoteness (HHS, 234; MV, 196/249).

The second step schematizes the new similarity into an image (which anticipates the identity of a concept). In other words, the emerging meaning based on the similarity is a formula for the construction of the image. "Time is a beggar," for Ricoeur, is a sort of imperative ("Imagine this!") which commands a reader to see time (the tenor) as a beggar (the vehicle). Upon this command the reader undergoes a variety of images. Some of these are wild or free, images which are arbitrary and which interrupt, divert or distort reading. One must allow oneself, however, according to Ricoeur, to be controlled by the similarity at the basis of the metaphor's emerging meaning. Guided by the emerging meaning the reader takes up the view points from which the tenor can be seen as the vehicle (MV, 212/269). Then the relevant aspects out of the variety of images can be actively selected and combined. This process, therefore, produces an image bound or tied to the emerging meaning.

The third step concerns what Ricoeur calls the moment of suspension or negativity which the image introduces into the referential field (MV, 239/301, 225/284).[33] For Ricoeur the image which arises from a metaphor is not a copy.[34] It is not a physical replica (like a passport photo), or a psychological replica of some absent thing (like a memory). Both types of replicas imply that the absent thing could be perceived elsewhere in its presence. Thus, the only difference between seeing an image-copy and perceiving the thing lies in their respective modes of givenness, absence and presence. This difference raises no specific question of the referent or original because presence and absence are the modes of givenness of the *same* reality. A copy simply refers to some sort of naturalistic (in Husserl's sense of the word) or positivistic object. The metaphorical image, however, is fictitious. A fictitious image has no model or already given original to which it could be referred. Even if we can refer the components from which it is constructed to corresponding things, we have not, according to Ricoeur, accounted for the new combination. The new combination has no referent or original of which it is a copy. Thus, according to Ricoeur, the original is not absent but unreal (or *irreal*). The original is a nothingness which is not reducible to the nothingness of absence. A fictitious image refers, therefore, to an unreality, not to a naturalistic object. It functions as a sort of imaginative *epoché* and questions our natural attitude about reality (Husserl) (MV, 209/266).

It still, however, refers. Ricoeur uses the word *icon* (*icône*) to stress that the fictitious image is bound to the emerging metaphorical meaning which redescribes reality, and to stress the similarity between the fictitious image and painting (MV, 209/265–66).[35] For Ricoeur, the fictitious image could be externalized in a material medium and, therefore, made public. Externalization implies that in the production of the icon, as in that of a painting, its referent or subject matter must be condensed and abridged in order to capture it in a limited space. Ricoeur points to the example of the fifteenth-century Flemish painters who enhanced contrasts and defined edges in opposition to ordinary vision which blurs edges and shades off contrasts. According to Ricoeur, however, these effects became possible only after the invention of oil paints which gave the Flemish painters an "optic alphabet." Then they could capture the universe in a web of abbreviated signs. Thus, for Ricoeur, by abbreviating to a finite set of discrete units, an increased power to generate new units by means of combination, or more precisely, synthesis, is achieved.[36]

In the fictitious image or icon this increased generative power transforms or reshapes naturalistic reality. Abbreviating and thereby stripping reality of contingency, an icon allows reality's essential features to present themselves. The unreality of the referent gives way to primordial reality. Always at this point Ricoeur appeals to Husserl's notion of the life-world or Heidegger's being-in-the-world (HHS, 118/60, 141/114, 192, 220/210; INT, 94; MV, 306/387–88); or like Kant, he says that imagination has the power of presenting an Idea (MV, 303/338).[37] Over and above the essential, the increased generative power also allows new features to present themselves. The new combination (or synthesis) of the metaphor's predicative structure induces an image in which the pertinent characteristics of the subject and predicate (that is, their categories) merge to disclose something new, something which we only dimly or unconsciously feel. The fictitious image is like a representative who not only pleads the case of the client as best as possible, but also brings to light features which the client himself never before recognized. "Time is a beggar" discloses not only the profoundly human reality of time, but also something entirely new which increases the reality of time. It is a sort of living image, a representative, in which reality does not become less but more. Ricoeur calls this ability to increase reality "iconic augmentation" (INT, 40).[38]

On the basis of this three step process a fictitious image, as Ricoeur says, "occurs" (*arrive*) (MV, 210/266). This event

> brings to concrete completion the metaphorical process. The meaning is then depicted under the feature of ellipsis. Through this depiction, the meaning is not only schematized but lets itself be read on the image in which it is inverted. Or..., the metaphorical sense is generated in the thickness of the imagining scene displayed by the verbal structure of the poem. Such is...the functioning of the intuitive grasp of the predicative connection.[39]

The image is the completion of the metaphorical process, a process at once predicative (or linguistic) and, therefore, bound to the whole context of the sentence, and imaginative, which itself is intrinsic to the predicative process. On the basis of the metaphorical process, and thus on the basis of the augmenting image, a metaphor's meaning is understood. For Ricoeur, this meaning has never occurred before. The new sense of the sentence's predicate has never existed before as a part of its polysemy or lexical code. It happens only in the present use of language, in *langage*, not in *langue*. The new sense is singular or unique. This is why Ricoeur can say that the paraphrase of metaphor is infinite. Quite simply, there is nothing else like it. The metaphorical event is an advent of meaning; it is a live metaphor (cf. HHS, 133).[40]

Metaphorical novelty, however, does not imply a lack of ideality. A metaphorical meaning, for Ricoeur, like the meaning of an ordinary sentence, is repeatable (HHS, 170). If "an influential part of the language community" adopts a metaphor, its meaning becomes "everyday" (HHS, 170). The previously novel, metaphorical meaning is now taken as a standard acceptation of a word. Hence, dead metaphoricity for Ricoeur is polysemy (INT, 52/148; HHS, 170). As we saw earlier, dead metaphoricity, for Ricoeur, is the basis for the conceptual work that constructs a system of categories. The similarity aimed at in the metaphorical process already anticipated this regulative univocity. The ideality of metaphorical novelty points to a horizon of identity.

3

As is well-known, the Ricoeurean symbol differs radically from live metaphor. Symbols according to Ricoeur are bound to life (*bios*) (INT, 59/153), to "primary experience (INT, 57/151); they possess a nonlinguistic element which cannot be reduced. Because of the symbol's irreducible connection to life, they "presents *gifts* to thought," as Ricoeur's well-known aphorism goes.[41] For Ricoeur, when we sleep and dream, when we experience religious ceremonies, when we view the cosmos, humans belong immediately, if only for a moment, to the infinite, to the total, to what Ricoeur calls the totally other.[42] By making contact with that which is totally other, the symbol for Ricoeur is actually the transgression of human finitude; it is completely unlike any mundane reality. By being totally other from the mundane, however, what the symbols presents cannot be conceived. The symbol, therefore, for Ricoeur possesses an inexhaustibility not rooted in human finitude.

The symbol transgresses the human limit; therefore, we cannot say that Ricoeurean inexhaustibility is equal to what Hegel would call the bad infinite; the sheer number of symbolic occurrences does not repeatedly throw us back into our finitude. Yet, conversely we cannot equate the Ricoeurean transgression with what Hegel would call the good infinite; being nonconceptual, the symbol remains finite, an experience. At best, we can say that Ricoeur occupies a quasi-Hegelian position in regard to the relation of the finite and infinite, a position moreover that he shares with Gadamer.[43] In the experiences of symbols, Ricoeur describes the finite transgression of finitude.[44] Our only response to such symbols can be faith, not knowledge or reflection, Ricoeur says.[45]

Symbols, therefore, unlike live metaphors, as Ricoeur explicitly says, "cannot be exhaustively treated by conceptual language,... there is more in symbols than in any of its conceptual equivalents" (INT, 57/151). As Ricoeur says, "Metaphor occurs in the already purified universe of the *logos*, while the symbol hesitates on the dividing line between *bios* and *logos*. It testifies to the primordial rootedness of Discourse in Life. It is born where force and form coincide" (INT 59/153). Although metaphors imaginatively unify sense and sensibility, sensibility is, so to speak, "sandwiched" between two moments of sense. The metaphorical image comes out of polysemy and results in a new meaning. The image lies between the two interpretations. In contrast, symbols, according to Ricoeur, function at the "crossroad" of sense and sensation. Indeed, the life from which they occur, according to Ricoeur, is the very principle of the symbol's "dissemination" (*dissémination*) (INT, 54/149) into dispersed and heterogeneous methods of investigation (INT, 57/151).

Despite the difference between live metaphors and symbols, Ricoeur speaks of "intermediary degrees between them." On the one hand, this means that one can extend Ricoeur's discussion of symbol to live metaphor. Certain persistent metaphors such as fire, water, sky, are as powerful as symbols (INT, 65/158). These living representative can present the totally other; within them humans can find the experience of the finite transgression of finitude. Metaphors such as these can be inexhaustible in the same way as symbols. They resist conceptualization more than other metaphors because life is the basis of their increase, their augmentation, their excess.

On the other hand, the intermediary degrees imply that one can extend Ricoeur's discussion of live metaphor to the symbol. Although the symbol is bound to life, it does not lead to something like obscurantism (cf. INT, 57/151).[46] Ricoeur's famous aphorism also says that "The symbol presents a gift *to thought*." Hermeneutics attempts to bring incoherent symbolic discourse into philosophical or speculative coherence.[47] Anticipating the "Eighth Study," Ricoeur says in *The Symbolism of Evil*, that "we are going to explore a third way—a creative interpretation of meaning, faithful to the impulsion to the gift of meaning from the symbol, and faithful also to the philosopher's oath to seek understanding."[48] In *Interpretation Theory*, Ricoeur says that, because metaphor marks the emergence of conceptual thinking without being conceptual thinking as such, it leads the theory of symbols

into the neighborhood of the Kantian theory of the schematism
and conceptual synthesis.... There is no need to deny the concept in order to admit that symbols give rise (*donne lieu*) to
endless exegesis. If no concept can exhaust the requirement of
"thinking more" borne by symbols, this idea signifies only that
no given categorization can embrace all the semantic possibilities of a symbol. But it is the work of the concept alone that can
testify to this surplus of meaning. (INT 57/151)

Thus, we must conclude that being like metaphorical distanciation,
indeed like dialectical mediation, symbolic dissemination for Ricoeur
maintains something like a regulative horizon of identity. It, too, passes
through the Kantian productive imagination.

The Historical Present

Defined by the phrase "the dialectic of event and meaning," distanciation focuses on the present. The present, we saw, is the instance at which discourse is uttered and understood. As a singular instance, it is divided from the past and the future. Involving repetition, however, this instance is not discrete. Connected to the past, productive imagination appropriates polysemy even as it singularizes itself and deviates. Anticipating the future, productive imagination produces a universal meaning whose openness is regulated by an idea of identity and univocity. Distanciation's present then extends into an infinite future and into an unrecoverable past. What is this Ricoeurean present of discourse? Or, to appropriate the "Eighth Study's" terminology, what is "the historicity of discourse" (cf. MV, 298/377–78)? In works such as *Interpretation Theory*, Ricoeur provides no theory of the historical present. In *Time and Narrative*, III, however, he sketches a theory of historical consciousness which culminates in the notion of the historical present. As we shall see now, the historical present recapitulates all of distanciation's characteristics: universality and singularity, continuity and discontinuity, productive imagination, a regulative idea, no absolute knowledge.

1

Ricoeur defines the historical present not as intuitive presence but as a combination of action and language which he calls initiative (or beginning) (TNIII, 230/332–33). Rejoining his earlier theory of discourse, Ricoeur states, "In a broad sense, every speech act (or every act of discourse) *commits* (*engagent*) the speaker and does so in the present" (TNIII, 232/335, my emphasis). When he speaks, a speaker then is engaged in action. As speech act theory has shown, words do things.

A promise, of course, exemplifies initiative for Ricoeur (TNIII, 233/336). By its lack of completeness, a promise commits or engages a speaker, myself, explicitly; it obliges me to do something (TNIII, 233/336). In order to fulfil this obligation, I must, according to Ricoeur, be aware of what I can do (my bodily abilities). I must be able to reason about how to carry out my promise. As either "calculations" or "practical syllogisms" (TNIII, 231/222), my reasoning must concern the systems and circumstances that surround me. As Ricoeur says, "By doing something,... agents learn to isolate a closed system from their environment and discover the possibilities of development inherent in this system" (TNIII, 232/334). Thus, when I start to fulfil my promise, I set the system's resources in motion, interfere in them, produce something, cause something to happen, have an effect which comes to completion only when the promise is fulfilled.

Described in terms of a promise, initiative, for Ricoeur then, mixes the two traditional and polar interpretations of the present, the present measured as a discrete point "broken off" from the past and future and the present lived as the thickness of the near past and the imminent future. Moreover, for Ricoeur, the initiation of a promise is not "solipsistic" but is based upon and establishes a "we-relation" (*être-en-commun*) (TNIII, 234–35/337–38). The historical present then is based upon what Ricoeur calls "public space," a basic agreement about speaking the truth. This basic agreement implies that all social contracts will be kept and all violations forgiven. Borrowing terminology from Nietzsche, Ricoeur says the historical present consists of forgetfulness and hope (TN, 240/346). The historical present, therefore, for Ricoeur is both "intervention" and "continuation," discontinuity and continuity, difference and identity, singularity and universality.

2

Simultaneous continuity and discontinuity can be seen most precisely within Ricoeur's notion of traditionality, the past aspect of the historical present (TNIII, 217/314).[49] According to Ricoeur, the past is something we suffer, undergo, or to which we are submitted. The correlate to "being affected by the past" is "effective history" (a phrase Ricoeur borrows from Gadamer). Effective history is the history that happens to us. It is exterior to us, different from us, temporally distant from us (TNIII, 220/318). Temporal distance, however, for Ricoeur, is not an unbridgeable gap, but a space of mediation, which turns affectivity into an active reception of the past. Thus, the "antinomy" between continuity and discontinuity turns into "the dialectic between distance (*éloignement*) and undistanciation (*dédistanciation*) (TNIII, 220/319, cf. 144/206).

Although traditionality, for Ricoeur, is a formalistic description of our relation to the past, this relation can also be described in terms of content. The addition of content transforms the dialectic of distance and undistance into one of question and answer, interpretation and reinterpretation. Abstract temporal distance is now construed as a heritage (TNIII, 221/320). This transformation of temporal distance is possible for Ricoeur because traditionality possesses a lingual (*langagière*) structure. Traditionality becomes traditions because many languages, many documents and monuments, many texts constitute it.

In this shift from traditionality to traditions Ricoeur explicitly recapitulates his theory of the text, in particular, the text's omnitemporality. Traditions are constituted by traces (TNIII, 222/321, 124/182). Borrowed from Levinas (and bearing similarities to the Derridean trace [cf. TNIII, 29n12/46n1]), the Ricoeurean trace is a vestige of the past that remains. Drawing upon the play within the word *passer*, Ricoeur characterizes the trace as a passage. While the passage is dynamic (passing through, passing away, passing on, the past), it is "written" on a durable support, which Ricoeur calls the mark, the trace's static aspect. The dynamic-static mix implies "paradoxically," as Ricoeur says, that the trace signifies the past without presenting it.

There are two obvious responses to the trace's paradox of identity and difference, according to Ricoeur. We can respect the past's difference, the absence signified by the trace; we can even emphasize its lack of coincidence with the present. Or, we can reenact the past and identify the present with it; we can traverse the distance. Ricoeur, of course, suggests a dialectical response which combines identity and difference. Here he draws explicitly upon his metaphor theory.

As Ricoeur stresses, when an interpreter of a trace (a historian) constructs a narrative, this narrative *corresponds* to what really happened (TNIII, 151/219). As Ricoeur says, "The work of the historian thus consists in making narrative structure into a 'model,' an 'icon' of the past, capable of 'representing' it" (TN, 152/220). Ricoeur's use of *icon* here indicates that the narrative is something more than the original; the icon is, we recall, a living representative. Because of iconic augmentation, the historian's narrative could not be a scale model or exact duplicate. Moreover, the original events are gone. The narrative is more than the past events and yet bears a resemblance or similarity to them. It is an "image" which is the same as the original despite difference. The correspondence, therefore, is a "metaphorical relation," essentially tropological. As Ricoeur says,

> In sum, the theory of tropes, through its deliberately linguistic character, may be integrated into the table of modes of historical imagination without thereby being integrated into its properly explanatory modes. In this sense, it constitutes the deep structure of the historical imagination. (TNIII, 153/222)

For Ricoeur, Kantian productive imagination mediates every relation to what is different or distant and is the bases for everything which can be different or is distanciable; it always points to identity.

Thus, unlike the theory of tropes concerned with understanding the past, historical imagination's "properly explanatory mode" concerns, for Ricoeur, the legitimacy of traditions' contents. Because traditionality possesses a "lingual" structure, imagination can produce diverse tropological correspondences. For Ricoeur however, all tradition's diverse contents and interpretations—the "rival traditions to which we belong in a pluralistic society and culture" (TNIII, 224/324)—make a claim to truth. Yet, as Horkheimer and Adorno have shown, interests animate traditions' statements (TNIII, 225/326–27).[50] An interest such as domination even distorts and dissimulates itself in its very expression. Thus, the interpreter or the historian must decipher and evaluate traditions' contents: Are these statement true and objective? The answer to this question elevates traditions to tradition.

Again following Gadamer, Ricoeur first rejects methodologism as a way of describing the specific mode of interpretative explanation (TNIII, 223–24/324–25; cf. INT, 71–88). Methodologism attempts to dominate and master the text or trace, to turn it into a manipulatable tool. Instead, Ricoeur speaks of a critical moment characterized as historical research or, of course, as distanciation, the ability to recognize the temporal distance that the trace has traversed, the temporal distance that implies objectivity. Temporal distance for Ricoeur as for Gadamer, "filters" traditions; what remains seems to be true.[51] The authority of tradition is based in these persistent statements. For Ricoeur, however, unlike Gadamer, the question of why certain contents persist demands an answer.[52] By means of what criteria can we judge a prejudice based in traditional authority; what nonideological tribunal can distinguish ideology from truth? As Ricoeur says,

> This tribunal has to consist in the self-positing of an ahistorical transcendental, whose schematism, in the Kantian sense of the term, would be the representation of an unfettered and unlimited communication, hence of a speech situation characterized by a consensus arising out of the very process of argumentation. (TNIII, 226/327)

Ricoeur's explanatory mode, therefore, recapitulates his theory of discourse. The ahistorical transcendental is the very intention we saw animating the dialogical situation described in the dialectic of event and meaning: the undistorted transfer of a univocal meaning from one to another. In fact, in *Time and Narrative*, III, Ricoeur states that "the transcendence of the idea of truth, inasmuch as it is immediately a dialogical idea, has to be seen as already at work in the practice of communication" (226/328). As in the theory of discourse, here in the question of our relation to the past, this idea functions for Ricoeur, on the one hand, as a "negative limit idea" excluding cases of distorted messages (equivocity), and, on the other, as a "regulative idea" directing the conversation between the present and the past towards agreement (univocity) (TNIII, 226/328).[53]

3

The movement from abstract traditionality to concrete but diverse traditions to the unified tradition illuminates for Ricoeur only the historical present's past aspect. Initiative bases itself upon the dialectic of distance and undistance; a promise arises in a context we did not make but understand. Initiative, for Ricoeur, however, also begins to do something; the promise will fulfill itself. The present then advances towards a future. The addition of the futural aspect to the interpretation of the past shows us, according to Ricoeur, that the present dialectically combines "the space of experience" and the "horizon of expectation."[54]

According to Ricoeur, the phrase, "space of experience," aptly describes our past-relation because, on the one hand, experience refers to the undergoing of something implied by the German *Erfahrung* (TNIII, 208/302). Thus, it captures our being affected by the past. On the other, "the space of experience" is apt, according to Ricoeur, because "space" expresses the past as a place with different possible traversals and levels. Thus, it captures the diversity of traditions. For Ricoeur, however, experience is the key to our past-relation. Through experience we form habits which are the "integration" and "gathering together" into myself of what is alien and diverse (TNIII, 208–09/302).

"Horizon of expectation" aptly describes our future-relation, according to Ricoeur, because " 'expectation' is broad enough to include hope and fear, what is wished for and what is chosen, rational calculation, curiosity" (TNIII, 208/302). Like our being affected by the past *in the present*, expectation is the future *in the present*; it refers to the present as the "not yet." Ricoeur, of course, contrasts the phenomenological concept of horizon with situation. Where a situation suggests a limited perspective, horizon expresses that the perspective has been surpassed (TNIII, 208–09/302, 220/319).

Thus, the horizon of expectation, for Ricoeur, is the space of experience's polar opposite. Where "space of experience" suggests integration and gathering together, the "horizon of expectation" suggests an unfolding and a breaking open (TNIII, 209/302). Because the horizon of expectation is always surpassing itself, for Ricoeur the space of experience never determines it completely; we have expectations for what never happened in the past. Yet, and conversely, Ricoeur says that "there is no surprise so wonderful (*divine surprise*) for which the baggage of experience is too light; it could not know how to desire (*souhaiter*) anything else" (TNIII, 209/302). Thus, the horizon of expectation and the space of experience for Ricoeur mutually condition each other. They form a dialectic in which the horizon of expectation consists in the hope (or fear) of a surprise that unfolds a habit beyond itself; when the surprise happens, it is happily integrated into its proper location and level in the space of experience.

Like traditionality, the space of experience and the horizon of expectation are, as Ricoeur says, "metahistorical categories" (TNIII, 214/309). Nevertheless, as promising implies, they have ethical and political implications; they are prescriptive as well as descriptive. In general they prescribe, according to Ricoeur, that "the tension between space of experience and the horizon of expectation must be preserved..." (TNIII, 215/311). If the space of experience becomes a rejection of the past in favor of the future, and if the horizon of expectation becomes a utopia without past precedent, then the tension between these two poles becomes according to Ricoeur a schism.[55] History becomes distance without distanciation, universality without singularizations or singularities without universalization. In short, history becomes undialectical.

Ricoeur specifies this general prescription in terms of two imperatives. First, utopian expectations cannot become entirely abstract. If they are to be attainable, they must maintain their link to experience. Without the experiential link, utopias, as Ricoeur says, "make us despair of all action" (TNIII, 215). While Ricoeur does not identify the experientially based utopia with the state of right (*droit*) first envisioned by Kant, he does not deny the relevance of Kant's kingdom of ends for it (TNIII, 216/312–13). There is still a regulative idea of peace, concord, consensus, the regulative idea mentioned earlier. Second, we must keep the space of experience from narrowing. For Ricoeur, the past is not done and over with; it is open to ever new revitalizations. Historical events can and must be imaginatively construed otherwise; polysemy can and must be imaginatively reused; texts can and must be imaginatively reinterpreted.

The tension between these two imperatives implies, on the one hand, that our attempt to realize a utopia directs our revitalizations of the past. By means of future expectations, we may open up "forgotten possibilities, aborted potentialities, repressed endeavors in the supposedly closed past" (TNIII, 227/329). On the other, as Ricoeur says, "…the potential of meaning thereby freed from the solid mass of traditions may contribute to determining the regulative but empty idea of an unhindered and unlimited communication" (TNIII, 227/329). In other words, the past may help us understand what intermediary steps must be taken to fulfill the utopic vision. Thus, the first imperative helps the second for Ricoeur and the reverse.

Taken together, Ricoeur's metahistorical categories describe not a Hegelian historical totality but prescribe an "incomplete mediation." History for Ricoeur does not summarize itself "in a mode of thought that would encircle (*embrasserait*) past, present and future as a whole" (TNIII, 193/280); its image is not that of a closed circle but that of "an endless spiral" (*une spirale sans fin*).[56] There is always more to be thought. By resisting what he calls the "Hegelian temptation," Ricoeur recapitulates the victory of misunderstanding and the failure of textual absolute knowledge.[57] Rather than an eternal present capturing all of history in lucid concepts, the dialectic between the space of experience and the horizon of expectation prescribes (for the historian, for the reader, for the individual and communal agent) totalization. Totality becomes for Ricoeur an idea, an infinite task, for distanciation.[58] This task is the imaginative elevation of the universal from the singular and appropriation of the universal to the singular, an elevation and appropriation regulated and limited by ahistorical truth and identity, even univocity.

This task remains incomplete, for Ricoeur, because of the efficacity of the past (TN, 228/330). He admits that "the effort of a constituting consciousness [attempting] to master the relation of the known past to the actual past" lies in the background of his dialectic of distance and undistancing (TNIII, 228/330). No matter how well, however, one can imaginatively reconstruct the past, the narrative one writes is not the past. The past is always exterior because I have not made it. All constituting consciousness for Ricoeur first of all *belongs* (*appartient*) to the past by being affected by it (TNIII, 227/329). While the past always eludes our attempts to appropriate it, the future, according to Ricoeur, also escapes our attempts to control it. When I initiate an action, even an action as common as an utterance, I can never be sure of its consequences. Unforeseeable effects stem from our best conceived plans (TNIII, 213/308). Combining the past and future limits, Ricoeur says,

> Above all, the vulnerability of the theme of mastering history is revealed...on the level where it is called for, the level of humanity taken as the sole agent of its own history. In conferring on humanity the power to produce itself, the authors of this claim forget one constraint that affects the destiny of great historical bodies as much as it affects individuals—in addition to the unintended results that action brings about, such action only takes place in circumstances it has not produced. (TNIII, 213/308–09)

In relation to history, to language, to itself, constituting consciousness, for Ricoeur, is finite. Finitude is an irreducible characteristic of Ricoeurean distanciation, a characteristic that cannot be stressed enough.[59]

Ricoeur's Interpretation of Husserlian Temporalization

Finitude for Ricoeur, however, is not a rigid limit. Because distanciation is defined by productive imagination, human experience can always transcend the limit. Imagination's interplay between the finite and the infinite leads to distanciation's dialectical mixture. In the "Eighth Study," we saw this mixture as the intersection of speculative and metaphorical (or poetical) discourse. On the one hand, distanciation as elevation produces universality or identity or continuity, in a word, meaning; on the other, as appropriation, it produces singularity or difference or discontinuity, in a word, an event. While mixture suggests indeterminacy, Ricoeurean distanciation is regulated by an idea. Whenever imagination produces discontinuity, there should be continuity; whenever it produces singularity, there should be universality; whenever it produces difference, there should be identity; wherever there is mediation, it aims at immediacy; whenever the present becomes distant as the past, the present should be once more. Thus, for Ricoeur the notion of an Idea in the Kantian sense prioritizes the present, immediacy, continuity, identity, and universality. Even the radical discontinuity that Ricoeur claims for speculative discourse is based in the continuity of meaning that underlies metaphorical transformation. We cannot forget that Ricoeur says, quoting Derrida, that "No philosophical discourse would be possible...if we ceased to assume...'the sole thesis of philosophy,' namely, 'that the meaning aimed at through these figures is an essence rigorously independent of that which carries it over'" (MV, 293/372).

We can see Ricoeur's prioritization clearly in his reading of Husserlian temporalization in *Time and Narrative* III. Ricoeur's reading of Husserl discovers that immediacy and continuity precede spatial separation and discontinuity. Mediation or distanciation, traces or absence, derive for Ricoeur from immediacy and should return to it. Immediacy, as we shall see, supports all of Ricoeur's theories; mediation for Ricoeur is a "third." Thus, by briefly examining Ricoeur's interpretation of Husserlian temporalization, we shall be able to crystallize the difference between Ricoeur and Derrida. As we know already from our reading of "White Mythology," for Derrida, mediation, space, discontinuity, and traces are prior to immediacy, time, continuity, and perception. In contrast to Ricoeur, mediation for Derrida is a "fourth."

1

As is well-known, Ricoeur's entire enterprise in all three volumes of *Time and Narrative* is to reconcile, by means of narration, the subjective experience of time with objective or cosmological time. Husserl is for him a philosopher of subjective time. Ricoeur aims his criticisms at Husserl's failure to reconcile his subjective descriptions with irreversible temporal succession, at his failure to return out of the reduction to objective time. In short, Husserl does not, and seems unable to show, how the structure of the living present matches up with causality. Thus, Ricoeur uses Kant as a counterbalance to Husserl. This sort of criticism, however, implies that Ricoeur affirms Husserl's discovery of the subjective flow of time. Like Augustine, Husserl shows us, according to Ricoeur, that the present is not an instant or mere point (TNIII, 23/37).

Husserl's problem in the *Phenomenology of Inner-Time Consciousness* lies in duration. How does a temporal object such as a sound endure; how does the present as lived come about? Husserl's solution to this problem, according to Ricoeur, is the notion of retention (TNIII, 27/44). Retention, for Husserl, is the past intentional phase of an immanent object, a phase always compounded with the primal impression or now point and protention or anticipation. Retention "thickens" the now point into a present; it permits the object to remain or to be there *still*. Retention is Husserl's great discovery (cf. TNIII, 26/43), and the issue for Ricoeur (as for Derrida) is to determine its relation to primal impression or immediate presence.

Following Husserl's stated intentions, Ricoeur asserts that this relation is one of modification (TNIII, 29–31/48–50). The notion of modification implies, as Ricoeur says, that difference does not lie between the primal impression and retention but between the recent past and the past properly speaking. As Ricoeur says,

> it can be asserted that the present and recent past mutually belong to each other (*s'appartiennent mutuellement*), and that retention is an enlarged present that ensures not only the continuity of time but the progressively attenuated diffusion of the intuitive character of the source point to all that the present instant retains in itself or under itself.... Beginning is beginning to continue (TN, 30/48)

The notion of retention as a modification of presence implies that presence's originary character extends to the recent past, that difference, alterity, and negativity are no longer primary (TN, 30–1/50). Imagination and recollection, traces and signs are for Ricoeur entirely derivative. For Ricoeur, there is no space between retention and the primal impression, but rather a "continuous passage" from primal impression to retention (TNIII, 33/53). There is only space (distance) between retention and recollection. Indeed, Ricoeur criticizes Derrida for overlooking in *Speech and Phenomena* this exact difference between retention as modification of presence and recollection or imagination as absence and discontinuity. As Ricoeur says,

> To preserve [Husserl's] discovery, we must not place on the same, under the common heading "otherness," the nonperception characteristic of recollection and the nonperception ascribed to retention, under the threat of cancelling out the essential phenomenological difference between retention, which is constituted in continuity with perception, and recollection which alone is, in the strong sense of the word, a nonperception. (TNIII, 29n12/46n1)

Mediation, for Ricoeur, functions, therefore, in its most traditional position, as a middle arising out of a simple origin and directing itself towards a simple end or purpose; to place mediation anywhere else according to Ricoeur "remains a pious wish."[60] Immediacy supports the entire Ricoeurean edifice. We can see this in two ways.

On the one hand, because Ricoeur himself suggests that an almost perfect symmetry exists between Husserlian temporalization and his own theory of historical consciousness (cf. TNIII, 32/52–3), immediacy supports Ricoeur's historical present, which itself supports his entire theory of discourse. In Ricoeur's interpretation of Husserlian secondary memory or recollection, we can see for instance the seeds of Ricoeur's discussions of traditionality and of the trace. Ricoeur stresses that recollection's intentional mode is that of the "as if"; the past is remembered as if it is present. The "as if" implies not only that recollection and imagination are similar activities; they differ according to Ricoeur only by means of the thetic or nonthetic character of the mode of presentation (TN, 35/56). The "as if," however, also implies that recollection differs from retention. Between retention and recollection there is distance, distance between what was and what is being recalled; recollection is the representation of something that was. Thus, in recollection there is the mediation of a replica (TN, 35/56). Retention is production; recollection is re-production.

The difference of intentional presentation (the "re-" or "*wieder-*" of recollection), however, does not mean that the recollection is *radically* different from retention. As Ricoeur notes, Husserl calls both recollection and retention modifications (TN, 37–8/59). As it passes from primal impression to retention to forgetfulness and then to its recollection, the experienced content remains the same. Like all dialectical phenomena, inner-time consciousness and recollection, in Ricoeur's interpretation, function by means of the continuity of content. The content can always be made present "once again," as Ricoeur says (TN, 33/54). On the basis of this "once again," then, a coincidence is possible between the past and the present. An object can be identified (TNIII, 34/55); in other words, distance is overcome, "undistanced."

On the other hand, we can see how Ricoeur's interpretation of Husserlian temporalization supports his theory of mimesis developed in *Time and Narrative*, volume I, even though his theory of mimesis seems to imply primordial mediation or discontinuity. Ricoeur's theory of mimesis attempts to reconstrue the traditional hermeneutical circle of self-understanding. For Ricoeur, the circle consists in a triple mimesis: a primary mimesis (mimesis$_1$) within experience (which is irreducibly temporal), a secondary mimesis (mimesis$_2$) which configures, distances, or narrates temporal experience, and a third mimesis (mimesis$_3$) which refigures or renarrates temporal experience. In *Time and Narrative I* Ricoeur entertains a possible objection to this formulation of the relation of narrative to temporal experience. This objection, according to Ricoeur, would say that narrative puts consonance where there is only dissonance, that mimesis$_2$ does violence to temporal experience.[61] Ricoeur counters by saying

> our experience of temporality cannot be reduced to simple discordance. As we saw with Augustine, *distentio* and *intentio* mutually confront each other at the heart of our most authentic experience. We must preserve the paradox of time from the leveling out brought about by reducing it to simple discordance.[62]

To this we must add that when Ricoeur recognizes the filial relation between Augustine and Husserl, he stresses in volume III that "...we can see in the phenomenology of retention and in that of primary and secondary memory a subtle form of the threefold present and of that of *intentio/distentio animi*, and even the phenomenological resolution of certain paradoxes in the Augustinian analysis" (TNIII, 57–8/87–8). Thus, we must say that the Husserlian resolution in terms of immediacy supports Ricoeur's theory of mimesis. To say this again, as we move to Derrida—indeed as we move not only to Derrida's reading of Husserl, but also to his theory of mimesis (in his reading of Mallarmé)—immediacy supports the entire Ricoeurean edifice.

PART III

Derrida's Notion of *Différance*

8 ◆
The Primordial Unity of Essence
and Fact: A Reading of Derrida's
Introduction to Husserl's The Origin of Geometry

Derrida's thought consists in a critique of the philosophic desire for mastery, the desire to reduce absence, difference, and alterity down to mere negative modes of presence, identity, and sameness.[1] Derrida's critique, however, does not oppose philosophy (or metaphysics) from the outside (from another region like rhetoric); it works from inside. As we saw in our reading of "White Mythology," Derrida opposes Aristotle's hierarchization of the proper and the metaphorical by stressing incongruities within the Aristotelian corpus. When the solar examples disclose the priority of metaphor over propriety, Derrida "detours" the metaphorical away from the analogical to the homonymic (or catachretic). Derrida's turn, however, does not merely refer metaphor to a linguisticality more fundamental than meaning; metaphorization designates the very movement that produces presence, identity, and sameness in the first place. Derrida's thought, therefore, turns philosophy into an unqualified affirmation of this totally other metaphorization, *différance*.

Consisting most simply of genesis and structure (or of force and form), *différance* is mediation;[2] it is the ability to repeat factual and singular differences as an essential and universal sameness.[3] To borrow the almost classical definition from the "Différance" essay, it is the ability to let past and future moments be absent—temporalize—and simultaneously to make these absences coexist in the present—spatialize (MAR, 8–9/8–9). It is passive activity: passive because it is conditioned by given moments or differences that disappear, active because it synthesizes or repeats something that remains. *Différance*, however, differs from the dialectical notion of mediation because it is irreducibly inadequate to itself.[4] (As we have seen, supplementarity and *différance* over-

91

lap.[5]) *Différance* produces a structure infinitely iterable beyond my finite existence. Because the structure exceeds my force, it is always just outside my reach. Between the iterable form and the content, there is an interval that cannot be closed. The grasping of it, then, must be deferred to another person; the structure must be externalized.

When iterable structures are made intersubjective or public, *différance* becomes the basis of history and tradition for Derrida.[6] It becomes the sending and receivings of structures (most basically linguistic structures). This circulation consists, on the one hand for Derrida, of purposive use. History consists of communication and imaginative creation. On the other hand, circulation consists of what Derrida calls the aleatory.[7] Accidents can befall a structure in circulation. Although catastrophes come from outside the structures, they are for Derrida essentially connected to them because of the structures' iterability.[8] When misfortune strikes, the structure deviates in an unintended and unimaginative way. This unfortunate abuse is a difference, according to Derrida, totally unexpected; it is beyond conceptualization. Involving such essential accidents, tradition or history, therefore, for Derrida cannot be conceived as a straight line or as a circle; it can be conceived only as a zigzag.

While Derrida's notion of *différance* has diverse traditional sources, Heidegger's influence is unquestionable and well-known.[9] Just on the basis of *Being and Time*, we can see this in three ways. First, Derridean *différance* springs out of an interpretation of temporalization; Heidegger in *Being and Time* defined Dasein's being as time. Second, as Derrida points out frequently, *différance* bears affinities with Heidegger's ontological difference. Being, like *différance*, is a middle or mediation; Dasein exists (being) "between" subject (a being) and object (a being). Lastly and most importantly, Derridean *différance* is defined as the primordial unity of essence and fact. Heidegger described Dasein's being in just this way in *Being and Time*.

Heidegger's influence can even be seen as early as Derrida's 1962 *Introduction to Husserl's* The Origin of Geometry.[10] According to Derrida's *Introduction*, Husserl, without perhaps realizing it himself, shows in *The Origin of Geometry* that difference, contingency, equivocity, singularity, and fact (*fait*) are inseparably interwoven with identity, necessity, univocity, universality, and essence (or *droit*). This unity is implied by Husserl's description of the structure of history, historicity, which is itself dependent upon the structure of time, the living present. For Derrida, as we shall see, both historicity and temporalization are defined as "passage," a sending, of an object or a sense from *arche* or origin to *telos* or end. Within this passage, according to Derrida, there is "the absolute of a danger." It is this dangerous notion of temporalization that Derrida first calls *différance*.[11] Thus, we must read Derrida's *Introduction to Husserl's* The Origin of Geometry.[12]

———
1
———

Derrida stresses that the singularity of *The Origin of Geometry* among Husserl's writings lies in the fact that Husserl's "two denunciations of historicism and objectivism [have never] been so organically united" (INF, 26/4). In a unique way, *The Origin of Geometry* unifies critiques of geneticism and of structuralism.[13] The extraordinary organic unity of these two critiques leads to Derrida's insight that Husserl has two organically united projects in *The Origin of Geometry*. On the one hand, Husserl engages in a new type of historical reflection aiming at reactivating the original acts that produced geometry; Husserl attempts to "question back" (*rückfragen*) to the subjective genesis of geometrical knowledge. On the other hand, he attempts to describe historicity or traditionality, the condition for the possibility of reactivation; Husserl tries to describe the structure of history or tradition. As Derrida's *Introduction* brings to light then, Husserl's enacts in *The Origin of Geometry* a zigzag movement (*mouvement en vrille,* Derrida says, literally, a tendrillic movement), a zigzag between the genetic and the structural project, between the specificity of the geometrical science as a cultural product and culture in general, between a posteriori and a priori, between finally origin and end (INF, 33/14).

By comparison to Kant, Derrida shows how "hazardous" Husserl's *genetic* project is (INF, 38–46/20–30). In the Preface to *The Critique of Pure Reason*'s second edition, Kant says that geometry arises as a historical event. The Kantian historical event, however, is only revelation (and not creation). The birth of geometry, for Kant, is only an "*extrinsic* circumstance for the emergence of truth (which is itself always already constituted for any factual consciousness)" (INF, 41/24). Kant's thought seems to be a barely altered Platonism, which implies "a world of ideal constituted objects." Thus, for Kant according to Derrida, geometrical science only apparently evolves; history remains merely external to sense (INF, 41n30/24n2).

In contrast, for Husserl, the origin of geometry happened for a "first time" (INF, 47/31). Even though, as Derrida stresses, this act includes a strata of receptive intuition, it is still a production (*Leistung*) (INF, 40/22).[14] Even though, for Husserl, geometrical ideal objectivities such as triangularity must arise out of non- or pre-geometrical objectivities, they did not exist as such before this "experience." This experience is not equal to a becoming conscious of something already implicitly possessed. The first time for Husserl, therefore, is an inaugural and institutive act. As Derrida notes, in comparison to Kant, Husserl's "freedom with respect to empirical knowledge is more difficult to justify at first sight" (INF, 42/25).

As nonrevelatory, geometry's original experience cannot not be a "total fact." It must bear the characteristics of singularity or oneness (*unicité,* as Derrida says), irreversibility, and irreplaceability (INF, 30/8, 47/31; cf. INF, 47n39/31n1); a creation happens only once. As Derrida points out, however, and this is how Husserl avoids providing empirical descriptions, this nonrepeatable fact must have in principle (*en droit*) conducted into history what can be willfully and indefinitely repeated, an "essence-of-the-first time" (*Erstmaligkeit*) (INF, 46–8/30–2). Husserl describes this type of essence, according to Derrida, in *Ideas I* as ultimate material essences or eidetic singularities.[15] Such essences exclude empirical individuality, the *tode ti* of brute existence, while including the individuality in general of a particular thing; they refer to "the sense of the fact," the repeatability of the nonrepeatable (INF, 48/33).[16] The essence-of-the-first time, therefore, consists in the exemplarity of the factual example. By creating in a singular historical event this very specific type of universal essence, "this experience," Derrida says, "remains, de jure as well as de facto (*en droit comme en fait*), first" (INF, 46/29).

From this initial description of the specific type of origin he seeks Husserl zigzags, Derrida shows, to his structural project. Thanks to the production of this very specific type of universal essence, geometry according to Husserl exists for everyone. Geometry's essence has been delivered; this delivery in turn makes a return inquiry possible. *Rückfrage*, like Derrida's translation of it, *question en retour*, has a postal resonance (INF, 50/36). Geometry's essence, as Derrida stresses, makes a reference back (*renvoi*) to its first sending (its *premier envoi*), to its first time (INF, 50/36). Thus, tradition is like a postal service. By reading the letter sent through the mail we should be able to determine who the sender is.[17]

What is the essence of geometry according to Husserl? Derrida tells us that Husserl in *The Origin* applies an eidetic reduction to "ready made geometry," to the factual geometry in circulation and delivered over to us. This reduction separates geometry's ideal sense from historical contingency and opacity. The reduction discloses geometry's sense (or *noema*) as a unity "infinitely open to *its own* revolutions" (INF, 52/38, Derrida's emphasis). In order to be essential or a priori, this unity must be able to account for every possible future development in geometry and mathematics. No historical stage of geometry should be able to limit it. As Derrida points out, even Goedel's discovery of undecidable propositions should not be able to alter the unity of this sense (INF, 53–5/38–42). Geometry's sense, therefore, is nothing but the pure openness of an infinite horizon; it is the unity, as Derrida says, of a tradition (INF, 52/38).

Having described the conditions for the possibility of his specific *Rückfrage*, Husserl zigzags again, according to Derrida. He now tries to describe the origin of geometry, its specific *Erstmaligkeit*. What Husserl provides, however, are only the formal or general conditions for the constitution of an object: "grasping an existent in the consciousness of its original being-itself-there" (INF, 62/51). In other words, the origin of geometry must be based in making the object immediately present before me. As Derrida points out, Husserl's description "recalls the 'principle of all principles' defined in *Ideas I*." This type of immediate, intuitive presence is the source of all authority and evidence for Husserl.

Thus, according to Derrida's *Introduction*, Husserl first zigzags from his genetic project, a description of the type of origin he seeks, to the conditions for the possibility of his specific "questioning back," to his structural project. Then he performs the specific questioning back, but the origin discovered turns out be merely formal or general. Now Husserl, according to Derrida, zigzags back to his structural project. Derrida calls this zigzag a detour and a surprising turnabout (INF, 62/51, 76/69). Husserl attempts to describe the conditions for the possibility of questioning back *in general*; he describes the structure of tradition, tradition's "ether" (INF, 49/34), the postal system. In other words, he attempts now to answer the question of "[how]…subjective egological evidence of sense become objective and intersubjective," becomes for everyone at all times (INF, 63/52).

2

Husserl's answer to this question is: language or "literature in the broadest sense" (INF, 66/56–7). Husserl's answer may appear surprising because, according to the terminology of *Experience and Judgment* (INF, 72/63),[18] geometrical objects are entirely free idealities, while language is bound. Although linguistic units possess a degree of ideality—their phonetic and graphic forms and their intentional content are repeatable (INF, 67/58)—they cannot be understood without referring to facto-historical linguistic systems and to real sensible things in this world (INF, 70/62). A geometrical object, however, such as circularity (as Plato knew) is intelligible, entirely noetic and, thus, not bound to the real and contingent world. Geometrical propositions then, like the Pythagorean theorem, can be translated an infinite number of times; they are supra- or a-temporal and supra- or a-spatial. Geometrical ideality seems to lie beyond all language and sense content as such (INF, 75/68).

Husserl's reliance on language as the essential condition for absolute objectivity should not, however, surprise anyone according to Derrida (INF, 79/73). From the *Logical Investigations* on, Husserl always insists that ideal objectivity must be communicated to others in order to be constituted as such. Without language, geometrical idealities would remain imprisoned in the inventor's head, in his psychological subjectivity (INF, 77/70).[19] While oral communication frees ideal objectivity for the protogeometer's institutive community, ideal objectivity does not become "for everyone" until someone writes it down (INF, 87/84). This is the "decisive step," Derrida says, through which alone ideal objectivity achieves its complete constitution, its "indefinite perdurability" (INF, 87/83–4).

The *Introduction's* entire seventh section is devoted to describing the "ambiguous value" of writing's virtual communication. "The graphic possibility," as he says, is ambiguous because it possesses "…an original spatiotemporality that escapes the alternative of the sensible and the intelligible, or the empirical and the metempirical" (INF, 90/88). When someone inscribes a geometrical truth, its absolutely free ideality penetrates into less and less free ideality. It finally resides in a real event composed of "vague morphological types" like letters and sensible matter such as ink and paper; it resides, as Derrida stresses, in a book (INF, 90–1/88–90, 89n92/86n3). The inscriptive event consists of an incessant synthesis that not only binds the ideality of sense to a factual sign, but also, however, frees the sign from its nonrepeatable character. Other books can be made; its *morphe* can be reproduced (INF, 90n93/88n1). Writing not only "localizes and temporalizes" ideal objectivity, but also "unlocalizes and untemporalizes" it (INF, 89/86). As a necessary condition for knowledge and truth, writing, therefore, primordially interweaves essence (or *droit*) and fact (*fait*) (INF, 92/90; cf. 46/31). This primordial unity of essence and fact implies that writing is, according to Derrida, simultaneously the condition for the possibility and impossibility of knowledge and truth. It is simultaneously the possibility for discontinuity and continuity, loss and gain, forgetfulness and recollection. As Derrida says, writing is dangerous—dangerous in two ways (INF, 92/91).[20]

The first corresponds to writing's factual or sensible side. Because "first sense *must be able* to be recorded in the world and be deposited in sensible spatiotemporality" (INF, 92/91), it seems that sense is subject to "a universal conflagration, a worldwide burning of libraries, or a catastrophe of monuments or 'documents'," all of which are part of what Derrida calls "the terrifying foreseeable risk (*risque*)" (INF, 92–7/91–7). If we look at *Ideas I*, we see, however, that for Husserl such a possibility has nothing to do with ideal meaning; to associate the possibility of factual destruction with meaning (which must by definition transcends every fact) is nothing less than a confusion of ontological regions. According to the analyses of *Ideas I*, writing should be nothing more than a *Körper*, a constituted, factual, sensible body. Derrida points out, however, that in *The Origin of Geometry* Husserl calls writing a *Leib*, a lived or constituting body. Thus, Husserl himself in *The Origin* associates essence and fact. It's hard to understand, as Derrida, therefore, suggests, how truth could escape the possibility of factual destruction and forgetfulness (INF, 97/97–8). Death would seem to be transcendental, irreducibly connected to the indefinite perdurability of sense, to the very completion of its constitution, to life (cf. INF, 88/85).

The second danger lies in writing's ideality. For Husserl, according to Derrida, the real danger of inscription lies in passivity. The reader's first awareness of the meaning of printed words is associative; he arbitrarily follows threads of equivocations. Such associations for Husserl are irresponsible. The reader must be active (not passive) in his reading. However, the reader's associations are possible according to Husserl only because the writer has left surfaces upon which sedimentations have been able to be deposited (INF, 100/101). In other words, equivocations can be followed only when they have been sewn into the text (INF, 100/101). For Husserl, as Derrida points out, "Responsibility for reactivation is co-responsibility" of the author and reader (INF, 100/101). Forgetfulness is, therefore, for Husserl merely a modification of consciousness, "a lapse more than a defeat" (INF, 98/98). By imposing an imperative of univocity on readers and writers (INF, 100/101), Husserl believes the entanglement of *Leib* and *Körper* should be able to be overcome.

According to Derrida, Husserl's devotion to the reduction of equivocity can be seen as both a refusal of history and a deep fidelity to history. "On the one hand," univocity seems to take meaning or truth out of history's reach. Univocity involves no virtual or potential meanings; it has mastered the dynamic of sense. Univocal language, therefore, remains the same; it is an ahistorical structure or essence. Yet, "on the other hand," as Derrida points out, univocity guarantees the exactitude of translation; thus, it is the condition for the possibility of communication, historical transmission, and reactivation. As Derrida says, "Univocity only indicates the limpidity of the historical ether" (INF, 102/104). Husserl's imperative of univocity can be seen then as only a reduction of empirical and factual language towards historicity.

Derrida recognizes however—and we've seen this already in "White Mythology"—that the structure *of* history must include univocity (sameness) *and* equivocations (changes); without one or the other we would not have history. Derrida, therefore, endorses Husserl's imperative of univocity, and yet he opposes to it an imperative of equivocity. He says, "Such a reduction [to univocity] should (*doit*) be recommenced indefinitely, for language neither can nor should (*doit*) be maintained under the protection of univocity" (INF, 102/104). Derrida is endorsing neither "radical equivocity" nor "absolute univocity." Radical equivocity would "preclude history by plunging it into the nocturnal and ill-transmissable riches of 'bound' idealities"; similarly, "absolute univocity would itself have no other consequence than to sterilize or paralyze history in the poverty of an indefinite iteration" (INF, 102/104). In order, therefore, to have history, there must be a reciprocal dependence between equivocity and univocity.[21]

Derrida, however, does not merely bring a new imperative of equivocity into symmetry with Husserl's imperative of univocity; Derrida instead argues for a dissymmetry: equivocity is absolutely irreducible. According to Derrida, there are only two limit cases in which absolute univocity can be imagined (INF, 103/105–06). The first case concerns propriety or the proper. We could imagine that the designated thing was singular or unique, precultural or natural. A singular name then could correspond to it and be univocal. As Derrida stresses, however, the word itself must be ideal or universal. The notion of univocity itself implies that the meaning must remain the same across a transmission; the characteristic of univocity is translatability. The project of univocity itself, then, necessitates the word's utterance; if the word is not communicated, I would never know that it was univocal. Sharing places the singular word, as Derrida says, "in a culture, in a network of linguistic relations and oppositions, which would load the word with intentions or with virtual reminiscences" (INF, 103/106). Thus, in this first limit case absolute univocity defeats itself.

In the second Derrida starts from universality, not singularity. Here the chance for univocity does not lie in a precultural object but in a transcultural one, an absolutely ideal objectivity such as a geometrical object. Derrida argues, however, that an ideal object in principle is "always inscribed within a mobile system of relations and takes its source in an infinitely open project of acquisition" (INF, 104/106). In other words, an object is indefinitely iterable and systematic. Indefinite iterability implies, therefore, that an ideal object or a true proposition can always fall into "some singular placings in perspective, some multiple interconnections of sense, and, therefore, some mediate and potential aims" (INF, 104/106). An ideal object can be singularly recontextualized, mediated by lateral relations, animated by unforeseen intentions. Iterability and context dependence, however, define all language, not just absolutely ideal objectivities. Thus, as Derrida says,

> If, in fact, equivocity is always irreducible, that is because words and language in general are not and can never be absolute *objects*. They do not possess any resistant and permanent identity that is absolutely their own. They have their linguistic being from an intention which traverses them as mediations. The "same" word is always "other" according to the always different intentional acts which thereby make a word significative. There is a sort of *pure* equivocity here, which grows in the very rhythm of science. (INF, 104/106–07)

To understand this pure equivocity that grows from the very rhythm of science, in other words, to understand Derrida's criticism of both limit cases, we need only think of the word *I*. This word possesses a different or singular referent (and thus a different meaning) every time someone else generates it. Yet this word's meaning must have some sort of identical meaning—without it transcendental philosophy, for example, would be impossible—some sort of universal structure that makes it available for more singularizations and equivocations. In contrast to Husserl himself (and to Ricoeur), the horizon of language for Derrida is not univocity but equivocity, not communication but noncommunication (cf. INF, 82/77).

3

Dependent upon writing, the success of Husserlian reactivation, according to Derrida, seems then to be uncertain (INF, 105/107). Finite, as Husserl recognizes, the phenomenological investigator is outstripped by writing which is infinite, infinitely equivocal, different, other. Husserl's response to the problem of finitude is to speak, however, of the possibility of removing the "limits from our capacity, in a certain sense its infinitization" (INF, 106/109). According to Derrida, this secondary reactivating operation is the same as geometry's originating subjective act for Husserl (INF, 106/109–10). To turn to geometry's *specific* (not general) *Erstmaligkeit* is Husserl's penultimate zigzag in *The Origin of Geometry* (INF, 117/123–24).

For Husserl, the origin of geometry lies in the invariant structures of the life-world.[22] We know a priori, according to Husserl, that within the life-world things are laid out in anexact space and time. While things consist in a number of determinations (aesthetic, ethical, etc.), things are also corporeal and have spatial shapes. We also know that under the pressure of pragmatic needs these shapes can be perfected; imaginative variation produces morphological shapes such as roundness. Finally, we know that the art of measurement must have been developed. This art, according to Husserl, points the way to univocity and exact objectivity.

The origin of geometry itself then is based on these life-world structures and yet leaps away from them. This passage away is prepared, according to Derrida, by the philosophical act (INF, 127/136). The philosopher, according to Husserl, inaugurates the theoretical attitude which overcomes finitude (INF, 127/136). Some ideal "Euclid" (under the influence of Platonism) opens up the horizon of knowledge as an infinite task. The theoretical attitude, Derrida says, "makes idealization's decisive 'passage to the limit' possible, as well as the constitution of the mathematical field in general" (INF, 127/136). In other words, the theoretical or philosophical attitude outlines mathematics with a boundary or a limit within which infinite developments are possible.

According to Derrida, Husserl's initial description of idealization as the passage from the finite to an infinite limit complicates the Husserlian notion of origin. Derrida recognizes that Husserl must consider the life-world invariants not as immediate conditions for the origin of geometry, but as preconditions. If they were conditions, Husserl would fall into an infinite regress of origins (INF, 125/134–35). Derrida, however, also recognizes that the inaugural infinitization based in the theoretical attitude which opens up mathematics is only the first stage of infinitization. The "Greek" infinitization is not entirely open; it is limited to mathematical content within which or about which there is the possibility of infinite developments. In the modern age, however, there is another infinitization, one which extends mathematical infinity to all fields of research; this infinitization is not limited to content. This is *The Crisis*' mathematization of nature. According to Derrida, this second infinitization is a "resurrection" or "rebirth" of geometry—Derrida uses the phrase *à partir de* frequently in this discussion—because it is based on the first. It actualizes something latent in the geometry's origin, something only announced or indicated there. Moreover, as Derrida stresses, Husserl's vision of philosophy being transformed into phenomenology itself develops on the basis of the inaugural infinitization. Phenomenology, however, thematizes subjectivity's anexact essences. Why have, as Derrida asks then, the origin of geometry begin with the idealization of exactitude; why not place the origin in the imaginative variation producing morphological shapes (INF, 131/142)?

Each revolution based on geometrical or mathematical infinity, then, implies that we must rethink the origin's composition. The development itself is infinite; therefore, we must conclude that the origin recedes with every upsurge or revolution. The infinite openness of the geometrical tradition itself implies an infinite regress of origins. Derrida, therefore, wonders "if it is legitimate to speak of *an* origin of geometry" (INF, 131/141). Geometry, as Derrida says, "is on the way to its origin, not proceeding from it" (INF, 131/141). This problem of the reciprocal implication of end and origin brings Husserl, and Derrida following him, to his ultimate zigzag. The geometrical traditional line, for Husserl, is only a fragment of and relative to the absolute, "universal teleology of Reason" (INF, 131/142). The idealization that Husserl describes, therefore, as the specific origin of geometry—the passage to the limit[23]—is really the origin of all knowledge, tradition, and culture.

According to Derrida, a passage to the limit is defined for Husserl by the *immer wieder* and the *und so weiter,* by iteration (INF, 134–35/146–48, 135n161/148n1). Geometrical idealizing iteration, for example, bases itself upon morphological shapes such as roundness. If a passage to the limit is to produce, however, an absolutely free ideality such as circularity, it must "leap," according to Derrida, "from every descriptive mooring" (INF, 133/145). Ultimately idealization can take no aid from sensibility or imagination; it cannot be equivalent to *Wesenschau* which determines an object in intuition. Yet, taking no aid from sensibility, the geometrical passage to the limit cannot be arbitrary (INF, 135/147). Geometrical iteration must be regulated by the unity of an object; the infinite approximation to complete ideal objectivity must be prescribed already to idealization. The perfectly intelligible geometrical object, according to Derrida, is simultaneously created and re-cognized (INF, 134–35/147). Husserl would call this object guiding and produced by idealization an Idea in the Kantian sense.[24]

According to Derrida—and here he follows Ricoeur—an Idea in the Kantian sense in Husserl bears two characteristics, totality (or completeness) and infinity (or openness); the word *horizon* combines these two. In *Ideas I*'s phenomenology of reason, to which Derrida turns, Husserl says that because a transcendent thing possesses infinite profiles and iterations, complete or total determination of it is impossible for finite consciousness; nevertheless completeness is prescribed to it as an Idea (cf. INF, 139/152). We should try to approximate the transcendent thing's complete or total determinations, even though approximation will be infinite. According to Husserl, we know about the Idea's prescription by means of a specific sort of evidence or presence. According to Derrida, this cannot be adequate evidence because of the Idea's infinite iterations, because of its openness, its "again and again." We have evidence only of the Idea, not what it is the Idea of. In the Idea of infinite determination infinity itself, that is, its content, does not appear.[25] All possible appearances of the thing are not evident; only that there will be more is present. The infinite Idea, therefore, possesses, as Derrida says, a "strange presence," merely formal or finite presence (INF, 139/153).[26]

Derrida interprets this strange presence as the mediation of a sign. Indeed, opposing himself to what Ricoeur says in his essay "Kant and

Husserl,"[27] Derrida says that the Idea in the Kantian sense is an empty or unfulfilled meaning intention (INF, 139–40/153–54). Our only access to what Husserl calls "pure thinking" (cf. INF, 134/145) is through language, through the *logos* (INF, 140/155). The Idea's content is absent or nonpresent but the form refers to it across future distance. As Derrida says,

> [Husserl] locates the *space* (Derrida's emphasis) where con-
> sciousness notifies itself (*se signifie*) of the Idea's prescription
> and thus is recognized as transcendental consciousness
> through the *sign* (my emphasis) of the infinite: this space is the
> *interval* (Derrida's emphasis) between the Idea of infinity in its
> formal and finite (yet concrete) evidence and infinity itself out
> of which there is the Idea. (INF, 140/154)

This is Derrida's criticism of Husserl's intuitionism.[28] There is no immediate (or adequate) evidence of an object's total structure, of a total cultural object or of a science, because of the spacing between the finite
form and the infinite content. The finite form functions like a sign (or a
trace) of what is to come.[29]

The Idea then "announces itself"—Derrida uses this word frequently throughout the *Introduction* (*s'annoncer*, cf. for example INF, 86/82,
130–31/140–41)[30]—as a sign; simultaneously, it is produced by iteration and presupposed by iteration as its guide or imperative. Because of
its infinite iterations, and thus because of its infinite differentiations or
equivocations, the Idea that results can be nothing more than a minimally the same form, a letter, a mere X. In turn, the Idea dictates—this
is an imperative parallel to Husserl's univocity imperative—that this
minimally the same form should become completely determined, filled
in with the content of all possible subjectivities. The Idea is, as Derrida
says, objectivity in the broadest sense. Similarly, the intention, of which
the Idea forms a pole, is empty of every determined object; it is nothing
but pure directedness. As Derrida says, its being is intentionality (INF,
139/153) or Reason (INF, 140/154).

Reason and Idea must, for Husserl, be the beginning and end of history. As Derrida stresses however, although Husserl calls Reason and

Idea eternal, eternality for him is a mode of temporality. Reason and Idea are *arche* and *telos of* time and history (INF, 141–42/155–56, 148–49/165). According to Derrida, this genitive is simultaneously subjective and objective. If the genitive were only subjective, then the Idea would be a mere static value standing outside factual history ("Being or History," as Derrida says),[31] descending down into it only for empirical embellishment. This subjective interpretation would result in objectivism. In contrast, interpreting the genitive objectively would result in psychologism or historicism. Then Reason and the Idea would be relative to empirical genesis. However, since the genitive is simultaneously subjective and objective, Derrida can conclude that "The *Absolute is passage*" (INF, 149/165). Passage or mediation, for Derrida, is primary in every sense of the word.

The Absolute *of* passage means first that all sense arises out of a series or iteration of singular, factual, or empirical events. Conversely, however, an iterable structure cannot come about through an arbitrary series; therefore, the series itself must have presupposed some structure as its guide. Structure conditions genesis; genesis conditions structure. Second, the Absolute of passage implies the reciprocal implication of end and origin. A sense or structure can approximate its complete constitution only because of its infinite iterability; in turn, however, because the *telos* of totality is only approximate, the *arche* withdraws or recedes. There are infinite *tele* or destinations for this letter; therefore, there are infinite *archai* or senders. Historicity, therefore, can be conceived neither as a straight line nor as a circle but only as a zigzag. Third, for Derrida following Husserl, the Absolute of passage means linguistic iteration. Being graphic, passage is both sensible or material, factual, and intelligible or intangible, essential. As irreducibly interwoven, essence is necessarily subjected to catastrophes and fact is necessarily subject to the abuse of "mediate intentions." Language, therefore, for Derrida, is simultaneously the condition for the possibility and impossibility of objectification and return inquiry. The passage of writing is the Absolute, the Absolute, however, "of a Danger" (INF, 149/166).

This phrase, *the Absolute of passage,* is not, however, restricted merely to historicity for Derrida; it refers beyond intersubjective passage to Husserlian temporalization or the living present. The living present is

the absolute of all experience (INF, 150/166); therefore, the three implications of historical passage must be enrooted in it. This Absolute means
for Derrida first that empirical genesis conditions transcendental structure and simultaneously that transcendental structure conditions empirical genesis. The living present is the structure or form of all experience,
of all temporal genesis, from which objects or structures come. As a
structure, however, the living present itself must be subject to this generation. It must come about in a series of temporal moments in order to
attain a level of ideality and objectivity (cf. INF, 136–37/148–50). Thus,
the living present is simultaneously constituting and constituted. Second, like that of any structure, the completeness of the living present's
structure can only be approximated because it too can be infinitely iterated. In turn, however, because the *telos* can only be approximated, the
arche recedes; in other words, the original subjective experience of the
living present withdraws as time marches on. The living present, like
historicity, contains a reciprocal implication of end and origin.

Third and most importantly, however, the living present's passage
is also dangerous. The form of the living present, like any structure or
meaning, is recollectively identified according to Husserl; it is for Derrida nothing more than a sign. As recalled and identified, this sign can be
iterated indefinitely. The form of the living present is an Idea in the
Kantian sense; Husserl in *Ideas I* indeed speaks of its unity as an Idea.
Being recalled in recollection and anticipated in protention, this finite
sign of infinite content implies intersubjective circulation within me; it
is being communicated among others within myself. That each now
always fades away into retention and can only be recalled recollectively
in a sign implies "the transcendental sense of death"; that the now is
always conditioned by an open protention portends mediate intentions
and equivocations. The interval between the idea's form and its content
can never be closed. Displacing Husserl's imperative of completeness
(univocity and communication), and yet based on it, is a Derridean
imperative of inadequation (equivocity and noncommunication). The
living present, therefore, is always deferred to another and delayed by
another. As Derrida says, "the Absolute is present only in being *différant*
without respite" (INF, 153/171). Husserlian temporalization, according
to Derrida in the *Introduction*, always includes both alterity and same-

ness, singularity and generality; it is, according to Derrida, "the necessarily *one* root" of "all the instances dissociated by the various reductions: factuality and essentiality, worldliness and nonworldliness, reality and ideality, *empeiria* and transcendentality" (INF, 148–49/164–65; cf. INF, 57–8/45–6, 85–6/81–3). Based in a unity, this precursor of *différance*, therefore, is "dialectical through and through" (INF, 143/157).

4

Our reading of Derrida's 1962 *Introduction* seems to bring to light more similarities with Ricoeur than differences. Husserlian temporalization is the precursor of both Ricoeurean distanciation and Derridean *différance*. Derrida's definition of living present as the primordial unity of fact and essence seems to overlap completely with Ricoeur's definition of distanciation as the dialectic of event and meaning. Even the *Introduction's* discussion of "the passage to the limit" matches Ricoeur's discussion of imagination and the speculative act in *The Rule of Metaphor*.[32] Passage for Derrida, too, has a horizonal structure. More striking, however, is Derrida's use of the word *dialectic*; the word occurs repeatedly in the *Introduction* (INF, 58/46, 86/83, 143–44/157–59, 152/170). Moreover, the word *passage* itself refers to dialecticity, as both Ricoeur and Derrida know; when Hyppolite translated Hegel's *Phenomenology of Spirit* into French, he used it to render *Übergang* (transition). We must conclude, therefore, that in the *Introduction différance* is a dialectical notion of temporality not unlike Ricoeur's notion of distanciation.[33]

We must, therefore, turn to Derrida's later texts in order to differentiate clearly between Derridean *différance* and Ricoeurean distanciation. *Speech and Phenomena* (1967), as we know from our earlier reading of "White Mythology," is one of the crucial texts in the development of Derrida's thought, in particular, its famous (if not infamous) chapter 5.[34] Here, where the entire issue is the immediacy of self-intuition, Derrida focuses on the descriptions in the *Phenomenology of Internal Time Consciousness* where Husserl calls retention a nonperception. Retention as nonperception, for Derrida, is not a modification of primal impression. Rather, almost unconsciously, Husserl seems to have recognized that retention must be different from primal impression in order for it to be characterized as the past. This difference implies that the possibility of "a simple self-identity" within the living present is destroyed.[35] Lacking self-identity, the living present for Derrida must be conceived, therefore, as a relation; retention is the "fold" (*pli*) of a return, of a repeatability.[36]

According to Derrida, the "folding" that is the living present grounds all replicas, all representation, all recollection, all reflection; it is "the constitution of a trace in its most universal sense."[37] How else, Derrida asks, "can it be explained that [for Husserl] the possibility of reflection and re-presentation belongs in essence to every lived experience...?"[38] Even a reflection upon the form of presence itself, upon the living present, must be grounded in it. The infinite repeatability of the form of presence itself must arise from the marking of a limit (finitude) between primal impression and retention. The form of the living present must be represented in retention before it is reproduced in recollection. A blink, an empty space, or an abyss, therefore, makes the ideality of the present appear; an *écart,* as Derrida says, conditions the Idea of the living present.[39] The very basis of what Husserl would call a "phenomenology of phenomenology" lies in an interval.

A series of implication follows from the interval. In *Speech and Phenomena*'s chapter 6, Derrida can describe temporalization as auto-affection. Then, Derrida can conceive *différance* itself as "the same" (*le même*).[40] Sameness is another way, like the fold, through which Derrida refers to the relation. In chapter 6, however, he interprets the relation not as temporalization but as "spacing" (*espacement*);[41] the relation is a "space between." Chapter 7 then introduces the notion of supplementarity on the basis of spacing. The mediation between one "fold" and another remains inadequate. The space that joins and divides a trace to itself cannot be closed; a trace is always more and/or less than itself.

Thus, in direct contrast to Ricoeur's interpretation of Husserlian temporalization, Derrida's interpretation in *Speech and Phenomena* prioritizes space, distance, discontinuity, and mediation over temporalization, proximity, continuity, and immediacy. Indeed, the undecidability of the trace (supplementarity) seems to make the rupture from dialectic and from Ricoeurean distanciation complete for Derrida. Nevertheless, Derrida must take one more step in order to separate clearly différance from dialectic (and from imagination). Even in *Speech and Phenomena*, Derrida associates différance with dialectic;[42] even in *Speech and Phenomena* Derrida associates his liberation of the sign with a liberation of imagination;[43] even in *Speech and Phenomena* he speaks of repetition as the "common root."[44] He must take one more step towards the aleatory; he does this in *Dissemination* and, in particular, in "The Double Session" (1972). Here, Derrida articulates the nondialectical notion of dissemination. Dissemination is a genesis based not in temporalization and imagination, but rather in spacing and the aleatory. For Derrida, chance alterations are radically discontinuous, totally unexpected, even though they are based in the continuity of a minimal form such as a letter.

Before turning then to "The Double Session," we must recognize that Derrida's development of thought is not merely discontinuous. In a number of ways, the *Introduction* says the same as *Speech and Phenomena* and "The Double Session." This is one reason why our reading of the *Introduction* is so important. First, suggesting auto-affection, Derrida in the *Introduction* calls temporalization "auto-temporalization" (INF, 152/170).[45] Moreover, Derrida's interpretation of "the Idea of history" as containing simultaneously a subjective and objective genitive implies auto-affection. Second, because the "double envelopment of the living present," as Derrida calls it (INF, 137/149), is auto-affective, Derrida can say in the *Introduction* that the living present is "the consciousness of Difference" (INF, 153/171). Third, when Derrida describes Husserlian idealization, he speaks of the "interval" within the Idea in the Kantian sense, the "space" between the form of infinity and its content. Although Derrida turns to temporalization as the "necessarily *one* root" of idealization, of reason itself, he shows that the living present itself is given as a Kantian Idea. Thus, even in the *Introduction* spacing can be seen to function prior to temporalization. Fourth, the interval implies that the Idea is the *logos*, language, a sign, literature. Fifth, when Derrida describes in the *Introduction* the catastrophic fires that can always befall writing, he implies that the aleatory can interfere with any postal sending. Indeed, Derrida concludes his discussion of Husserlian historicity in the *Introduction* by explicitly mentioning chance: "[Intentionality] is also nothing but the Absolute of a living Movement without which neither its end nor its origin would have any *chance* of appearing"

(INF, 150/166, my emphasis). Sixth and last, in the *Introduction*'s penultimate paragraph Derrida says: "Without such a consciousness [of Difference], without its own proper *dehiscence*, nothing would appear" (INF, 153/171, my emphasis). *Dehiscence* means dissemination (cf. DIS, 215n27/243n21).

The Displacement of Imagination by Chance:
A Reading of "The Double Session"

Between the publication of the *Introduction* (1962) and that of *Dissemination* (1972), in which "The Double Session" appears, Heidegger's thought exerts new pressure on Derrida. As we know, Derrida comes to question the so-called metaphysics of presence, idealism (Platonism and phenomenology).[46] Heidegger's thought, however, in particular his "Moira" essay, seems to influence Derrida in another, less obvious, way (DIS, 192n19/219n13). According to Heidegger, Parmenides's poem speaks of an original doubling (*Zwiefalt*) of thought and being.[47] From Parmenides, there is a falling away (*Wegfall*) and unfolding (*Entfaltung*), and finally a sending (*Schickung*) into history, in which there are many (*vielfältige*) signs, according to Heidegger, of the original doubling. Heidegger's thought in this essay, therefore, a thought of an original spacing and throw into historical multiplicity, a thought "utterly foreign to the Hegelian approach," allows Derrida in "The Double Session" to determine différance not as temporalization, not as imagination, not as dialectic, but positively as spacing, as a dice throw, as dissemination, in a phrase, not as one root but as two.

"The Double Session" then arises out of this "development" in Derrida's thought.[48] Overall, "The Double Session" expressly concerns literature, but not literature in a limited sense. Rather, it concerns literature in a general sense, literature as constitutive of presence. For Derrida in "The Double Session"—and the *Introduction* implies this already—literary theory is transcendental theory; Mallarmé's short theatre review *Mimique* is a "handbook" of literature as *différance* (cf. DIS 221/250).[49] In each of the two sessions, Derrida "sews" literature and *différance* together. Rather than follow Derrida's discussion of *différance* and literature "fold by fold," I am going to treat the two separately. Thus, the first section will focus on Derrida's interpretation of Mallarmé's *Mimique* as a book about the "inside," about reflection. Here we shall see the determination of *différance* as spacing and its separation from temporalization. The second section then will turn to the "outside" (cf. DIS, 236/267), to the consequences Derrida draws from Mallarmé's *Mimique* for literature. Here we shall see literature separated from dialectic. Being determined instead as dissemination, a text multiplies its effects in the most surprising ways, in ways that no one could imagine.

1

First appearing in 1886, collected in *Crayonné au théatre, Mimique* is a very short (less than one page) review of a pantomime booklet, Paul Margueritte's *Pierrot Murderer of his Wife* (also 1886) (DIS, 195–96/222). In order to provide background for Derrida's discussion of *Mimique*, we need to assemble first what he says about *Pierrot*; Derrida analyzes it at length (DIS, 198–205/225–33). According to Derrida, Margueritte wrote the booklet in which Pierrot seems to speak after he himself performed the mute pantomime; *Pierrot* then implies that gesture precedes voice (DIS, 199/227). The mimodrama itself reproduces a past event, Pierrot's murder of his wife, Columbine. The mime, however, not only reproduces the event but also Pierrot's deliberations about how to commit the crime; *Pierrot* also implies that the crime is yet to be done. On the basis of his deliberations, Pierrot decides to tickle his wife to death. When the mime acts out the crime, this "sleepwalker" (as Margueritte calls him) plays both roles, husband and wife, murderer and murdered. The play ends, however, with Columbine reappearing to Pierrot, who is then himself overcome with laughter and dies (DIS, 201–02/229). *Pierrot* finally implies, therefore, that the "supreme spasm" is doubled.

Derrida's starting point shows immediately that he is concerned here not merely with literature but also with reflection; he begins his analysis of Mallarmé with this passage from *Mimique*: "The scene illustrates the idea, not any actual action" (DIS, 194–95/220–21). This passage according to Derrida could lead one to say that Mallarmé's *Mimique*'s proposes something like a theory of representation (more

Cartesian in this case than Hegelian). According to this interpretation, the mime signifies not the representation of an actual thing or an empirical reality. The "content" of his *scène* (staging, the theatre) would be "the ideality—*for* a subject—of what is" (DIS, 194/221). The mime would be representation as passive receptivity of a transcendent idea.

Mallarmé's *Mimique* then could be described as a "work of writing against time." According to Derrida, this is how Jacques Scherer interprets it in his *Le "Livre" de Mallarmé* (DIS, 230–31/260–61). For instance, Scherer says, and Derrida quotes this, that "the elimination of [actual] action necessarily entails an elimination of time." Mallarmé's "stage" implies, according to Scherer, that "theatre takes us out of the flow of time, by introducing us into time regained, or eternity." In other words, in this idealistic interpretation, the mime signifies, as Derrida says, "an eternal present" (DIS, 231/261).

Another sentence in *Mimique*, however, leads to another interpretation according to Derrida (in the first session): "Such is this *Pierrot Murderer of his Wife* composed and set down by himself, a mute soliloquy." This implies that the mime is an active producer. *Pierrot* implies, as we already noted, that gesture precedes voice. The mime obeys no verbal order; he follows no verbal discourse, no diction or dictation (DIS, 195/221–22). Derrida says, "The mime produces, that is to say makes appear *in praesentia*, manifests the very meaning of what he is presently writing: of what he *performs*. He enables the thing to be perceived in person, in its true face" (DIS, 206/233/234). Therefore, one might interpret the mime not in terms of representation but as the "scriptural production" of presence. Thought would be conceived as unveiling, monstration, manifestation, presentation. This interpretation, too, would be, according to Derrida, idealistic (more Hegelian than Cartesian). It would locate the origin of ideality in subjective productivity; *Mimique* would be about idealization.

Mallarmé's *Mimique* could then be described as "a work of writing by time." According to Derrida, this is how Jean-Pierre Richard interprets it in his *L'Univers imaginaire de Mallarmé* (DIS, 231–33/262–64). For instance, Richard says, and Derrida quotes this too, that "What the theater indeed aims to abolish in each of its creations is actuality as well as materiality. The work of unrealization and vaporization is henceforth entrusted to time itself: ...the mime oscillates within a double call to the imagination, a call both from the future and the past." In this interpretation then, according to Derrida, the mime signifies the temporal production of presence; he signifies "*our own* transcendental truth."

Mimique, however, contains this sentence as well: "a mute soliloquy that the phantom, white as a yet unwritten page, holds in both face and gesture at full length to his soul." The mime according to Derrida makes gestures in (to his) white face; he "writes" on the white page which is himself. The mime signifies then, for Derrida, auto-affection. As the passive recipient of this writing, the mime is representation ("illustrates the idea"); at the same time, however, he is actively producing ("composed and set down by himself"). The mime is representation and creativity at once (*à la fois*, as Derrida says [DIS, 198/225]). *Mimique*'s content, Derrida shows, cannot be reduced down to a subjective idealism of representation (truth as adequation) or a subjective idealism of creativity (truth as *aletheia*, of course)[50] because it is both at once.

Because of the simultaneity found in Mallarmé's *Mimique*, the mime's "operation," according to Derrida, cannot be conceived as temporalization (DIS, 208/236). Temporalization always presupposes a complete present (immediacy) as origin and outcome of its process. As Derrida stresses, however, Mallarmé also says, "here anticipating, there recalling, in the future, in the past *under the false appearance of a present*." The mime, as an "illustration of the idea," is an image of a model, a present joined or synthesized to the past; the mime, as "writing" himself, also creates himself without a model, a present separated or differentiated from the past. Simultaneity means that while identification keeps creation from completely producing a present separated from the past, difference keeps synthesis from completely reproducing a past in the present; simultaneity keeps the relation inadequate. Derrida uses the word *mimicry* (*mimique*), not mimesis, to indicate this simultaneity of the mime's operation (DIS, 206/234). Temporalization presupposes either representation or creativity (continuity or discontinuity) but not both together.

The simultaneity signified by the mime's operation is Derrida's "Double Session" transformation of the "primordial unity" that we have seen in the *Introduction* characterize *différance*. The mime irreducibly represents; the hyphen here implies—and this at least make explicit what was only suggested in the *Introduction*—that two comes before the one, that something is always already missing to which the present refers, that mediation has always already been inserted into immediacy (DIS, 221/250). According to "The Double Session," the mime's operation functions because of a "between": "Whether it names confusion or interval, the 'between' (*entre*), therefore, carries all the force of the operation" (DIS, 220/250). *Entre*, according to Derrida, is a syntactical, formal, or mathematical term (DIS, 222/251); it signifies "a semantic quasi-emptiness...the spacing relation" (DIS, 222n36/251n29). For Derrida, therefore, an interval divides and joins (*écarte*) re-flection: "...in *inserting* a spacing into interiority, [the mime's operation] no longer allows the inside to close upon itself or be identified with itself" (DIS, 234/265). In "The Double Session," therefore, Derrida determines différance not as temporalization but as spacing, not as immediacy but as mediation.[51]

Mallarmé himself calls spacing a hymen: "in a hymen (out of which flows Dream), tainted with vice yet sacred, between desire and fulfillment, perpetration and remembrance." Hymen implies that the mime's operation (the sleepwalker) marries dream and wakefulness. According to Derrida, Mallarmé's capitalization of the word *Reve* indicates a fiction that is neither mere dream because, as creativity, it deviates from any past referent nor mere wakefulness because, as imitation, it refers to something absent (DIS, 210–11/239). Simultaneity as hymen also implies the marriage of event and memory. Even as it breaks with the past, an event never completely takes place because it always repeats something absent, something to which the event can be compared. Desire is never completely fulfilled because the perpetration changes the object that was desired. Desire always returns because the hymen remembers. The mimodrama implies all of this. Pierrot deliberates about something in the future that was supposed to have already taken place in the past; Columbine reappears again after her murder-marriage. The hymen, therefore, as Derrida says, does not take place insofar as "event" means the present (DIS, 213/241).

Finally, the hymen, as the marriage of opposites, annuls, according to Derrida, the difference between difference and non-difference, distance and nondistance, imitator and imitated, signifier and signified, appearance and thing itself.[52] What the hymen "removes" (*leve*) is "the decidable exteriority of the differing terms" (DIS, 210/238). All of these differing terms, as Derrida says, "amount to the same (*reviennent au même*)" (DIS, 209/238). The same, however, unlike the word *marriage,* does not imply according to Derrida neutralization (DIS, 207n24/ 235n18).[53] Neutralization means that one of the opposing terms had negated the other, elevated (*releveé*) the other, consumated the marriage. For Derrida, identity and difference, distance and nearness, all the oppositions that make thought (or reason) possible, themselves derive from the same. Thus, none of the opposing terms related in the same remain.

What remains (*reste*), according to Derrida, is a "*milieu* in the sense of middle, neither/nor, between, *and* in the sense of element, ether, whole, medium" (DIS, 211/239, 239/269; my emphasis). The *milieu* refers for Derrida, on the one hand, to a line drawn between the two, a characteristic, a fold, or mark that simultaneously divides and joins them. On the other, it refers to an element that "reflects" upon the trait between the relata, a relation related to the relation; it is auto-affection turned towards itself, a metaposition. As Derrida says, the element "remarks" the mark (DIS, 238/269). Following Mallarmé's use of the word *scène,* Derrida also says that the *milieu* consists of four surfaces, the surface of each relata facing each other, the surface that runs along the back of the stage connecting them, and a fourth surface, the element, that points to the three "walls" and exposes its reverse side to the audience.[54] It is as Derrida says, a "reflecting screen" (DIS, 202/229), a sort of see-through mirror.[55]

This "tain" is, as Derrida says—and we saw this in our reading of "White Mythology,"—"a supplementary double" (DIS, 238/268). This fourth, too, is separated by space; it constitutes another relation. If the fourth as a reflection, however, is supposed "to conceive and class all" self-relations, then one needs to remark this relation as well, etc. The field, however, will lack the relation that encloses it and the relation will exceed the field it makes possible. Every self-relation will participate in without belonging to the area it is supposed to enclose. Thus, every meta-position insofar as it is a closing, a limit, is an infinite opening; it is an asymmetrical relation insofar as it remarks itself. The *milieu* as middle and as element then will always have the structure of a neither/nor, the structure of more and/or less than itself (DIS, 258–61/291–94). Separated by a space that makes the metareference itself possible, an element infinitely generates itself (cf. DIS, 242/272–73); based in a "no more," the fourth is more than the relation or any of the relata. An element such as mimicry, fiction, or ether (atoms of air), therefore, must be characterized by the locution *plus de* (DIS, 274/307).[56] Only an infinite number of traces remain when the decidable exteriority of different terms has been removed (DIS, 211/239).

The logical structure of the same (of the hymen, of *différance*), for Derrida, therefore, is relation not unity (DIS, 208/236), a relation that, being none of the relata, being nothing but empty space, establishes the relata out of itself. Mallarmé's sentence, then, "The scene illustrates the idea not any actual action," means that the scene illustrates—represents—nothing (DIS, 196/224, 206/234). Mallarmé uses the word *idea*, in fact, to indicate that no real or actual thing is being imitated; the idea is no-thing. Being no-thing, however, the Mallarméan idea is not purely ideal. Rather, the word *idea* for Mallarmé retains what Derrida calls "the nothing" (DIS, 208/236). It refers to the space between two characters (the mime related as Pierrot and Columbine, as active and passive, as subject and object, as real and ideal). By referring to the *milieu*, Derrida says, words such as "'Book,' 'Spirit,' the 'Idea'—the most spectacular examples of this grand scene—begin to function like signifiers unhooked, dislodged, disengaged from their historic polarizations" (DIS, 236/266). Traces such as these, therefore, "illustrate," make visible, like "the faceted multiplicity of" a chandelier, "a *lustre*," as Derrida says (DIS, 208/236); they "stage," factualize or materialize, the nothing.[57]

2

Through the same sentences in *Mimique* Derrida also shows that literature as such cannot be defined by the present; it *is* not. Or, as Derrida says, "there is no essence of literature, no truth of literature, no literary-being of literature" (DIS, 223/253). Literature, like thought, cannot be reduced down to either a theory of imitation (imitation of actual things or of the idea) or to a theory of creativity. Instead, literature "is" the simultaneity of imitation and creation, of identity and difference, of marriage and virginity. Again just as the simultaneity that constitutes thought is based in spacing, literary simultaneity is based in spacing, the "whites" between the words (difference, diacriticity, laterality, syntax). Thus, as Derrida says, "We must determine the structure of Mallarmé's spacing, calculate its effects, and deduce its *critical* consequences" (DIS, 236/266–67).

As is well-known, for Derrida, thematic criticism exemplifies modern literary criticism. Exemplary of thematic criticism is Jean-Pierre Richard's *L'Univers imaginaire de Mallarmé* (already mentioned). Richard's thematic criticism is concerned with establishing a dialectic of a text's multiple valences, a dialectic based on an unity posable, disposable (or available), transposable, based on a theme (DIS, 249/280–81). Explicitly influenced by Ricoeur, Richard conceives the aim of thematic criticism as a text's system of polysemy, as an analogy grounded on one determinate, decidable, present meaning (DIS, 245/276, 249/280–81). According to Derrida, the thematic aim arises from what "has remained profoundly inseparable from metaphysics, from Plato to Hegel": a desire for totality (DIS, 248–49/280). Indeed, Richard entitles one of his sections: "Towards a Dialectics of Totality." Thematic criticism—"the phenomenological, hermeneutic, dialectical project of thematicism" (DIS, 249/281)—admits that its perspective is finite, that the lexical richness of a text cannot be mastered. Nevertheless, even if polysemy is infinite, thematic criticism projects a future perspective, a horizon, from which it will be possible to determine all possible textual valences.[58]

One of Mallarmé's terms that Richard tries to thematize is *blanc* (white or blank) (DIS, 251–54/283–286). Within Mallarmé's text, the word *blanc* refers literally to empirical white things, and metaphorically, by means of resemblance, to virginity, purity, *etc.* To the thematic reading then, the *blanc* appears as "the inexhaustible totality of the semantic valences that have any tropic affinity with [whiteness]" (DIS, 252/283–84). *Blanc* appears as infinite polysemy, something akin to what Hegel calls the bad infinite; the mere infinity of occurrences or iterations—an incomplete series—throws us back on our finitude. As Hegel knew, however, the bad infinite still allows one the hope of the total, the dream of the sum.

According to Derrida however, Mallarmé's *blanc*, although inserted into the series, refers to the "totality, however, infinite, of the polysemic series" (DIS, 252/284). The totality of semantic valences, no matter how distantly projected, is possible only on the basis of the diacritical space, the whites or blanks between each occurrence. By remarking the mark between each occurrence, by referring to the *milieu*, by reflecting the "fanlike form of the text," this fourth word, *blanc*, is conditioned by the more and/or less structure. *More* because, even as it extracts or subtracts itself out in order to remark the whole, the blank is an extra or another *blanc* of the series. *Less* because, even as it is an extra member of the series, it cannot be included in what it defines or makes possible. It is, as Derrida says, a "representative or a delegate" of the series itself (DIS, 252/284). Thus, if the *blanc* is supposed "to conceive and to class all" the *blancs,* then another is needed in order to grasp the fourth. This "tropic movement" will of course, as we know from "White Mythology," go on incessantly (cf. DIS, 258/290). This is the law of supplementarity: the number of whites cannot be counted.

The law of supplementarity (différance) produces a very specific type of inexhaustibility: formal or structural (cf. 250/281). The generation of *blancs* begins with the outlining of a form, the drawing of lines, the marking of limits, the insertion of blanks; it begins with the attempt to encircle a totality. Then, however, Derrida takes a further step; he remarks the mark once more; he looks for what makes this encircling possible. This condition is another white space, another mark, another trait. These steps can go on forever. The further steps redraw, remark, "bleach out" the encircled totality. What has become infinite, unlimited, therefore, for Derrida in "The Double Session," is finitude, the limit itself (DIS, 253/285).

Thus, on the basis of the blanks, Derrida demonstrates that:

> the sum is impossible to totalize but yet it is not exceeded by the infinite richness of a content of meaning or intention; the perspective extends out of sight but without entailing the depth of a horizon of meaning *before* or *within* which we can never have finished advancing. (DIS, 251/282)

Derridean inexhaustibility is noncontent-based and nonhorizonal because the so-called master word itself, "the blank proper, the transcendental origin of the series" (DIS, 252/284), is more than "just one extra valence, a meaning that might enrich the polysemic valence" (DIS, 252/284). It is more because the *blanc* is less. It refers to no meaning, theme, or content; it refers instead to the very possibility of meanings and themes, to the nonthematic, asemic space that generates meaning or thematic effects. The empty space between can provide no *sens* or *Sinn*, no direction, towards which one could progress or return. Lacking a core, Derridean inexhaustibility cannot be conceived as perspectivism; there is no central object around which an infinite number of perspectives could radiate. Although différance or the law of supplementarity produces a nonfinite number of effects, Derrida's infinity does not equal the infinite determinations of a central meaning; such an infinity is what Hegel had in mind with the bad infinite. Likewise, although Derridean inexhaustibility resembles what Hegel calls the good infinite because it begins from encircling a totality, from the delimitation of what makes the bad infinite possible (cores of meaning), Derrida reflects one more time on what makes this encirclement or delimitation possible; this further reflection opens the possibility for an infinite number of steps back. Derrida's infinity, therefore, is not that of the bad or good infinite; quite simply, it does not make sense. If there is no guiding sense, no horizon towards which one could move, then, for Derrida, all one can do is move according to a certain rhythm. If, as Derrida says,

> there is thus no thematic unity or total meaning to reappropriate in an imagination, an intentionality or lived experience beyond the textual instances, then the text is no longer the expression or the representation (felicitous or otherwise) of any *truth* that would come to be diffracted or gathered in a polysemic litera-ture. It is this hermeneutic concept of polysemy for which the concept of dissemination must substitute. (DIS, 262/294)

Polysemy always maintains an horizon of expectation, an outline of an order, based in a semic unit that can be imagined. In contrast, as non-horizonal, as noncontent-based, as formal, différance in "The Double Session" is not defined as dialectic; it is defined as dissemination (DIS, 235/266).[59]

Mallarmé's "genius," then, for Derrida—if we can speak this way (cf. DIS, 274/306)—is dissemination. When Mallarmé forms his writing, undoubtedly, he appropriates polysemy's semic order. He also, however, according to Derrida, plays on linguistic contingency and haphazardness, on his chances. On the basis of the given "phonic and graphic affinity"—words and letter look and sound the same—he divides language up and recombines it again. He reforms the spaces, the *blancs*, as Mallarmé himself would say. Mallarmé breaks the codes, transforms the forms, deviates from the norm. Based in chance, his writing can seem to be totally arbitrary. His writing, however, cannot be entirely arbitrary. Otherwise it would be mere noise; it would not rhyme. Mallarmé, as Derrida points out, must guarantee intelligibility or better the functioning of the terms, a minimum of grammaticality in order to have an effect (DIS, 278n75/310n63). The new form must at least obey, copy, imitate, the forms of letters. His versification must "stamp" matter with form, "fire" singularity with universality, "vitrify" the nonrepeatable with the repeatable.

If we focus on the chance in Mallarmé's play, then someone like Richard can say that Mallarmé's writing results in new words "totally foreign to language (*langue*)" (DIS, 256/288), in totally new associations of meaning, even complete arbitrariness. If, however, we focus on the necessity in Mallarmé's play, as Derrida does, then we must say that "the total new word foreign to language also returns to language, recomposes with it according to new networks of difference, becomes divided up (*morceler*) again, etc...." (DIS, 256/288). By possessing at least the minimally identifiable form of letters, these morcels of Mallarmé's language can come to echo each other otherwise, to imprint themselves upon one another again, to establish more phonic and graphic affinities; something else can be "thrown into the bargain." By being iterable, these letters can fall into different configurations of space. By remaining, Mallarmé's writing can be exposed to danger, sprayed like a jet of water.

For Derrida, therefore, Mallarmé's "genius" is not imagination but chance; dissemination is *rhythmos* (DIS, 279/312). *Rhythmos* originally combined (according to Benveniste) both *schema, morphé, eidos* (form), and *diastemata* (intervals).[60] According to the *rhythmos*, Mallarmé's writing is, as Derrida says, "the folding together of an identity and a difference…a game of chance forever new, a play of fire forever young…a play of luck with necessity, of contingency with law. A hymen between chance and rule" (DIS, 277/309).[61] The chance graphic and phonic affinities on which Mallarmé plays are relations of the same. Every form, the minimal unity of a letter, according to Derrida, is divided and divisible.[62] Mallarmé's forming of aleatory affinities only exposes form to more chances. Because an atom is divisible—it swerves, even zigzags— an atom does not burn out, but remains warm. Like an atom, every text, every word, every letter, is out of our control. Made possible by the same, a roll of the dice gives a totally different idea, a totally other idea; lacking the arrow of meaning, the results for Derrida cannot be expected, foreseen, or anticipated. For instance, Derrida reproduces without emphasis the following constellation of words in Mallarmé: *moire, memoire, grimoire, armoire, miroir, hoir, soir, noir, voir* (DIS, 277/310). The graphic affinities between *air* and *oir*, between *moire* and *moira*, all of a sudden produce the surprise that Mallarmé stands between Heidegger and Democritus, and perhaps among others.[63]

CONCLUSION ◆
The Difference Illuminated

So close together that they are almost indistinguishable: Ricoeur and Derrida. Ricoeur, too, speaks of the "between," of simultaneity, sameness, traces, nothing, space. Derrida, too, speaks of dialectic, passage, horizon, letters, ideality, time. Both distanciation and différance derive from Husserl's theory of intentionality. Both distanciation and différance derive from the traditional notion of mimesis. Repeatability defines both types of mediation. Both Ricoeur and Derrida are devoted to finitude. Finally, the fact that neither Ricoeur's hermeneutics nor Derrida's deconstruction takes up positions simply opposed to philosophy (or metaphysics) indicates their proximity. Indeed, we can make the difficulty of distinguishing them even greater. Although Ricoeur's and Derrida's respective characterizations of historicity provides a clear difference—Ricoeur in *Time and Narrative I* describes it as an endless spiral while Derrida in the 1962 *Introduction* describes it as a zigzag—Derrida probably borrowed this phrase, "*une mouvement en vrille,*" from Ricoeur, who had already used it in his 1950 Introduction to his French translation of Husserl's *Ideas I*.[1]

Despite these blurring similarities, we have seen a difference emerge. Like a crisscross, the difference can be divided into four. First, we can focus on the origin of mediation in Ricoeur and Derrida. We have seen that Ricoeur over and over again focuses on the present. The basis of Ricoeur's discourse theory is the present; the center of his meditation on time and narrative is the historical present. While we have seen Ricoeur's notion of the present overlap occasionally with what Derrida calls presence—Ricoeur, for instance, speaks of discourse's "mode of presence"—we cannot equate it with *Vorhandenheit*; Ricoeur explicitly characterizes the present as action, as promise, as question, all of which imply openness and absence. Over the course of our analysis, however, it became clearer and clearer that the present for Ricoeur could only be characterized as some sort of immediacy. For Ricoeur, belonging to is unreflective and unmediated; mimesis$_1$ is consonance; retention in the living present is the continuous passage from, the modification of, the primal impression. For Ricoeur, the attempt to make mediation absolute "remains a pious wish." This is the first difference: unity is prior for Ricoeur; duality is prior for Derrida.

We have seen that for Derrida mediation itself is prior to presence or immediacy. Our reading of Derrida's *Introduction* disclosed that the living present for Derrida is "the consciousness of Difference." Although this is not explicit in the *Introduction*, passage turned out for Derrida to be discontinuous, except for the minimal continuity of form. All passage implies death; what remains is the tomb. We saw this more clearly in our brief considerations of *Speech and Phenomena*.[2] Derrida's analysis of Husserlian temporalization (like his analysis of Aristotelian time in "Ousia and Grammé") shows that spacing precedes the present. Lastly and most clearly, our reading of "The Double Session" disclosed the logical structure of *différance* (of supplementarity, of mimicry, of the hymen, of the same) as relation not unity, a relation that, being none of the relata, establishes the relata out of itself. For Derrida, the absolute is nothing but empty space. This emptiness is not a void, a mere negative determined by the positive full, but rather the emptiness between two. The Derridean Absolute is white like the background of a the printed page or black like that of the Milky Way.

Second, from the origin we can turn to middle itself. For Ricoeur, the distanciation of meaning from the immediate event is dialectical. Ricoeur characterizes the dialectical movement as repeatability. Ricoeur separates his notion of repeatability from that of French structuralism; therefore, we were able to interpret it as based in content. Meaning not form comes about. This implies, as we saw, that the speaker's (or writer's) singular intention is simultaneously cancelled and preserved in a universal structure. Structure, as in a sentence, for Ricoeur is synthetic; the sentence is supposed to equal a whole context capable of reducing polysemy—or of augmenting it.

Our examination of Ricoeur's metaphor theory, then, showed that imagination produces an image referring not to the nothingness of absence but to the nothingness of ideality. Because the novelty of live metaphor results from imagination's "work"—we might say, from its serious play—imagination must be defined for Ricoeur, as a work of negativity. Imagination must negate polysemy (which itself possesses the outline of an order), contingency, and chance associations, if its product is going to be understood; passage for Ricoeur must be safe. In fact, we saw over and over again that all forms of distanciation for Ricoeur aim to be univocal, even turned into concepts. Historical traces, for instance, found within the space of experience are supposed to be "undistanced" or "unspatialized," in other words, temporalized and made present. Based in intentional content, distanciation cannot not prioritize continuity. Mediation for Ricoeur is a mere means to be negated; it is truly or merely a "between." This is the second difference: mediation for Ricoeur is content-based, continuous, imaginative, dialectical negativity; mediation for Derrida is formal, discontinuous, aleatory, disseminational affirmation.

Derrida's thought of mediation, as we saw, emanates from Husserlian historicity (as well as from Husserlian temporalization). Husserlian historicity, as Derrida interprets it, implies the inseparability of genesis and structure; the genitive in the phrase, "the genesis *of* structure," must be interpreted as simultaneously subjective and objective. Although in the *Introduction* Derrida explicitly interprets the genesis of structure (idealization) dialectically, by the end of our reading we came to realize that certain elements of Derrida's early thought were already undialectical. The passage through this "of" is dangerous; as both material and ideal, language, the sign in general, is irreducibly subject to both catastrophes and equivocations. Writing, as tradition's "ether," cannot not imply discontinuity. In "White Mythology" we had already seen Derrida break with dialectical mediation by reinscibing metaphor first as catachresis, then as homonymy. Then, like "White Mythology," "The Double Session" showed us, by means of Mallarmé's mime, that auto-affection can never be adequate; a joining and division (an *écart*) disrupts the relation.

In "The Double Session" we saw that the irreducibility of this deviation opens up dissemination's frivolous play. Dissemination implies for Derrida that every form, every letter, every atom of language, air, is divided and divisible. Mallarmé, we saw, according to Derrida, forms the chance divisions of language, and in turn exposes this form to more. He writes not according to polysemy's content but according to the *rhythmos*. Thanks to Mallarmé's "genius," therefore, Derrida was able to show that dissemination affirms the aleatory, even affirms it twice.

Third, from the middle we can turn to the end. Because Ricoeur's starting point is belonging to, the positive expression of finitude, we saw that he is able to resist the Hegelian temptation of totalization. While distanciation for Ricoeur is the abstraction of universality, the atemporality of meaning, belonging to concretizes and temporalizes it. Ideal meaning for Ricoeur keeps presenting more "perspectives"; there are always more events. Live metaphors, too, provide a surplus that outstrips finite understanding. In symbols, however, we encountered a limit in Ricoeur more radical that perspectivism. Unlike live metaphor, the Ricoeurean symbol exceeds conceptualization because it bases itself in the nonlinguistic, in *Bios*. We even saw Ricoeur appropriate the Derridean term, *dissemination*, to characterize the symbolic gift. Here we had to say that Ricoeur's discussion of symbolic inexhaustibility does not fit neatly into the Hegelian categories of good and bad infinite. While it would have been easy, therefore, to return to Derrida's well-known formulation (in "Structure, Sign, and Play") of totalization's two impossibilities in order to distinguish Derrida and Ricoeur, we cannot appeal to it here.[3] Perhaps we must even say that Ricoeur shares this quasi-Hegelian position not only with Gadamer but also with Derrida himself.

Nevertheless, from this quasi-Hegelian position Ricoeur always retreats to Kant. We saw Ricoeur assert intermediary degrees between metaphor and symbol. He interprets the symbol, therefore, in terms of the continuous passage of productive imagination. The symbol's gift resembles live metaphor's novel meaning. Based in sense (*sens*), Ricoeurean distanciation always points to a horizon of totalization, always in the direction of the complete identity of thought and being. As a promise, the historical present for Ricoeur points towards the keeping of it; as a question, it points towards an answer. It seems that even Ricoeur's so-called symbolic dissemination should renew the prejudices we already possess. We cannot forget that Ricoeur says in *Time and Nar-*

rative, III, that "there is no surprise so wonderful (*divine surprise*) for which the baggage of experience is too light; it could not know how to desire anything else." The Ricoeurean radical alterity, therefore, is expectable. This is the third difference: for Ricoeur, distanciation is horizonal, telic; for Derrida, différance is nonhorizonal, atelic.

We saw otherwise in Derrida. Even as early as his *Introduction* Derrida attempts to reconceive the relation between the finite and the infinite. Reason itself, the eternal, we saw, was subject to the finitude of time. Again, although this was not explicit in Derrida himself, we were able to see that the gap Derrida discovered in time is unclosable. The implication of this we had already started to see in our "White Mythology" reading; it became explicit, however, when we examined "The Double Session." Here Derrida shows that the hymen, the joining and deviation, the same, the relation between, spacing, *différance*, all or any of these imply a very specific type of inexhaustibility. For Derrida as we saw, a trace signifies neither a determinate referent nor a unit of meaning, neither a factual thing nor an ideal essence. Rather, it illustrates the white spaces themselves, the asemic possibility of meaning. In order to make this reference, a word such as Mallarmé's *blanc* must abstract itself from the series in which it nevertheless participates. It becomes then an extra *blanc*, but one not belonging to the series. As we know well from our "White Mythology" reading, the adoption of this metaposition makes any attempt to totalize the trace's relation to the relation, any attempt to account for all the white spaces, infinite; the field cannot be saturated. Thus, we saw that Derridean inexhaustibility also does not fit neatly into the Hegelian categories of good or bad infinite. Although the law of supplementarity produces an infinite number of effects, its infinite quantity does not result from the iterations of one meaning; although the law of supplementarity begins from the encirclement of the totality, the totality withdraws.

Derrida, therefore, is quite explicit in "The Double Session": dissemination does not project a horizon. Referring only to white spaces, a trace lacks the direction of meaning. Lacking the direction of *sens*, its trajectory is unexpectable. It neither moves ahead and fulfils a desire nor does it renew what we already believed. It neither answers a question nor does it keep a promise. No one can predict into which constellation an atom will fall. No matter what we wish, a letter can institute a revolution within the tradition. When it does, this can only be called a surprise, a surprise so wonderful that it cannot be packed into the baggage of experience, a surprise so divine that it is totally other.

Finally, we can turn to the opening, the fourth, the Idea. We saw for Ricoeur that an Idea in the Kantian sense is defined by totality and openness. The Idea's openness, its infinity, results from the endless possibility of concretion, instantiation, factualization. There is always more content to be added to infinity's form. Because of the infinite possibility of new events, the circulation of the Idea never closes. Even in the "Eighth Study" Ricoeur kept the Idea open. He does not organize speculative discourse as a generic unity, but rather determines it as a regulated polysemy of being; its "logical space" is analogical. Both of these terms, *polysemy* and *analogy*, imply plurality, difference, and equivocity. This is why we must characterize Ricoeur's hermeneutics as a revival of the most generous instances of Western metaphysics.

Nevertheless, we also saw Ricoeur, following Aristotle and then Hegel, refer this polysemy to "one thing." Ricoeur's polysemy, as a plural identity, cannot not be regulated by unity. The one, we saw, determines for Ricoeur all interpretation, and, therefore, all "middle" discourses, as "a struggle for univocity." Indeed, we were able to say at different points in our analysis that the Ricoeurean Idea imposes an imperative of univocity; an end is still dictated. For Ricoeur, the point of all discourse is to fulfill the intention of an "unhindered and unfettered communication"; "the kingdom of the similar" should return to a "kingdom of the same." Ricoeur, therefore, conceives the relation between the totality and infinity, the Idea itself, as a dialectic; the Idea must arise in unity and point towards unity, even though peace is never achieved. What illustrates the Ricoeurean Idea, therefore, as we know, is an incomplete circle, an endless spiral. Although it never quite adds up, the formula for the Ricoeurean Idea is: origin + mediation + end = Idea. This is the fourth difference: for Ricoeur, the Idea is a third; for Derrida, it is a fourth.

The formula for the Derridean Idea is: origin + mediation + end + the "+" = Idea. This formula was already intimated in Derrida's *Introduction*. Here we saw that, for Derrida, the Idea's "strange presence" arises in Husserl from the *space* between the Idea's form and content, between totality and infinity, between intention and fulfillment. Even in the *Introduction* then, we were able to call the Idea a trace; this minimal *X* remarks the mark. In "The Double Session" we saw Derrida define the Idea as the fourth "wall" representing the three sides of the stage (Mallarmé's *scène*). Because it refers literally to nothing, to no origin, to no one, the Derridean Idea points to nothing, to no end, to no one. Lacking this one (or even "we"), the Derridean Idea—we should say Derridean Ideas—cannot be conceived as polysemy or analogy. As we saw in the *Introduction*, the imperative of univocity is displaced by one of equivocity; in "The Double Session" we saw this imperative reappear as the law of supplementarity, as the law of *plus de*. The trace must remain as the flickering back and forth between two; the marriage between Pierrot and Columbine must remain violent.[4] Therefore, what illustrates the Derridean Idea is the zigzag.

This is why we must say that Derridean deconstruction is a perversion of philosophy. The Derridean Idea, which is différance, reflects the triadic action of the Platonic, Cartesian, Hegelian, or Husserlian Idea. By making mediation prior, the very notion of priority or origin is distorted; by recognizing that the Idea lacks a horizon, the very notion of end or purpose turns. The Derridean Idea refers to what makes idealism in all its forms, including that of Ricoeur, possible and yet to what idealism cannot and must not attempt to totalize: the empty space between two. The empty space between, in which writing zigzags like a drunk, is what provides the chances that cannot be imagined.[5] The empty space between, what Ricoeur's hermeneutics, perhaps hermeneutics in general, does not account for; empty space, what Derrida's deconstruction, perhaps deconstruction in general including that of Heidegger, counts on. This brings us to one more difference between the thought of Ricoeur and Derrida: hermeneutics, the endless questioning of the one principle, of the monarch; deconstruction, the infinite response to the lack of a principle, to anarchy.

Philosophy and Communication:
Round-table Discussion Between
Ricoeur and Derrida

This is a translation of the round-table discussion following the presentation of Derrida's "Signature événtement contexte," Ricoeur's "Discours et communication," and Roland Blum's "La perception d'autrui" at the Fifteenth Congress of the Association of the Society for Philosophy in the French Language, Montreal, in 1971. The English translation of "Signature événtement contexte" appears in Derrida's Margins of Philosophy *(trans. Alan Bass [Chicago: University of Chicago Press, 1982], 307–330). As far as I know, no English translation of the Ricoeur piece exists; there is, however, a German translation in* Neue Hefte für Philosophie, *11 (1975): 1–25. As far as I know, Blum's essay has never been translated into English either. The transcription of the discussion was published without revision in* Actes du XVe de L'Association des Sociétés de Philosophie de Langue Francaise, *Université de Montreal, 1971, volume 2, pp. 393–431. The conference was organized by Venant Cauchy, who authorized this translation. Besides Derrida, Ricoeur, and Blum, Ernest Joos, Gilles Lane, Yvon Gauthier, Claude Panaccio, Clément Légaré, Roger Marcotte, Thomas de Koninck, Henri Declève, and Jeanne Parain-Vial participated. René Schaerer was the moderator. Occasionally I have inserted phrases to eliminate some ambiguity; these are indicated by square brackets. I would like to thank Kevin Thompson who first told me about this discussion and Jacquie Baertschi for her help on the translation.*

—Leonard Lawlor

René Schaerer: We've heard three great plenary sessions on the basis of which our discussion will now proceed. If I would have had the time, I would have tried to order the principal themes so as to be able to put them in a series and perhaps provide a better orientation for this discussion. That is not possible; it is, therefore, up to you to do it.

Although the three papers presented in the sessions revolve around only one theme, they differ from one another. It seems to me that they can be grouped in the following way: the first treats communication in terms of discourse; the second in terms of writing; the third in terms of perception. We might have thought that the third paper should have figured at the beginning. But since our speaker [Blum] has shown that perception is in fact a mystery that no system can capture, we might wonder whether perception is not precisely what is least immediate in all of this.

[Scherer instructs the audience on asking questions.] I now turn the floor over to whomever wishes to speak.

Ernest Joos: In the preceding session, there was a discussion concerning the foundation of the problem of communication. Presuming that the papers were concerned with this, at least implicitly, I would like to continue in the same vein and ask now at least two, if not all three, speakers the same question but in a concrete form. Although philosophy raises more questions than it answers, this uncertainty in philosophical matters guarantees a continuity to our work. With this in mind, I hope my remarks don't appear unusual. Derrida's beautiful analyses have led us to the edge of another question, the question of the possibility of repetition, of the iterability of writing, or, we might say, the autonomy of writing. It seems to me that Derrida stranded us at this point, probably because of time. Permit me, then, to raise the problem of the origin of iterability. I had the impression that we were bent on metaphysics. Derrida asserted in *Speech and Phenomena* that metaphysical phenomenology is the metaphysics of presence because of the form of the eidetical. He also showed that those who wanted to destroy communication, linguistics, or philosophy themselves run up against metaphysics. Hence, we have Austin. Blum asks: Is there a common sense to which we can reconnect all the senses? I think Blum appeals to Wittgenstein. Ricoeur says already in his wonderful writings that symbols present a gift to thought and that illusion lies not in the attempt to look for a starting point but in the attempt to look for a presuppositionless beginning; he says, there is no presuppositionless philosophy. Thus, in order to break out of the hermeneutic circle, Ricoeur says, it's necessary to turn towards a wager. The wager throws us out of phenomenological description because we have to remember—returning with the aim of beginning, Ricoeur says—on the basis of the medium of speech. In light of the density of Ricoeur's text, I myself wouldn't dare say what his wager was. I would like him, however, to reveal it to us, to reveal the presupposition underlying his work. Thus, I am asking all three speakers the same question, a question which is neither one of method nor of linguistics, but a question concerning the foundation of communication.

René Schaerer: All three speakers are going to respond. Professor Ricoeur, I believe that you were mentioned last. So, perhaps you would like to say a few words.

Paul Ricoeur: The question is: what are my presuppositions? I haven't at all organized my paper around the idea of a wager. Fundamentally I attempted to see how far the method of analytic philosophy could go when applied to the themes of discourse. What I made use of was more detailed and more complex in the analytic tradition, namely, the subordination of logic within a theory of utterances to a theory of discursive acts. In this theory of discursive acts, I attempted to complicate what's mistakenly called the mental. I called this the noetic, which allowed me to hook up with the phenomenological theme of intention, but now freed of its psychologizing confusions. If there was a wager, it occurred at the beginning of my conclusion, namely, that we cannot meditate on communication, if we haven't looked upon the abyss of incommunicability. Therefore, there's a boundary between communicability and incommunicability; this boundary is probably what my work rests upon. To bring this to light, however, I had to make a second-degree reflection. Did you notice that in relation to discourse I used the word *wonder* or *miracle* twice? This means that communication does not in principle work; communication is not a fact. Conveyed by discourse, communication is an extremely precarious result. If there was a metaphysical aspect or layer to my paper, it was that communication rises out of a fundamental incommunicability that I called, in the conclusion, the psychical. My paper contains a certain monadic vision. Communication is a sort of struggle, precarious and rarely successful.

René Schaerer [to Joos]: I would be pleased if Derrida and Blum would like to say something, after which you can follow up.

Ernest Joos: I understand Ricoeur's position when he says that he takes incommunicability as his starting point. As Ricoeur indicates, to look now for metaphysical roots other than this would be another task.

Paul Ricoeur: Yes, I'm ready to discuss what's in my paper but not what's not. I believe the most I can say then is that what would have to be questioned is the concept of monad. This was apparent to me at the beginning [of my paper], but as an operative concept, operative in the sense Derrida used this morning following Fink. In every paper there are operative concepts, concepts with which we work and with these concepts we work "upon" other concepts which become thematic. You're asking me to engage in a second-degree discourse and work, which would make the operatory emerge in order to be rendered thematic. This is what I would have really liked to reflect upon, but it's extremely difficult. It's a question of the status of monadism in philosophy, a monadism we verify constantly in the extremely precarious character of communication. Ethical problems arise there, but I wanted to keep them at bay because I only wanted to present the relation of logic to discursive operations and to the boundary of the intentional which analytic philosophy has revived in some way, nothing more.

Jacques Derrida: I would like to make neither a too cryptic response to the question nor dismiss it. In regard to the question of the origin of iterability, as you've asked it, I will say simply, however, that if there is an iterability in general, as I tried to show, not only in writing in the strict sense but also in signification in general, even in what we call spoken language and even in prelinguistic experience insofar as there is no experience separate from chains of differential marks—and as soon as there are differential marks, there is the trace, identifiability, iterability, etc.—insofar, therefore, as this iterability is general, the origin no longer exists. Or at least the question of origin is discovered, in its turn, to be questioned or disturbed in its philosophic presuppositions. The form of the question of origin has a history; what are we asking for in a question of origin? In philosophy, each time that we ask this question we presuppose, it seems, that at least a simple point exists, an uncomplicated source, a "stigma," if you like, an instant or a point, something which will not allow itself to be precisely divided; a divisible origin is no longer an origin. Thus, every question of origin implies that a simple origin existed. With the notion of general iterability I tried to propose a general structure in which the origin no longer exists or, at any rate, exists only as a secondary effect. Being an effect means as well being dependent on a cause or being an appearance within a system which it no longer commands. Therefore, origin-like effects exist, but there is no ontological, archeological, theological, etc. origin. This is the sense, if you like, in which I will not object to the question of origin. When I have the chance, I will question what it metaphysically presupposes.

May I be permitted to diverge and reopen the question that our speaker [Joos] just asked Ricoeur? In regard to the monad, more precisely to the problem of monadism, I found myself asking the following; and it will follow up on what I just said. Each time that the concept of monad appears in the history of philosophy, notably with Leibniz and Husserl, the multiplicity of monads has always been regulated in some way, conceived as regulated, by a law. In Leibniz's case this law was the divine understanding which dominates, for example, the expressivity or expression among all the monads. Although the monads do not communicate with each other, their harmony is regulated by a law the concept of which the divine understanding contains. With Husserl, the multiplicity of monads is regulated by a polar *telos*, a *telos* of rational communication. Thus, I would like to ask Paul Ricoeur the following question: when he makes use of the concept of psychic monad, has he freed it from this theological or teleological horizon that dominated Leibniz as well as Husserl?

Paul Ricoeur: That will depend upon the type of discourse within which the question is posed. In a philosophic discourse the problem of the horizon of incommunicability certainly remains an absolutely, indeterminable horizon. The brute fact of incommunicability is in some way verified every time that we don't happen to hit it off with someone, when a discussion doesn't ensue, when our discursive marks of recognition don't happen to coincide. There is a sort of incommunicability behind us and, secondly, before us there is a task of communication. And I think that this idea of incommunicability behind and a task of communication in front cannot be overcome philosophically. In other species of discourse such as poetic discourse, mythic discourse, religious discourse, a different problematic could come about, and we could then ask whether it can be freed from metaphysics, for example, themes like those of the communion or of the participation of all in a mystical body. These are perfectly understandable problems, problems which humans have understood and which they continue to understand. Such problems, however, do not belong to the same problematic as I just alluded to, which is regulated by the discourse. Now, I would like to ask you a question which is the opposite of the one you asked me. It seems to me that in your paper you somewhat excessively inflated the problems of writing because you tackled problems which had not been treated in their correct place, which were problems of discourse. Discursivity, in fact, possesses all the characteristics you recognized in writing. You, however, were compelled to refer to writing because, in my eyes, you remained in a semiology and never in a semantics, that is, you remained in a semiology concerned with the conditions of the sign. Since these conditions are not satisfied in the phonic order, you had to investigate another order, that of the trace, distanciation, spacing, etc. I say, however...precisely because there is a gigantic hole in your whole enterprise, because you have no theory of meaning. Then you are compelled to inflate the theory of writing, all of which has not been constructed in its proper place, within a theory of discourse. If you construct this theory of discourse, it can account for the characteristics of writing that you've demonstrated. It can do this because all the characteristics that you attributed to writing can be found within discursivity itself. This is a little of what I would like to discuss with you concerning the problem of discourse.

René Schaerer: We would be pleased if Derrida would like to say something in response.

Jacques Derrida: Without a doubt, the lack, among others, of a theory of discourse is very noticable, not only in the paper I delivered this morning but also in propositions I've risked elsewhere. In an entirely preliminary way, what's interested me in a theory of discourse, which in fact is necessary, is simply to record all of what is presupposed, in short, all the things left uncriticized, which, it seems to me, restrain right up to the present the attempts at a theory of discourse witnessed in linguistics as well as in philosophy. These presuppositions are the ones I very schematically outlined this morning, namely, that something like the event, for example, was obvious, that we would know what an event was. Now a theory of discourse presupposes a theory of the event, a theory of the act, a speech act theory, a theory of the act as singular event. I tried to mark in the theory of event, for example—but this concept is connected to a whole group of other concepts—I tried to mark what prevents every supposed event from being constituted as an event in this philosophic sense (singular, actual, present, irreplaceable, unrepeatable, etc.). The event's singularity is divided by the simple fact that the event was a genre of discourse, simply, a semiological event. And when you say that...

Paul Ricoeur: That's not the same thing.

Jacques Derrida: Yes, I'm going to try...

Paul Ricoeur: This distinction between semiology and semantics...

Jacques Derrida: exactly...I'm coming to it...

Paul Ricoeur: appears to me absolutely fundamental...

Jacques Derrida: I'm coming to it.

Paul Ricoeur: and mixed together in a theory of writing. In lots of ways this theory is semiological, but it aims to resolve semantic problems with semiological resources.

Jacques Derrida: Yes, which brings me then to this point. In a certain way—I want to be precise—in a preliminary way, I have also attempted a critique of semiology. Therefore, it seems to me hard to enclose what I do in a semiology. Nevertheless, it seems to me just as hard to do away with the semiological strata in a theory of discourse; it cannot be erased there. Whether we like it or not, a discourse will remain caught in a chain, in a lattice of what we would traditionally call signs. And whatever the originality or specificity of discourse would be in relation to the chain of signs, we have to take account of the fact that discourse cannot exist without semiotic marks. Thus, I have not at all tried to reduce discourse to a set of signs, but I have tried to keep us from forgetting that there are still signs in discourse, that discourse exists with the sign, with the differential chain, with spacing, etc. This is all of what we...

Paul Ricoeur: Yes, but I believe we really have to distinguish what we understand by spacing. The spacing found in discourse is not the same as what you find in the semiological order when a sign is distinct from another sign. This is the semiological spacing that may be phonic or graphic. Discursive spacing is something else entirely. For example, Strawson distinguishes the subject function and predicate function. You have spacing there, but this is entirely different because you have to start from the "symploke," from the internal connection. If you lack a theory of the sentence, you can never distinguish the characteristics proper to semantics from the semiological ones. I agree when you say that discourse is always caught in signs, but discourse can also change this lattice. This is what translation does. Then the problem is to know what we translate; what we translate is the discourse's meaning. You make it pass from one semiological system to another. What's transferred? The characteristics of meaning. If you, however, lack a theory of meaning, you can't construct a theory of translation either.

Jacques Derrida: Was I mistaken about your restricting difference to the semiological as if semantic difference doesn't exist, as if difference doesn't also constitute the semantic?

Paul Ricoeur: Yes, but I don't capitalize the word *difference*...

Jacques Derrida: You've often complained about my capitalizing *differ-ence*...I've never done it....

Paul Ricoeur: but [you write it] with an "a"...

Jacques Derrida: But that gives the word another meaning...

Paul Ricoeur: That does give the word another meaning. There are dif-ferences between signs. Then there is the fact that the subject is not the predicate. Finally, there are differences everywhere. But what's important is that discourse produces, by its own differences which are not semio-logical differences, effects of discourse which are not effects of signs.

Jacques Derrida: I agree entirely. That's why I never said that difference might have to be restricted to the semiological element. I said that dif-ference itself is "essentially" or "by definition" differential. This means that there are differences, there are different types of difference, and that there are semiological differences and differences in the semantic order.

Paul Ricoeur: Then [difference] is entirely within the semiological precisely because there are only differences, while it's a functional instrument in discourse. Then it cannot be overestimated.

Jacques Derrida: It comes down to this question: Can we erase or reduce the differential element in the semantic order or in discourse?

Paul Ricoeur: But who wants to reduce it? We have to see how it works. We have to construct a theory of discourse in order to know this. Only by constructing a theory of discourse will we come to know this. We will know, for example, how the identifying function works with the predicative function, how the predicative function is going to be articulated in terms of characterization, in terms of classification. All of these are differences, but these are differences which are differences of discourse. And we have to know what the discursive dimension is in order to know how these differences work. There is not only difference; there is also the same. For example, when I speak to you, I hope that you understand the sentence just as I pronounce it, because even if you disagree with me, we have to be disagreeing about the same thing.

Jacques Derrida: That's what I called iteration this morning. Iteration implies same and difference, same and other, if you like. The difference between same and other is what I call *différance*—precisely with an "a." *Différance* implies that alterity would not simply be the screen between the different things, but that there would be an economic system of differences which in fact presupposes the intervention of the same. This is why I will never oppose, as you seem to do, difference to "symploke." I believe that difference in fact implies and is implied by "symploke."

Paul Ricoeur: What is absolutely important for me is the recognition of the discursive order as being settled by no discussion concerning the semiotic order and [as] calling for its own analysis. My problem consisted in discovering the discipline within which all the characteristics of discourse can be inscribed. I said that it is not linguistics—not even a linguistics of discourse—because it's still too bound up with discussions of language as a system (*langue*). Precisely in the manner of speech, it treats only the residues of *langue*. The flaw in a theory of speech is that it is always a residue of a theory of *langue*. The discipline is not logic either because logic is only bare propositions. It's not a philosophy of spirit because it implies mentalism. Consequently, this is the place where speech act theory has appeared to me to be a certain unifying structure. But then whether this discourse is spoken or written has appeared to me to be relatively indifferent because the fundamental characteristics of semantics are relatively indifferent to this difference. I said *relatively* because I believe that we can justify the transition to writing made by all cultures entirely by the fact that material inscription is done only in order to get into print what was already in discourse, namely, its distanciation from its speaker and what that is is the meaning. Only a theory of meaning and not a theory of signs can provide an account of precisely this difference. Moreover, my discourse can go beyond me and reach you. The cure for monadic solitude to which all of us aspire is there, and this, in fact, would be the place to ask why we want to communicate, why we're not satisfied with being just ourselves but want in a certain way to be another by means of discourse. This would be the ethical and theological, but I haven't spoken of these.

Jacques Derrida: I'd like to say that I agree entirely with you about the task of a specific theory of discourse, even if the horizon or the foundations of this task can be conceived differently. I agree entirely that it's necessary to develop a specific theory of discourse. On the other hand, I agree entirely—and I indicated this in passing this morning—that a certain imperialism of linguistics in this domain has to be criticized. And it seems to me—here I also agree with you—that Austin's theory is interesting in regard to this point. Therefore, we're in complete agreement there also. Finally, in regard to the distinction between speech and writing that you mentioned at the end, I would like to note simply that, as the traditional distinction, it has never interested me, and I don't subscribe to it at all. What interests me is a transformation of the concept of writing. I'm not at all interested in writing as notation or as the reproduction of a discourse, in any case not as something vis-à-vis speech. If this sort of writing interests me, it does insofar as it can provide a certain number of guiding threads along which we can read the history of philosophy concerning this point.

René Schaerer: Ladies and gentlemen, I don't mean to put an end to this unique, friendly debate, but I would like to give Professor Blum the opportunity to respond to the question.

Roland Blum: I don't know if I'm going to respond to the question, but I would like to speak with Derrida a little. It seems to me that you place yourself somewhat on the opposite side of all the other philosophers discussed today, whether it's Levinas or Strawson or Searle. I believe that all of them want to keep in touch with the world of common sense. And it seems to me that in your semiotic theory—moreover, I think this is what Ricoeur objects to—you reduce or eliminate this world that all of us accept and on the basis of which we live. There's a paradox there because [we have to ask], as Wittgenstein or perhaps Strawson would say: what relation or connection exists between the world you've created (the world of differences) and the world from which you started, the world of events, at the end of the account? For example, a speech act is an event. We all know that we can speak, that we can start [to speak] and that we can stop. This is a speech act, and the issue is to analyze it; this is what Searle has done, what Strawson as well tries to do, and Levinas. You, however, make this vanish, like a magician, if I can say this. What, therefore, is the connection between your starting point and what you discover? This is what I don't understand.

Jacques Derrida: Heaven help me if I've created, as you said, a world, especially if it's one of differences!

Gilles Lane: I would like to ask Professor Derrida a question, a question which is simultaneously an objection. I would like to hear his reactions concerning this subject. It's clear that we can't blame someone who's in the midst of investigating something for not being able to say immediately what he has discovered. It seems to me, however, that there is room in a paper, above all in a philosophy conference, to express at least what one hopes to discover, what one might catch a glimpse of discovering, or perhaps at least what one hopes won't be discovered. Otherwise, it lacks the absolutely basic components without which papers are descriptions which appear to us like noises absolutely insignificant for what constitutes communication itself.

I would like to ask now the question that will perhaps provide the opportunity for Derrida to say something about this or to indicate why he doesn't want to say anything about it. I'm referring to the last remark of his paper this morning, a rather mysterious remark at that, a remark about something like an improbable signature. I didn't understand exactly. But what I believed I grasped, in a rather vivid impression, was that, on Derrida's part, there was a certain irritation with something or someone. If I'm mistaken, Professor Derrida will be able to say that there was absolutely no irritation, that everything was very placid. Otherwise, this will perhaps be an opportunity to respond to this objection or to say why he's not responding to the objection.

Jacques Derrida: Are you asking me a question about irritation?

Paul Ricoeur: About the improbable.

Jacques Derrida: In the draft that I sent to Professor Cauchy, this rather elliptical conclusion on the improbable signature was followed twice by my signature, the handwritten version, and then, as we usually do, the typed version below it. This continued some propositions concerning the in some way divided—I am going to return to the word *divided*—character of every signature. Austin and along with him common sense—and here I'm returning to your [Blum's] question—see the signature as the written equivalent to the source event of discourse. [It's believed that] when a signature is affixed somewhere, the origin of discourse, of written discourse in this case, is in some way stapled, marked, identifiable, and, in this sense, event-like, absolutely singular. Now, prior to this elliptical conclusion, I tried to show that [Austin] could not have the signature functioning there as a signature, because there are signatures which function as such on checks, in political treaties, in letters, etc. And I didn't allow myself an easily skeptical comment about the value of a lot of signatures at the bottom of checks, at the bottom of political treaties, and at the bottom of letters; I didn't make an argument out of it. I simply made the comment that in order for these signatures to have signature effects in the best cases (that is, the cases in which the check is honored because there's money in the account or in which the pact is honored because the peace treaty is respected), in all of these best cases the signature must be identifiable or readable in order for the signature to work as such. Its form would have to be recognizable, repeatable. A signature that would take place just once in a noncoded, unreadable form would not be a signature. Therefore, in order for a signature to take place once, it must have taken place many times already or it must have been able for it to take place many times already. This is what I call the division of the event of signature. There is no pure signature event, no pure signature. Like every event of discourse or of writing, a signature is in itself dubitable, imitable, and, therefore, falsifiable. And a theory of the signature that does not take account of this falsifiability can in no way render an account of what can be the so-called authentic effect of the signature. This is what I had suggested previously as a signature's improbability. The irony of this conclusion, of this fall upon the improbable signature, is that: when you get right down to it, who would really believe that, during the course of a unique event, a singular and irreplaceable individual signed the text that I presented this morning? If this had happened and if it really constituted a unique and irreplaceable event, would this event have been readable, would communication have taken place? I don't believe so. My communication, therefore, could have some chance of being communicable only insofar as its signature was altogether improbable.

Paul Ricoeur: I'm not at all satisfied with this analysis of the signature because it lacks its support. This support is twofold, and only a theory of discourse provides it. First, a theory of the proper name is needed. There are fifteen years of literature in the analytic tradition on the proper name. If there's no proper name, there's no signature. The signature is the mark of the proper name. Material spacing is nothing next to the problem of the expression of a proper name. The way a proper name works in language is a problem of discourse; it's no longer a problem of the signature.

Jacques Derrida: That's the question I'm asking.

Paul Ricoeur: Secondly, you don't sign just anything. For example, the signature on your paper is not at all the same as the signature on a check. [You signed your paper] simply so that we wouldn't confuse yours with someone else's. But, in any case, I believe that we don't need to blow these things out of proportion. We have to proceed analytically. You have signing situations that are entirely incomparable. You don't want your text to be confused with someone else's. You happen to be correcting some transcripts that someone forgot to sign; because we don't know who wrote them, it's necessary to make an identification. What, then, is the identification function? Or yet again, you have some signatures that commit the signer [to something]. But then it's the code, not the signature, which states that if we signed a certain piece of paper in certain circumstances, then you've committed yourself [to something]. What does it mean to be committed? That description of the signature will not tell you what it means to be committed. [Commitment depends] on the play of a language in which the signature is inscribed. In the performative, the signature effectively plays the role of the first person subject. It doesn't matter whether there was or was not a signature of the subject. What matters is the play of language in which the signature testifies to a commitment. I find myself wondering how you can turn the signature into a theory of commitment if you lack a theory of intention. In particular, how can you reflect upon the meaning of honesty? I believe that we'd have to do a lot with jurisprudence here in order to see how a signature effectively functions in the cases where the signature has the value of commitment and not simply that of identification, of non-confusion as if I think it was all the same case. The signature on your paper was not an oath; it was there so that Cauchy wouldn't think that it came from someone else.

Jacques Derrida: I quite agree that a signature concerned with commitment has a specificity which doesn't correspond to a signature of a philosophic text. In fact, there's need to construct a differential theory of signatures. Nevertheless, the signature to a commitment wouldn't be possible if there wasn't a signature in general, [if there wasn't a signature] at a level we could call transcendental, at a level of the signature in general, a level of what defines a signature. The subject himself must be identifiable as the one who signed, etc. At this level I ask the question of the proper, of the proper name, etc. Here I believe the question becomes: Is there a proper?

Paul Ricoeur: That's something else.

Jacques Derrida: Yes.

Paul Ricoeur: It's exactly like Russell.

Jacques Derrida: I'm quite convinced of it.

Yvon Gauthier: I have two brief questions and I hope that the responses will also be brief. The first is addressed to Ricoeur. The intersection of analytic philosophy and phenomenology seems to be very problematic in regard to the point in your paper that is starting to look essential to me, that of incommunicability. It seems to me that analytic philosophy hasn't thematized incommunicability since Wittgenstein's thesis concerning the impossibility of a private language. The second question is for Derrida on the question of iterability. In an extreme case such as mathematical writing (which is also a type of writing), doesn't iterability complement recursion? Thus, for a recursive function you have a successor function. In this way isn't this iterability, being the mark and sign of a *telos* or of a destination, at the same time a recursion towards the same, that is, finally, whether in writing or in discourse, a recursion towards the word, the originary word, the writer or the speaker? Doesn't iterability complement recursion?

Paul Ricoeur: I'll be very brief in response to your question because it's extremely interesting. You said that there is a point at which perhaps phenomenology and analytic philosophy don't intersect, the question of incommunicability; I'm, however, trying to find an intersection even there. I'm very interested precisely in Wittgenstein's discussion of the problem of other minds, a problem which in the German tradition is called the problem of the other, of the alter ego. By means of the examples, you know that all the analytic discussions revolve around the question of pain, of suffering. How can I know that when I say to you, "I suffer," you can identify it as having the same meaning? If suffering is private, the other's suffering is not the same, and I shouldn't use the same word. This is a very interesting problem. And it makes me say that the example is well chosen because there we are perhaps at the point of incommunicability, namely, to suffer from it. This is what I had in mind when I spoke of a basic incommunicability, incommunicability as non-noetic, lived experience. A lived experience which is not noetic or which is not "noetizable," if you like, is one which cannot be conveyed discursively, and that is perhaps what it means to suffer from [incommunicability]. Maybe we have to look at the part of Michel Henry's work on passivity; we probably have the very root of incommunicability in a meditation on passivity. Finally, however, I don't want to say any more about it because the analytic philosophers, justifiably, wouldn't like that, saying more about it.

Jacques Derrida: Listen, I entirely agree with the proposition that made up the first part of your question on iterability and recursion in mathematics. But I swear I don't understand the second part about mathematical writing implying the return to the original word and the mark of a destination or *telos.* I swear I just don't understand it.

Yvon Gauthier: You first stressed iterability, that is, the movement towards an end or a destination.

Jacques Derrida: No, I didn't use those words...

Yvon Gauthier: You spoke of the other, of alienation, if you like.

Jacques Derrida: I spoke of the other, not of alienation. And I didn't align the other with the idea of destination or *telos*...

Yvon Gauthier: Let's talk about the general concept of iterability, of writing as iteration. Isn't this iteration simultaneously a return to the same, that is, a recursion towards an origin? Isn't it iteration in itself? Isn't it an index of an origin and not [the index] of the mark or sign of an end, of the trace of an end?

Jacques Derrida: It is perhaps, even certainly, the index of the origin. But, at the same time, [iterability is] the limit blocking the return to the origin. There's an indestructible desire to return to the origin, therefore, marked, in fact, in every trace and in every mark. The fact, however, that the mark is a mark prohibits, it seems to me, the return to the origin from happening fully. Therefore, if *index* means here the desire aiming or pointing nostalgically towards the origin or nostalgically towards a *telos* or "eschaton," that's fine. But what we especially have to remember is what at a certain point impedes and divides this path toward the origin, toward the *telos.*

Yvon Gauthier: I'm using the word *word* in the sense that Heidegger and Gadamer use it, in the sense that language is already wholly inscribed in the word.

Jacques Derrida: In the word?

Yvon Gauthier: Yes, in the word, that is, *das Wort*.

Jacques Derrida: Yes, but my paper this morning implies, at least in a very indirect and distant way, a great mistrust of the word, of this unit called the word. [This] mistrust is difficult to justify quickly here, but it concerns everything that philosophy has invested in this unit that linguists unanimously recognize as a unit completely relative to...

Paul Ricoeur: to discourse...

Jacques Derrida: yes, to discourse...

Claude Panaccio: My question is directed to Paul Ricoeur who, towards the end of his paper yesterday, asserted that promising involves the one promising being sincere and he generalized this condition called sincerity to every form of assertion and discourse. On the basis of this, my question is twofold. First, what is the status of this involvement? Basically, isn't it already the issue of a moral need that we've imposed upon discourse from the outside, and which might be irrelevant to the theory of discourse? Second, along the same lines, how are we to treat then sentences or assertions in which the speaker doesn't believe? I'm obviously thinking of lies, but also of fiction and of an example within the genre of fiction: suppose we discover that Descartes didn't believe his *Meditations*, that he wrote them in order to get a job or something like that. What happens to the meaning of his work?

Paul Ricoeur: Yes, that's very interesting. I want to make a slight correction. You said that I generalized the condition of sincerity to all the forms of discourse. No, I said that in all the language games which can be considered acts of discourse, there is a function comparable [to sincerity]. For example, in the case of assertion, there's belief. I can't make an assertion without committing myself. And this way of being committed in an assertion constitutes the noetic element of the act, which is not simply a logical act; it's likely it would be the support of moral predicates. And since all the acts are produced in a cultural *milieu*, we are not in an ethically neutral *milieu*. All the ways of being committed are marked by prior ethical structures. We don't know an ethically neutral world. There will perhaps be a world, for example, in which murder is allowed, but then something else will be forbidden. What I'm arguing, however, is that if the act supports a potential ethical structure, the act is not an ethical phenomenon as such. It's an act which refers to the subject. The act is an utterance related to the utterer, and it is this relation that is absolutely fundamental. In Grice's language, and all his work is based on this, this relation is the possibility of the transformation of what he calls "utterance," the transformation of the "utterance's meaning to utterer's meaning." I just noticed Derrida make use of it when someone made an objection. He said: "I didn't say that this morning" or better, "I never had that word in mind." There is always a moment in discourse when we return to our discourse in order either to defend or support it. This means that it refers to us. In other words, when we don't recognize ourselves in a discourse that someone attributes to us, we say, "I didn't say that." We're not content with saying, "My discourse didn't say that"; we say instead, "I didn't say it."

Discourse's reference to the utterer seems to me to be part of a theory of discourse as such. Discourse is self-referential. All known languages are, therefore, constructed such that they contain self-referential elements. In my work, I call them marks of self-referentiality. Some will be grammatical, some lexical; there are thousands of varieties. This is semiology, which is realized by diverse means. What's important, however, is the self-referential function. This, I believe, is Austin's great discovery.

Jacques Derrida: What can I say about the question? What status does this "commitment" or self-referentiality of the subject have in a so-called fictional discourse, in, for example, a literary form where we have to deal with effects of this type? If the issue is a more or less recent type [of fiction], a novel, for example, is it the case that there was no commitment here? Or what would be the relation between this commitment and what you take as real commitment, commitment in the world or in life?

Paul Ricoeur: But we'd have to construct a theory of commitment. This is the place where I would say the problem of writing is very interesting; it creates in effect disjunctions in which we no longer know who commits himself in the discourse. It's important, however, to see the thing all the way through. This means that if we construct a theory of writing, we also have to have one of reading. You can't construct an abstract theory of writing; you can only have a theory of both writing and reading.

And it has to be constructed in comparison to speaking and hearing; [it has] to show in what way it's the same and different. There are lots of differences between these two structures, but writing completes itself in reading. It's in reading then that someone commits himself in a certain way, even if he only commits himself "fictively," as a reader of a novel, by believing in it without believing in it. What emerges here are all the paradoxes of the comedian and of the reader. In this case, the reader is committed in an imaginative, not ethical, way; he's opened for himself one possible way of being. This is what Heidegger aptly called *Verstehen.* Something happens which opens its own possibilities. And in this opening of its own possibilities, in this act of reading, there is a "commitment," even if the literary act suspended it in some way.

Jacques Derrida: Don't take me at my word if I say that this morning I precisely associated the reader with the writer, that I think just like you, that a theory of writing is inseparable from a theory of reading. Now, concerning the issue of the literary phenomenon, you seem to subsume it under the category of the imaginary. Do you think that this category can account for the specificity of literary writing? Isn't it a traditional category or a category of representation which might correspond either to a certain form of literature or to a certain representation that literature has given of itself? Do you think that the concept of the imaginary can handle this theory of literature?

Paul Ricoeur: I don't conceive the imaginary at all as representative. The imaginary is exactly the complete opposite of a representation since it sketches possibilities, possible ways of being in the world. This is why I said that a text always has a reference. It's a type of world which is open, in which I could live or in which I would like to live or in which I would like to be. And thus within this sketch there is an opening of being. Moreover, I called this imagination in a rather Schellingean sense....I especially wanted to oppose the imaginary to the ethical because the analysis of the promise encloses us into the ethical too much.

Claude Panaccio: Must we go so far as saying that insincere statements are not statements at all?

Paul Ricoeur: No, but I think this would be the place where we would need to construct a whole theory of modifications. We can understand modifications only on the basis of an "Ur," on the basis of a primal form. If I don't know what pure and simple being is, I wouldn't know what possible or fictive being is. Through modifications I can produce the whole fictive series. Of course there'd be much more interesting examples concerning irony. In analytic philosophy there's been some very interesting work on commitment in irony.

Clément Légaré: The symbol has been frequently mentioned in the conference but we know little about it so far; it's been sort of a mystery. In earlier discussions, it was said that all words are symbols; moreover, we speak of mathematical symbols, logical symbols, etc. Then a question arises: Among all these symbols, which are more symbolic than others? I'm addressing my question to Ricoeur: what is the structural status of the symbol? And during the course of discursive expression what allows us to detect the symbol? Is the symbolic effect perceived in the semiological order of the semic kernal or is it rather in the semantic order of *classemes*?

Paul Ricoeur: I'm not very happy to have to improvise about something which is not in my field. I can only say what my analysis implies about this. You know that my earlier work was concerned with symbolic expressions. Today, however, I see that this was premature because it lacked a semantic foundation and precisely a theory of discourse. I don't want to go back over it but I no longer believe that the symbol is a phenomenon of words; it is a discursive phenomenon. This means that all words possess many meanings, and polysemy is general. All discourse, however, is not polysemous and that's where the problem of the symbol lies. In what types of discourse do certain words preserve more than one signification in order to create a certain meaningful effect that we call the symbol? Better armed, I would say, this is the way that I would now attack the problem of the symbol. The symbol is a discursive effect based on the general polysemy of all words in ordinary language. However, you can make two types of discourse with polysemous words. You can make univocal discourses, discourses in which polysemy is reduced. This happens by all sorts of mechanisms which belong to the very nature of discourse, for instance, by the fact that only one dimension of one word's meaning sanctions only one dimension of the other words' meanings and by the phenomenon of co-optation which Greimas has described quite clearly. Next to this sort of screening of polysemy is the type of discourse in which polysemy is not only allowed but desired and maintained. There we have a certain effect, the symbolic effect. This comes about when many dimensions of meaning come into play simultaneously because a certain structure of the sentence has preserved them. The problem then becomes one of discovering the function of such a discourse, of discovering why we seek this discursive effect. By maintaining many dimensions of meaning, don't we preserve the possibilities of discourse to say the plurivocal aspects of reality, of being, of appearance disclosed by discourse's preserved plurivocity? This is how I would, therefore, attack the problem of the symbol today.

Roger Marcotte: I have a question for Derrida. Towards the end of your paper, you presented your conclusions as being able to be applied to every form of communication. It seems in the case of an artwork, which is a form of communication, iterability is impossible because, if an artwork is repeated, it's a copy. As different epochs come to know it, it changes value and it changes sense; it is better understood or worse than the first time. The person who made it cannot make another work exactly like the first in all respects. Therefore, how would the thoroughgoing iterability that you spoke about be applied to an artwork?

Jacques Derrida: Although I have to improvise my answer a little, I believe your question is quite fundamental. I'm going to refer to some very brief but very certain, it seems to me, Husserlian analyses and to certain examples Husserl provides of musical or visual artworks. He shows that an artwork cannot exist unless a certain ideality connected to the work's identity is constituted. If I cannot identify a painting, a sculpture, or a piece of music (which is itself repeated, interpreted, performed, etc.) as the same work, if I cannot identify it as the same, I cannot recognize in it the particular noematic content which identifies it as an artwork. How is this identity constituted? Clearly we are concerned with the identity of a singular event; there is only one statue, one painting, one exemplar, and the rest are copies. Well, this identity itself presupposes, that, in order to experience it, I can return to it, that I can retain the imprint of it. It is in the experience of iteration that the identity with its meaning as a singular event is constituted. I'm assuming here that you agree with me that an artwork, even though it might be a singular event, does not exist independently of my experience of it. It's not an object in itself. If it was an object in itself, it would not be posited as an artwork. It is defined as an event of art by means of a certain type of relation. On the one hand, [it relates] to its maker who is separated from it; on the other, [it relates] to the audience or spectator. We have to search within this experience for the root of iteration as the condition of the event's identity. If this event would be produced only once, and if I would see an object only in an absolutely fleeting instant, I would not be able to recognize it as an artwork, as the object and event of art. A certain return and repetition of my experience has to inscribe a trace structure, a structure of retention and anticipation, so that this ideal unity which makes the object the same as itself is constituted. This is why your question seems to me, in fact, to be altogether fundamental. In the case of these singular events, the type of iteration is not of the same order as the type of iteration found in other artworks, for example, in written art. There is iteration there but of an entirely other form. The multiplication of exemplars there doesn't maintain the same relation to the original as it does in music, which doesn't possess the same relation as painting, architecture, etc., either. Although we have here a differential typology of iteration, I believe that iteration exists in all the cases.

Thomas de Koninck: I would like to ask Ricoeur one question and Derrida one question. My question for Ricoeur is twofold: I would like to ask you to be specific about what Austin lacks and what Grice adds to Austin's position. And for Derrida: I would like to ask him also to be specific about or to recapitulate his critique of Austin?

Paul Ricoeur: From Grice's work, which is already considerable, I kept only the problem of the convertability of the significations of sentences into the signfications of the originators. This is what I was interested in. How is this play regulated? How can we make the transition from a "this means that" to an "I mean that"? Grice's problem is based on the fact that the verb, *to mean,* can have a personal subject or an impersonal one. What I was trying to say was that while analytic philosophy doesn't possess the means to resolve this problem, it does have the means to state that this transition constantly takes place in ordinary language and that ordinary language works on the basis of it. My claim is that—and you're right to think that I've added to Grice—we can give an account of the relation between what the analytic tradition calls extensionality and intensionality by means of another type of analysis which I called transcendental phenomenology. We can, therefore, introduce terms which appear to be psychological, terms like *believing* and *wanting*, into a logic which provides its proofs in quantification. Grice's problem resides here: how does quantification work when logic includes intensional operators? Russell tried to solve the problem by extracting the operators, by putting them in front. Thus, when we believe something, we go from the proposition 'P' to the proposition 'I believe that P.' While adding nothing to the meaning, it adds an intensional operator. The whole problem was to have a sort of formalization for the operators. In *Mental Acts*, Peter Geach tried to take the problem farther, and in a direction that would certainly interest Derrida because it is based on citation. We can say that interior discourse is a type of citation: "The Pharoah says to himself, 'the Jews may be destroyed'." "The Jews may be destroyed" is a type of citation as opposed to intensional operators. Here analytic philosophy seems to me to reach a sort of limit. As Grice says at the end of his "Utterer's Meaning, Sentence-Meaning and Word Meaning," I'm not going to deny myself the freedom of introducing intensional terms into a discourse nevertheless marked by extensional logic, formalization, quantification, etc.[1] ...For myself, I believe that it's really the task of a phenomenology to give a fundamental account of this possibility. In [phenomenology], I think, you have the support for the linguistics of discourse which shows that this transformation from the sentence's meaning to the originator's meaning depends upon the possibility of discourse's being appropriated by its utterer. [This possibility] is inscribed in the very structure of *langue* which provides indicators, which provides what we call "shifters." Through these shifters discourse designates itself.

---

1. The actual passage to which Ricoeur refers can be found on pp. 241–242 of Grice's "Utterer's Meaning, Sentence-Meaning, and Word Meaning," in *Foundations of Language*, 4 (1968).

Jacques Derrida: Your question concerns completely what you called my critique of Austin. To be specific, the issue was not one of a critique. Fundamentally, a critique is never very interesting. I was less interested in the critique than in a certain determination of what Austin's discourse implies and in what still remains to be carried out in his project. This is why I stressed a number of times what he says about the general theory, which, in him, is forthcoming. He says that "we have to develop a general theory," but at that moment he doesn't construct it. Now, what's remarkable is that the general theory concerns precisely all the phenomena of failure, all the phenomena of negativity, of what we call the nonserious, the anomaly, the parasite, etc. What seems to me unfortunate in this incompleteness is that the fact of taking account of a negativity— let's summarize all of these [phenomena] under the heading of negativity—coextensive with all of discourse would have led him to define this negativity not as an accidental fact in the sense traditional philosophy most often takes the negative, like an accident, but as a structural element of the law of speech acts. While developing this general theory, he wouldn't have been able to push all the parasites aside. Under the heading of the parasite we find precisely the phenomenon of citation which seems to be indissolubly linked to the structure of every mark. This means that I don't think a mark can be constituted without its being able to be cited. Therefore, the entire graphematic structure is connected to citationality, to the possibility of being repeated. And since a mark is repeatable, this means that it no longer needs me to continue to have its effects. Insofar as I make use of an instrument that bears within itself its repeatability, I am absented from what I use. And it's necessary to take account of this absence, even in spoken language. In spoken language, if I couldn't be absented permanently from the signs I emit, they wouldn't be able to function as signs, as marks. This is the kernal of what I think we have to add to Austin's theory insofar as it's to be generalized. Let me add also in passing what he says about intention as it organizes context—since speech act theory implies a theory of determinable context, the theory of the unconscious is a theory of consciousness, of consciousness actually present to what it utters—this appears to me to foreclose massively everything in language that doesn't depend upon consciousness. [This is the case] whether we determine the unconscious in a Saussurean way or by means of psychoanalysis, which moreover has been totally absent from our discussions since yesterday and which nevertheless cannot be left in the margins of a communication theory. Despite the interest it arouses in other respects and no matter how profound it might be, speech act theory seems to me to be rooted in a philosophy of consciousness which seems to me to have it limits.

Gilles Lane: I have a question concerning the notion of iterability. For awhile I've felt uneasy. I think I can be more specific about this uneasiness and ask Derrida himself to be specific about it as well. It seems to me that the claim that iterability would be essential to the mark is an hypothesis. There's no doubt that, in fact, given time we could repeat a lot of things. I'm wondering, however, whether iterability isn't rather a type of symbol of any sort of duality. What would be essential to the mark would be what takes place between the two poles. In any case, I would like Derrida to show us, by means of some examples, that the mark must be essentially iterable.

Jacques Derrida: If you don't mind, I'm going to throw the question back to you: show me a mark which cannot be iterated.

Gilles Lane: Well, the question of the artwork made me think of this.

Jacques Derrida: I've tried to respond to that question. Let's suppose— and I don't believe this—that the artwork is not iterable. Are you going to construct a theory of communication on the basis of the existence of artworks?

Gilles Lane: Of course not. I wouldn't construct a theory; I would want to pursue the experience and try to reflect upon it rather than start with the axiom that everything is iterable. If someone says, "Show me something that is not that," [and] if another person can't do it, it seems to me that this shows quite simply that [the second person] is wrong; it certainly doesn't show, however, that the first person is right.

Jacques Derrida: Look, I can show you thousands of marks which are iterable.

Paul Ricoeur: The adjective *iterable* is an adjective that is being applied to things other than marks. For example, I don't think that a citation would count as a mark because a citation is a sentence; a mark is a sign.

Jacques Derrida: That's an entirely arbitrary definition of the mark which is a sign...

Paul Ricoeur: A sentence is not a mark. The citation is a sentence to which we do not commit ourselves. We mention it, as the analytic philosophers say, we don't use it. [This is the] "use-mention" [distinction].

Jacques Derrida: Of course not. I'm using the concept of the mark in a very general sense in order to avoid being limited by the sign and all the connected concepts. If you want to define the mark simply as a notch in a piece of wood, then clearly my concept of mark is extraordinarily broad. I'm using the concept of mark, however, in the sense of the generalization I tried to define in my paper. As for the examples of iterable marks, the reason I'm allowing myself to ask you the question of the example of the noniterable mark is that there are plenty of iterable marks. Clearly, you receive or understand each word in my paper, each word that I pronounce only insofar as you recognize them, only insofar as we can repeat them, only insofar as I can repeat them, only insofar as you can repeat them, etc.... It wouldn't be hard to find iterable marks; the problem is with the existence of a noniterable mark. Again, give me an example of one.

Gilles Lane: You're demonstrating that iterability is essential to the mark?

Jacques Derrida: Yes, my argument is extremely simple and traditional. In order to demonstrate that a predicate is essential, traditional philosophy tried to separate it from the substance or thing. If you happen to separate iterability from a mark, you've demonstrated to me that it is not an essential predicate. If you can't separate iterability from the mark, then in the language of traditional philosophy it has to be considered an essential predicate. This is what I tried to demonstrate.

Paul Ricoeur: By means of iterability, we reidentify. Because there are nonreidentifiable iterables...

Jacques Derrida: For example?

Paul Ricoeur: That which is other.

Jacques Derrida: Noniterable identifiable.

Paul Ricoeur: No, nonidentifiable iterable.

Jacques Derrida: For example?

Paul Ricoeur: Well, I've heard two performances of a symphony and I don't recognize Beethoven. Somebody has, however, pretended to give me another performance; I say "no, it's not the same."

Jacques Derrida: You say that you didn't identify?

Paul Ricoeur: Yes, that's correct. That's why the essential problem with the artwork is not such that we repeat a performance but that I recognize the same.

Jacques Derrida: You have there two identifications: the identification of the original that you think you recognize enough in order to distinguish it from the nonoriginal [and] the identification of the bad performance. In the second case, however, there's iterability...

Paul Ricoeur: and of what?

Jacques Derrida: Of the original model that you know to be sufficiently repeatable in order to distinguish it from the bad copy, and then from this bad copy...

Paul Ricoeur: But it's necessary that it's the same in order for me to be able to say that we repeat it.

Jacques Derrida: Yes.

Paul Ricoeur: But that's what's in question.

Jacques Derrida: But in order for you to say that you don't recognize Beethoven, you have to have something of Beethoven, some fragment of him, a memory...

Paul Ricoeur: An original performance, a sort of expert witness.

Jacques Derrida: Yes, and one which is itself repeatable. [If it wasn't repeatable,] you wouldn't be able to distinguish it from what looks like a bad performance, an aberration...

Paul Ricoeur: Perhaps...

Henri Declève: Professor Derrida, if I really understand what's being discussed, they're objecting to your saying—which is not what I would object to—that because of its very iterability every mark bears a possibility of being considered nonserious, of being considered, as they said, a citation. I think that Ricoeur said exactly what you meant: as a mark, the citation can be abused and that is implied in the very idea of a mark. So far, I would completely agree. Likewise, a certain irony is implied in every type of signature, especially in the one at the bottom of a philosophic text which concerns communication. But the question could then be extended. Does the fact that philosophy must go through this exercise in irony and through this radical recognition of irony in the mark's iterability imply for you anything other than the expansion of what we've called since Kant the transcendental field? Can the ideas of consciousness, of the philosophy of an ineffable singular, etc., be overcome by simply overcoming a transcendental field with all the questions that were posed in regards to this field, to its logical structuration in diverse acts, etc.? On the other hand, do you see how [certain marks] would cling to such a theory; [how] this would be only in the explication of certain marks, their references and their ethical implications? Or is it, following what you said, too soon to speak of them? Or is all of ethics attached also to an idea of the mark which doesn't take seriously its possibility of not being entirely taken seriously?

Jacques Derrida: The nonserious was a citation. It's Austin who talks about the serious, who restricts himself to it, who thinks that the nonserious must be kept in the margins of his theory, at least for now. I didn't defend the nonserious.

Henri Declève: No, not at all.

Jacques Derrida: That tempts me sometimes! I'm not sure I've understood very well the point of your question about the transcendental. I don't believe in an overcoming of the transcendental. On the contrary, I think that the transcendental questions are indispensable, and that it's necessary to repeat them endlessly, even up to the point where we examine the questions themselves in the history of their forms. I don't think, however, that we can transgress the form of the transcendental question without all the well-known risks of empiricism, of positivism, etc. Now, at a certain strategically determinable moment in the discourse, we also have to examine what the form of the transcendental question signifies, what it implies. The last part of your question spoke of the ethical. This is an important and difficult question. Without doubt, everything that I proposed this morning or all the implications of what I proposed this morning do not lead immediately to the possibility of an ethics. We might even think that my propositions threaten ethics. A certain type of analysis is always dangerous for ethics and vice versa. I believe, therefore, that an ethical theory, a theory concerning the specificity of ethical acts, of ethical intentions, of moral laws, etc., is indispensable, that it has to be constituted. If, however, we haven't first analyzed or examined all the historico-transcendental underpinnings of the form of the ethical question, of what motivated ethics, etc, we will not be able to construct a rigorous ethical theory. Or, lacking that, ethics would be a sort of doctrinaire or interested violence. Here, I would take the Heideggerian line without making it the absolute final word. Heidegger says that the question of thinking is in some way prior—*prior* here must be understood neither in a chronological nor in a logical sense—to the division between ethics and logic, etc. For the moment, what interests me, what interested me this morning, is a type of questioning which has not yet coincided with the need for ethics. This does not at all mean that this questioning is immoral or anti-ethical; it means that this questioning must first delve into what is presupposed by all ethical motivation found in discourse. Have I answered your questions?

Henri Declève: I think one remains, that of the signature or that of the position of the one who signs. His signature is, nevertheless, not what you had earlier claimed, transcendental. You had even wanted that this end, this fall, might remain discreet. I think this is problematic.

Jacques Derrida: Yes, certainly. The signature is an event the density of which is not reducible... [Momentary interruption.]

Speaker from the floor: Professor Ricoeur has explained how a phenomenological analysis could help the analyses made by the speech act theoreticians. I would like to know what benefit he expects from using a phenomenological concept, which had been operative in the phenomenological movement, to resolve difficulties within the movement of analysis of analytic philosophy. In other words, why have recourse to a concept which is operative in a strictly phenomenological structure of thought? That's my first question. My second concerns, to use Benveniste's terms again, the formal apparatus of the utterance. Ricoeur reminded us that the formal apparatus of the utterance consists not only in the verbal paradigm, in the verb's person, but also in all the apparatus of "deixis." Can you imagine a machine that would exactly simulate statements in which deixis is apparent, a machine which would be able to say "me," which would be able to say "I," a machine which in the extreme case would be able to say "I think, therefore, I am"? I would like to know what trace of intentional consciousness according to a linguistics of utterance can never be simulated by a machine.

Paul Ricoeur: These are two entirely different questions. Perhaps not! You're asking me if the help offered by phenomenological concepts to analytic philosophy is not a sort of transfer from one sphere to another. I think that from the start the analytic tradition suffers from an initial difficulty. It doesn't know which discourse it speaks in when it speaks of ordinary language. This is why you'll find no definition of ordinary language anywhere. There is where I think—I agree entirely with Derrida—that there is a transcendental formulation which is fundamental at a certain moment, put off, as he pointed out, until another time and for someone else, until another strategic moment of our own philosophic discourse. The first strategic point, however, seems to me extremely important. The discourse in which we speak about ordinary language is not itself ordinary language. Then it's necessary to thematize the type of discourse in which we say "act." Finally we have to ask, what does the "act" in "speech act" mean? If the word *act* corresponds simultaneously to the three things of which Austin or Searle speaks—Searle has done this better—the locutionary act which is the proposition, the illocutionary act, and the perlocutionary act, how are we to know that they are three distinct acts? He tells us very simply that an act can be partial or complete. What does all of this mean? Part, whole! I think that a thematization of another level is necessary. It seems to me that phenomenology can provide this because it starts from the act of the reduction. The reduction is implicit in analytic philosophy because it always says: we don't add to the knowledge of the world; we only add to the discourse about the world. In order to divide the discourse of things, and, therefore, in order to constitute a logico-phenomenological field, we have to perform an act that withdraws out of what is natural. This is a phenomenological act. I would also say here that we add nothing to analysis. This is why I think there's more in analytic philosophy because it works [on things], while phenomenology remains programmatic. But phenomenology has the ability to define the field in which the questions arise that allow us to go from a simple logic to a speech act theory. I would not be surprised to see the word *intention* reappear there because I would be in a field where intention makes sense. The transition from extensional to intensional would be thematized by means of the concepts proper to this field.

Speaker from the floor: You're not unaware of the fact that intentionality says something different, even orthographically.

Paul Ricoeur: I've looked at a certain number of texts, in particular, in an American dictionary of philosophy where the word *intention* has two entries. In certain texts the word *intention* has replaced understanding, extension as opposed to intension. And then, the word *intention* is used to designate "believing," "wanting," etc.

Speaker from the floor: There's still, however, a step from intention to intentionality. Isn't there the infiltration of a philosopheme architectonically, certain authors say, foreign to the structure of investigation?

Paul Ricoeur: No, let's return to Husserl's *The Logical Investigations*. He introduces intentionality in a book called *The Logical Investigations*. I myself have looked for the connection to Frege since he says that we are not content with sense, that we want reference, and that we proceed from one to the other. At that moment he says this is the sign's intention. However, this cannot be thematized in a logic…

Speaker from the floor: You're not unaware either that the Frege-Husserl correspondence brings to light some differences between Fregean *Sinn* and *Gehalt*, the tenor of Husserlian sense. It implies that there will always be a split between this philosopheme borrowed from the phenomenological tradition and then an operative concept which could resolve the difficulties…

Paul Ricoeur: Let's take another example, Russell. Yesterday I left out two or three pages on Russell which are pertinent to what you're speaking about. It's a very interesting problem since Russell uses the following argument: If some entities don't exist, I can't talk about them. What is the nature of this proposition? It's not an analytic proposition. It's the same as the propositions that open the *Tractatus*; they're ontological propositions. Let's take Strawson's propositions. If there was no world containing bodies and persons, there would be no language containing proper names and, therefore, I wouldn't be able to make identifications. Without identifications, there would be no predication. Everything, therefore, is interrupted by some ontological propositions. If I don't inhabit a world, in the Heideggerian sense, in which there are persons and bodies, my language would not even be able to be constituted. These are what I would call some transcendental propositions that can help analytic propositions since the issue is to situate analytic discourse itself.

Speaker from the floor: I would say simply that these propositions are transcendental in a sense which is not specifically Husserlian and that the notion of the transcendental is expanded beyond its original territory.

Paul Ricoeur: Yes, but please understand what I'm saying. I'm not interested in an Husserlian archeology. I would say that we have to keep working; these things were written seventy or eighty years ago. We have to keep thinking; it's not necessary to repeat, even though iteration may be essential to thinking.

Jeanne Parain-Vial: I'm simply astonished that Derrida says that we have to see an artwork many times in order to identify it. It seems to me that we can identify a melody the first time we hear it. There's, therefore, no iteration. I would also like to ask him if he thinks that a process of iteration leads us to the certainties of the sort I have when I face a human being. This is a man; and even if he doesn't communicate, he tries to communicate. Even if I don't understand what he says to me, I read his will to communicate. It seems to me that this certainty is prior to every sign, every trace.

Jacques Derrida: No, I don't believe that what you describe as obvious—namely, the certainty, when I am before a man, that he is right there, that he wants to communicate—would be a certainty simple and prior to every trace or to every experience of a type of trace. I don't agree; I don't believe in something like a certainty immediate and prior to all experience of the trace. As for your first objection, what does it mean when you say "the first time that I hear a melody"? In the hearing of a melody, when do you identify the instant at which it is produced once, and when it, happening only in an instant, remains without having to be repeated? A precise description is indispensable there. What does the retention of a melody mean? [A melody] is already an extremely complicated whole, a system which is never perceived in only one of these instants and which presuppose a considerable chain of retentions, [which presupposes] therefore, an extremely complex organization of experience which we cannot categorize as a simple perception, as a unique sensation of which I preserve the memory after a single time. In order to preserve the memory of a melody that we hear just once, an experience is necessary—you doubtlessly know it, since I assume you're a musician—an experience already very sedimented. If I retain a melody I've heard just once, it has to be the case that this melody is connected to a musical world of a considerable, historical complexity. There, I believe we're already in a chain of very important traces...

René Schaerer: Ladies and gentlemen, this discussion has lasted almost two hours. Despite their good will and their mental perseverence, our speakers are human beings like you and me, and it would be inappropriate to abuse their strength. In closing, I would like to thank first of all the speakers, then those of you in the audience who spoke, and finally the audience itself whose inspiration was evident in the form of an entirely attentive presence.

NOTES ◆

Introduction

1. A number of books influenced me to organize the relation between Ricoeur and Derrida in this way: Rodolphe Gasché's *The Tain of the Mirror* (Cambridge, Mass.: Harvard University Press, 1986), Jean-Luc Nancy's *Le partage des voix,* (Paris: Galilée, 1982), and Manfred Frank's *What is Neo-Structuralism,* trans. Sabine Wilke and Richard Gray (Minneapolis, Minn.: University of Minnesota Press, 1989), also Frank's "Schelling's Critique of Hegel and The Beginnings of Marxian Dialectics," trans. Joseph Lawrence, in *Idealistic Studies,* 19: 251–268.

2. As far as I know, Ricoeur has made four other comments about Derrida. In *Interpretation Theory,* he says, "To hold, as Jacques Derrida does, that writing has a root distinct from speech and that this foundation has been misunderstood due to our having paid excessive attention to speech, its voice, and its *logos,* is to overlook the grounding of both modes of the actualization of discourse in the dialectical constitution of discourse" (26). In *Time and Narrative,* III, Ricoeur has a long footnote concerning Derrida's reading of Husserl on inner-time consciousness (III, 29n12/46n1); I shall return to this note in Part II, chapter 4. In *A l'école de la phénoménologie* (Paris: Vrin, 1986), Ricoeur speaks of Derrida's brilliant essay on Husserl's *The Origin of Geometry* (168). Finally, there is the round-table discussion between Ricoeur and Derrida concerning communication translated as the Appendix.

3. Jacques Derrida, *Positions,* trans. Alan Bass (Chicago: University of Chicago Press, [1972]1981), 45. Derrida has also made numerous other comments about Ricoeur. In *Limited Inc* (trans. Samuel Weber, [Evanston, Ill.: Northwestern University Press, 1988 (1977)]), he says, " 'Signature Event Context' analyses the metaphysical premises of the Anglo-Saxon—and fundamentally moralistic—theory of the performative, of speech acts or discursive events. In France, it seems to me that

these premises underlie the hermeneutics of Ricoeur and the archeology of Foucault" (p. 39). Derrida also makes a passing reference to Ricoeur in "Signature Event Context" (MAR, 326/388) and numerous passing references in his *Introduction to the Origin of Geometry*. Lastly, in "The Double Session," Derrida says during a discussion of Jean-Pierre Richard's thematicism that "In a recent study of the work of M. Eliade, Paul Ricoeur gives an excellent analysis of the different modes of comprehension at our disposal for dealing with the symbolic world: his remarks could be applied with little modification to a phenomenology of the theme. The theme, too, 'donates to thought'" (DIS, 249/280).

4. This book does not attempt to discuss hermeneutics and deconstructions as methods or theories of reading. Numerous books have already been written on this topic. Indeed this book presupposes the work done, for instance, by Rodolphe Gasché's *The Tain of the Mirror*, and Richard Palmer's *Hermeneutics* (Evanston, Ill.: Northwestern University Press, 1975).

5. Derrida's *Introduction* to Husserl's *The Origin of Geometry* is also important for understanding Derrida's thought in its own right. Derrida says in his 1980 thesis defense, "...all of the problems worked on in the *Introduction* to *The Origin of Geometry* have continued to organize the work I have subsequently attempted..." ("The Time of the Thesis," trans. Kathleen McLaughlin, in *Philosophy in France Today*, ed. Alan Montefiore [New York: Cambridge University Press, 1983], p. 39). Even as recently as 1987, Derrida reminds us of the importance of his *Introduction* to Husserl's *The Origin of Geometry*; see Jacques Derrida, "Some Statements and Truisms about Neologisms, Newisms, Postisms, Parasitisms, and other Small Seisisms," in *The States of "Theory"*, ed. David Carroll (New York, Columbia University Press, 1990), 90–91.

6. I am borrowing this phrase from Philippe Lacoue-Labarthe's and Jean-Luc Nancy's *The Literary Absolute*, trans. Philip Barnard and Cheryl Lester (Albany, N.Y.: State University of New York Press, 1988), 17.

Chapter 1

1. The following commentators have also been consulted: Gasché, *The Tain of the Mirror*; see also Gasché's "Quasi-Metaphoricity and the Question of Being," in *Hermeneutics and Deconstruction*, eds. Hugh J. Silverman and Don Ihde (Albany, N.Y.: State University of New York Press, 1985), pp. 166–90; Gregory Ulmer, *Applied Grammatology* (Balti-

more, Md.: Johns Hopkins University Press, 1985); Manfred Frank, "Die Aufhebung der Anschauung im Spiel der Metapher," in *Neue Hefte fur Philosophie*, 18/19, 1980, and *What is Neostructuralism*; Henry Staten, *Wittgenstein and Derrida* (Lincoln, Neb.: University of Nebraska Press, 1985); Paul De Man, *Blindness and Insight* (Minneapolis: University of Minnesota Press, 1986), and "The Epistemology of Metaphor," in *On Metaphor*, ed. Sheldon Sacks (Chicago: University of Chicago Press, 1979), pp. 11–28; Karsten Harries, "Metaphor and Transcendence," in *On Metaphor*, pp. 71–88; Allan Megill, *Prophets of Extremity* (Berkeley, Calif.: University of California Press, 1987); Hugh J. Silverman, *Inscriptions* (New York: Routledge, 1987); David Wood, *The Deconstruction of Time* (Atlantic Highlands, N.J.: Humanities Press, 1989); John Llewelyn, *Derrida on the Threshold of Sense* (New York: St. Martin Press, 1986); Jonathan Culler, *On Deconstruction* (Ithaca, N.Y., 1982); Christopher Norris, *Derrida* (Cambridge, Mass.: Harvard University Press, 1987); Sarah Kofman, *Lectures de Derrida* (Paris: Galilée, 1984); Luc Ferry and Alain Renaut, *French Philosophy of the Sixties*, trans. Mary H. S. Cattani (Amherst, Mass.: University of Massachusetts Press, 1990); Irene Harvey, *Derrida and the Economy of Différance* (Bloomington, Ind.: Indiana University Press, 1986), also Irene Harvey, "Metaphorics and Metaphysics: Derrida's Analysis of Aristotle," in *Journal of the British Society for Phenomenology*, vol. 17, no. 3 (October 1986), 308–330; Michael Ryan, *Marxism and Deconstruction* (Baltimore, Md.: Johns Hopkins University Press, 1982); Vincent Descombes, *Modern French Philosophy* (New York: Cambridge University Press, 1980); Francois Laruelle, *Les philosophies de la différence* (Paris: PUF, 1986); John D. Caputo, *Radical Hermeneutics* (Bloomington, Ind.: Indiana University Press, 1987); J. Degreef, "De la métaphore," in *Cahiers de literatture et de linguistique appliquée*, nos 3–4 (Kinshassa, Zaire: Faculté des lettres de l'Université National, 1971), 45–50; Herman Rapaport, *Heidegger and Derrida* (Lincoln, Neb.: University of Nebraska Press, 1989).

2. I have ignored Derrida's analysis of Bachelard's metapoetics because "*Plus de métaphore*" seems to captures the thrust of it.

3. Jacques Derrida, *Positions*, trans. Alan Bass (Chicago: University of Chicago Press, 1981 [1972]), pp. 41; Jacques Derrida, *Dissemination*, trans. Barbara Johnson (Chicago: University of Chicago Press, 1981 [1972]), 6–8.

4. For a short and very similar version of this "argument," see Jacques Derrida, "Limited Inc.," in *Limited Inc*, ed. Gerald Graff (Evanston, Ill.: Northwestern University Press, 1988), 70–72.

5. Cf. Jacques Derrida, "Structure, Sign, and Play in the Discourse of the Human Sciences," in *Writing and Difference*, trans. Alan Bass (Chicago: University of Chicago Press, 1978 [1967]), pp. 285–86.

6. Cf. Jacques Derrida, "The Supplement of the Copula," in MAR, 192/230.

7. Jacques Derrida, "The Law of Genre," in *Glyph* 7, trans. Avital Ronell, 212.

8. Jacques Derrida, *Speech and Phenomena*, trans. David B. Allison (Evanston, Ill.: Northwestern University Press, 1973 [1967]), 83–9. Cf. also Jacques Derrida, *Of Grammatology*, trans. Gayatri Spivak (Baltimore, Md.: Johns Hopkins University Press, 1974 [1967]); Jacques Derrida, *The Archeology of the Frivolous*, trans. John P. Leavey, Jr. (Pittsburgh, Pa.: Duquesne University Press, 1980 [1973]), 83–8/100–04.

9. Jacques Derrida, "The Pit and the Pyramid," also in *Margins*, 68–108/79–127. Derrida seems to have indicated the connection between metaphor and Hegelian thought first in "Violence and Metaphysics," in *Writing and Difference*, 112–15.

10. In "The Pit and the Pyramid," Derrida himself suggests a bridge between Husserl and Hegel: "Hegel evidently defines [independent representation] as an ideality, in opposition to the corporality of an intuitive signifier. This ideality is that of a *Bedeutung*. This word is usually translated as 'signification.' Having attempted, in commenting elsewhere upon the *Logical Investigations*, to interpret it as the content of a *meaning*, I would like to demonstrate here that such an interpretation is also valid for the Hegelian text. Such an extension is regulated by an internal and essential metaphysical necessity" (MAR, 82/94). See also below, Part III, chapter 1.

11. Cf. *Speech and Phenomena*, 85: "...temporalization here is the root of a metaphor that can only be primordial."

12. Cf. Rodolphe Gasché, *The Tain of the Mirror*, 314. For more on the question of the analogical unity of Being see Pierre Aubenque's "The Origins of the Doctrine of the Analogy of Being" in *Graduate Faculty Philosophy Journal*, vol. 11, no. 1, 35–46, and, of course, *Le problème de l'être chez Aristote* (Paris: PUF, 1966).

13. Aside from the thematic overlap between "White Mythology" and "Ousia and Gramme" (Aristotle and within Aristotle the question of *aisthesis*), in "Ousia and Gramme" Derrida cites "White Mythology." See MAR, 45n19/49n10.

14. Jakob Klein's *Greek Mathematical Thought* (trans. Eva Brann [Cambridge, Mass.: The MIT Press, 1968]) supports Derrida's interpretation of number in Aristotle. Klein says that for Aristotle (and for Plato) one can consider numbers, as such, without relation to that which is counted, without relation to the "content" of numbers. In Derrida's interpretation, the essence of time, for Aristotle, is the continuous and undivided "content" of the arithmetical divisions. The numbering (or divisibility) of time is an accident. Time defined by Aristotle as the "numbered number" of movement implies that time is not itself a mathematical (or divisible) thing.

15. Cf. Jacques Derrida, "The Supplement of the Copula," in MAR, 201/241.

16. Temporalization and spatialization, of course, is one definition Derrida gives to *différance*. Cf. Jacques Derrida, "Différance," in MAR, 13/14.

17. Cf. Ulmer, *Applied Grammatology*, 26–29.

18. Speaking not of metaphoricity, but of quasi-metaphoricity, Derrida is quite explicit about this redefinition in "The *Retrait* of Metaphor," 21/82.

19. For more one the relationship between deconstruction and *destruktion* see Gasché's *The Tain of the Mirror* and *Dialogue and Deconstruction*, eds. Diane Michelfelder and Richard Palmer (Albany, N.Y.: State University of New York Press, 1989). See also Herman Rapaport's *Heidegger and Derrida*.

20. See Derrida, *Speech and Phenomena*, chapter 4, where Derrida stresses the "Vor-" of *Vorstellung*, and chapter 6, where Derrida speaks of the ideal object as before (*devant*) the gaze (*regard*).

21. See below, Part III, chapter 1.

Chapter 2

22. Paul Ricoeur, *The Symbolism of Evil*, trans. Emerson Buchanan (Boston: Beacon Press, 1967 [1960]), 346.

23. Ricoeur, *The Symbolism of Evil*, 349.

24. Paul Ricoeur, *Freud and Philosophy*, trans. Denis Savage (New Haven, Conn.: Yale University Press, 1970 [1965]), 20–4.

25. Ricoeur, *The Symbolism of Evil*, 353. See also Paul Ricoeur, "On Interpretation," trans. Kathleen McLaughlin, in *Philosophy in France Today*, 187–97.

26. Cf. Paul Ricoeur, "Creativity in Language," in *The Philosophy of Paul Ricoeur*, eds. Charles E. Reagan and David Stewart (Boston: Beacon, 1978), 128.

27. See also below Part II, chapter 2.

28. Ricoeur also takes Aquinas's *Analogia Entis* as an example of the philosophical system that he has in mind. I have limited myself to Aristotle because he seems to play a more important and pervasive role in Ricoeur's most recent thought, from *The Rule of Metaphor* on. Ricoeur also discusses Aristotle in a lecture course from 1953–54 published as *Être, essence et substance chez Platon et Aristotle* (Paris: Societé d'Edition d'Enseignement Superieur, 1982), and in *Time and Narrative*, vols. I and III. He also discusses analogy in "History and Hermeneutics," in *The Journal of Philosophy*, vol. LXXIII, no. 19 (November 4, 1976), 683–695.

29. Cf. Paul Ricoeur, *Fallible Man*, trans. Charles Kelbley (Chicago: Henry Regnery, 1967), 60, 66–67; *Time and Narrative*, III, 60–96/90–144.

30. Here Ricoeur, like Derrida, cites Aristotle's use of the word *kurion*, MV, 291n66/369n1, cf. also MV, 19n24/27n2.

Chapter 3

31. In this respect "The *Retrait* of Metaphor" resembles Derrida's response to Searle in "Limited Inc." As we have noted, Derrida mentions Ricoeur there as holding propositions similar to those of Searle. But, in "Limited Inc," Derrida not only points out Searle's numerous reading errors, but also responds directly to Searle's proposition; in *"Retrait"* Derrida only points out Ricoeur's reading errors.

32. See below, Part III, chapter 2.

33. Cf. the following comment in *Speech and Phenomena*: "The dominance of the now is not only systematically connected to the founding opposition of metaphysics, namely, that of *form* (or *eidos* or idea) and *matter* as an opposition between *act* and potency.... It also assures the tradition that continues the Greek metaphysics of presence into the "modern" metaphysics of presence as self-consciousness, meta-

physics of the idea as representation (*Vorstellung*)" (62, translation modified).

34. Derrida always insists that Heidegger's text, like any other text in the metaphysical tradition, is divided against itself. Therefore, it can be read as assimilating itself to the tradition or as subverting the tradition. More clearly than any other analysis of Heidegger, Derrida's "*Geschlecht*: Sexual Difference, Ontological Difference," (in *Research in Phenomenology*, vol. XIII, 1983, 65–84, in particular, 79) demonstrates this division in Heidegger's text.

35. In "The *Retrait* of Metaphor," Derrida interprets Heidegger's metaphoricity in terms of intersection. Although it seems clear that Derrida intends this to refer to Ricoeur, the explication of the reference would demand a lengthy discussion of Heidegger.

36. Cf. Patrick Bourgeois and Frank Schalow, *Traces of Understanding: A Profile of Heidegger's and Ricoeur's Hermeneutics* (Atlanta, Ga.: Rodopi, 1990), pp. 67–87, in particular, p. 78. See also, Herman Rapaport, *Heidegger and Derrida*, 149–51.

37. See below, Appendix, 168.

38. See below, Appendix, 170–71.

39. See below, Appendix, 171.

40. See below, Appendix, 172.

Chapter 4

1. Paul Ricoeur, "On Interpretation," in *Philosophy in France Today*, pp. 187–197. Although it covers only Ricoeur's writings through 1969, Don Ihde's *Hermeneutic Phenomenology: The Philosophy of Paul Ricoeur* (Evanston: Northwestern University Press, 1971) is still the best introduction to Ricoeur's thought.

2. Cf. Paul Ricoeur, *Freud and Philosophy*, pp. 20–37.

3. The conquest of the concept of "belonging to" (*appartenance*, Gadamer's *Zugehörigkeit*), as Ricoeur wrote in 1977, marks the end of "un difficile combat avec l'idealisme husserlien qui n'etait pas encore entame par l'aveu precedent du caractere mediat de la réflexion" (quoted in *The Surplus of Meaning* by T. M. Van Leeuwan [Amsterdam: Rodopi, 1981], 25). Thus, the concept of belonging to stresses the fini-

tude of human experience, its incompleteness and surplus, and argues against the self-constitution implied by Husserlian idealism; as we shall see, it does not seem, however, to eliminate a certain basic notion of immediacy in Ricoeur. For more on the notion of belonging to, see Hans-Georg Gadamer, *Truth and Method* (second revised edition, trans. revised by Joel Weinsheimer and Donald G. Marshall [New York: Continuum, 1989]), 262, 295, 328.

4. In fact, here we could say that Ricoeur (not unlike Gadamer) uses Hegelian objective spirit against Hegelian subjective spirit.

5. Cf. Paul Ricoeur, "What is Dialectical?" in *Freedom and Morality*, ed. John Bricke (Lawrence, Kans.: University of Kansas Press, 1976, 173–189.

6. Cf. Hans-Georg Gadamer, "What is Practice?" in *Reason in the Age of Science*, trans. Frederick G. Lawrence (Cambridge, Mass.: MIT Press, 1976), 81.

7. Cf. Bourgeois and Schalow, *Traces of Understanding*, 88–91.

8. See also Paul Ricoeur, "Philosophie et langage," in *Revue Philosophique de la France et de l'Etranger*, 1978, 450–451; Paul Ricoeur, "Structure, Word, Event," in *The Conflicts of Interpretation*, ed. Don Ihde (Evanston: Northwestern University Press, 1974 [1969]), 81–83. For the best description of French structural linguistics, see Vincent Descombes's *Modern French Philosophy*, 75–109.

9. Cf. Ricoeur, *Fallible Man*, 30.

10. Ricoeur, *The Conflicts of Interpretation*, 86/87.

11. The same move is made by Gadamer in *Truth and Method*. Speaking of distance, Gadamer defines it by temporality (291–299).

12. See also Ricoeur, "Structure, Word, Event," in *The Conflict of Interpretations*, 87/87.

13. See also Ricoeur, "Philosophie et langage," 456; Paul Ricoeur, "Creativity in Language," in *The Philosophy of Paul Ricoeur*, 122–23.

14. See also Ricoeur, *"Philosophie et langage,"* 457.

15. Ricoeur's translation of Dilthey's *Zusammenhang* as *enchaînement* indicate the synthetic nature of structure; Ricoeur has also noted the connection of *Zusammenhang* in Dilthey to Husserl's notion of noema. Cf. HHS, 48–50/82–84. As Gadamer has shown, *Zusammenhang*

in Dilthey means structure, context, and continuity; see *Truth and Method*, 197–203, 223.

16. Cf. Ricoeur, *Fallible Man*, 50: "The verb is what makes the sentence 'holds together' *(tenir ensemble)*...."

17. The sentential structure could be called a singular whole in the same way as Ricoeur calls textual plots "singular totalities" *(totalités singulières)*. See *Time and Narrative*, vol. II, trans. Kathleen McLaughlin and David Pellauer (Chicago: University of Chicago Press, 1985), 10, 20.

18. Cf, Ricoeur, "Creativity in Language," in *The Philosophy of Paul Ricoeur*, 127–128.

19. Ricoeur, "Creativity in Language," in *The Philosophy of Paul Ricoeur*, 127.

20. Ricoeur, "Creativity in Language," in *The Philosophy of Paul Ricoeur*, 127.

21. Cf. Ricoeur, *Time and Narrative*, vol. II, 20/35.

22. Cf. Paul Ricoeur, "Schleiermacher's Hermeneutics," in *Monist*, 60 (1977), 188; Ricoeur, *Time and Narrative*, vol. II, 14–28/27–35.

23. Paul Ricoeur, "The Text as Dynamic Identity," in *The Identity of the Literary Text*, eds. Mario J. Valdes and Owen Miller (Toronto: University of Toronto Press, 1985), 175–186; cf. also Paul Ricoeur, *Time and Narrative*, vol. I, trans. Kathleen McLaughlin and David Pellauer (Chicago: University of Chicago Press, 1984), 68–71.

24. Paul Ricoeur, "The Hermeneutics of Symbols," in *The Philosophy of Paul Ricoeur*, 45; Paul Ricoeur, "From Existentialism to the Philosophy of Language," in *The Philosophy of Paul Ricoeur*, 90–1; Ricoeur, "The Metaphorical Process as Cognition, Imagination, and Feeling," in *Philosophical Perspectives on Metaphor*, ed. Mark Johnson (Minneapolis, Minn.: University of Minnesota Press, 1981), 243.

25. Cf. Ricoeur, "On Interpretation," in *Philosophy in France Today*, 194.

26. Paul Ricoeur, *Husserl: An Analysis of his Phenomenology*, trs. Edward G. Ballard and Lester E. Embree (Evanston, Ill.: Northwestern University Press, 1967), 98.

Chapter 5

27. Ricoeur, "Creativity in Language," in *The Philosophy of Paul Ricoeur*, 129–33.

28. According to Ricoeur, this interplay between sentence and word coincides with what Richards calls vehicle and tenor, Black's frame and focus, and Beardsley's modifier and principal subject (cf. *The Rule of Metaphor*'s Third and Fourth Studies).

29. Paul Ricoeur, "The Metaphorical Process," in *Philosophical Perspectives on Metaphor*, 229, 232.

30. Cf. Paul Ricoeur, *Time and Narrative*, vol. I, 52–77.

31. Ricoeur, "The Metaphorical Process," in *Philosophical Perspectives on Metaphor*, 228; Ricoeur, *Fallible Man*, 57–71. In *Fallible Man* Ricoeur calls Kantian imagination "the third term, the intermediate term" (57); Ricoeur, *Time and Narrative*, vol. I, 68. For other studies of the imagination, see Edward S. Casey, *Imagining: A Phenomenological Study* (Bloomington, Ind.: University of Indiana Press, 1976) and Richard Kearney, *The Wake of Imagination* (Minneapolis, Minn.: University of Minnesota Press, 1988).

32. Ricoeur, "The Metaphorical Process," in *Philosophical Perspectives on Metaphor*, 232–33.

33. Ricoeur, "The Metaphorical Process," in *Philosophical Perspectives on Metaphor*, 238–42.

34. Paul Ricoeur, "The Function of Fiction in Shaping Reality," in *Man and World*, XII (1979), 123.

35. Ricoeur, "The Function of Fiction," in *Man and World*, XII, 125.

36. Ricoeur, "The Function of Fiction," in *Man and World*, XII, 137.

37. See also Ricoeur, "The Metaphorical Process," in *Philosophical Perspectives on Metaphor*, 240.

38. Ricoeur, "The Function of Fiction," *Man and World*, XII, 136. Ricoeur and Gadamer share essential points on the relation of image (and symbol) and event. Thus, I have borrowed some Gadamerian wording to describe Ricoeur's notion of iconic augmentation. In particular, my use of the word *representative* derives from Gadamer, who uses the word *Repräsentation* not *Vorstellung*. See Hans-Georg Gadamer, *Truth and Method*, second revised edition, 138–144, 148–149, 423. Also

Hans-Georg Gadamer, "The Relevance of the Beautiful" in *The Relevance of the Beautiful*, ed. Robert Bernasconi (New York: Cambridge University Press, 1986 [1977]), 31–39.

39. Ricoeur, "The Metaphorical Process," 237.

40. Cf. Pierre Gisel, "Paul Ricoeur: Discourse between Speech and Language," in *Philosophy Today*, Supplement to vol. 4, no. 4 (Winter 1977), 46; Karsten Harries, "The Many Uses of Metaphor," in *On Metaphor*, ed. Sheldon Sacks (Chicago: University of Chicago Press, 1978), 170–171.

41. Ricoeur, *The Symbolism of Evil*, 348.

42. Ricoeur, *Freud and Philosophy*, 525.

43. Gadamer, *Truth and Method*, 469.

44. Since Ricoeur intends his discussion of imagination to resonate not only with Kant, but also with Schelling (see Appendix above, 149), perhaps Schelling also lies in the back of his symbol discussion; cf. *Freud and Philosophy*, 537. By allowing a certain reading of Schelling and German romanticism—one provided by Lacoue-Labarthe and Nancy in *The Literary Absolute*—inform Ricoeur's discourse on the symbol, one could make the difference we are trying to illuminate between Ricoeur and Derrida vanish. Nevertheless, Derrida himself has expressed reservations about Schelling's notion of imagination; see "Psyché: Inventions of the Other," in *Reading De Man Reading*, 57.

45. Ricoeur, *Freud and Philosophy*, 526. Cf. Jean-Luc Nancy, *Le partage des voix*, 15 n6.

46. Cf. Ricoeur, *Freud and Philosophy*, 528.

47. Ricoeur, *The Symbolism of Evil*, 350.

48. Ricoeur, *The Symbolism of Evil*, 348.

Chapter 6

49. Cf. Ricoeur, *Time and Narrative*, vol. II, 20.

50. See also. Paul Ricoeur, "Hermeneutics and the Critique of Ideology," in HHS, 63–100. See also John B. Thompson, *Critical Hermeneutics* (New York: Cambridge University Press, 1981).

51. Gadamer, *Truth and Method*, second edition, 291–300.

52. Ricoeur's relation to Gadamer is paradoxical. At times he seems to be Gadamer's best interpreter; at other times, he seems completely to overlook certain points. Gadamer, too, is concerned with the problem of criteria for distinguishing valid prejudices from invalid ones. This question animates his entire discussion of temporal distance; here he speaks of "foregrounding" (*abheben*: distinguishing) one's present prejudices from the past (299). Also his discussion of the parts-whole relation is animated by this question (294). Lastly in the discussion of effective history, he speaks of "testing" one's prejudices (306).

53. For other references to "Ideas in the Kantian sense," see Ricoeur, *Fallible Man*, 75; Paul Ricoeur, *Freedom and Nature*, trans. Erazim Kohak (Evanston, Ill.: Northwestern University Press, 1966 [1950]), 482–86; Ricoeur, "Hope and the Structure of Philosophical Systems," in *Proceedings of the American Catholic Philosophic Association*, 44 (1970), 55–69; Paul Ricoeur, "What is Humanism?" in *Political and Social Essays*, eds. David Stewart and Joseph Bien (Athens, Ohio: Ohio University Press, 1974), 86. Cf. also Patrick L. Bourgeois, *The Religious Within Experience and Existence* (Pittsburgh, Pa.: Duquesne University Press, 1990), 108–14.

54. Ricoeur appropriates these terms from Reinhart Koselleck (TNIII, 208/301).

55. Important background for this chapter is Ricoeur's 1975 lecture course published as *Lectures on Ideology and Utopia*, ed. George H. Taylor (New York: Columbia University Press, 1986).

56. Ricoeur, *Time and Narrative*, vol. I, 72.

57. Cf. Ricoeur, *Freud and Philosophy*, 527.

58. Cf. Paul Ricoeur, *Fallible Man*, trans. Charles Kelbey (Chicago: Henry Regnery, 1967), 26–75. Cf. also Bourgeois and Schalow, *Traces of Understanding*, 2–5. The importance of *Fallible Man* should not be underestimated for Ricoeur's thought. All the themes that he pursues later, his very theory of discourse in small, are contained here. In particular, Ricoeur's stress of the verb and synthesis as the central to language are already articulated here. In regard to the problem of finitude, in *Fallible Man* Ricoeur tries to reorient the opposition of finite and infinite along lines of receiving (perception) and doing (discourse) rather than those of quantity (cf. 52–55). Here, though, Ricoeur is more concerned with the sense of the infinite than that of finitude. Infinite, for Ricoeur, seems to mean a leap out of and based on temporalization into

omnitemporal objectivities or unities (cf. 58–73/55–63). Like Husserl, these unities are horizons of meaning, Ideas in the Kantian sense. Totalization, Ricoeur says explicitly is a task, a demand (*exigence*) (75).

59. Finitude (or fallibility) in Ricoeur is the "occasion" or the "possibility" for what he calls the fault (*faille*). There is a "gap" (*écart*) between the finite and infinite which defines man and a gap between the possibility of evil and its actuality. In *Fallible Man*, however, Ricoeur defines humanity itself as a "mixture" (*mixte*), a third term, mediation itself between finite and infinite (57); he speaks of transgressing finitude (38). In *The Symbolism of Evil*, he begins by trying to make the "transition" (*passage*) from the possibility of evil to its actuality by making use of images, symbols. See *Freedom and Nature*, 22–8, *Fallible Man*, 203–24, *The Symbolism of Evil*, 3–24.

Chapter 7

60. We should also keep in mind Ricoeur's refusal in *Fallible Man* to follow Heidegger's path in *Kant and the Problem of Metaphysics* (60). Ricoeur calls Heidegger's attempt to derive both sensations and concepts from the middle, from time, "a pious wish" (67). Indeed, Ricoeur proceeds in the chapter entitled "The Transcendental Synthesis" by first examining the beginning and end before turning to the middle. The middle, therefore, for Ricoeur is determined as the mixture of finitude and infinite.

61. Ricoeur in fact responds to two accusations. If there is a primary concordance, in temporal experience, as Ricoeur claims in his response to the first accusation, then one could in turn claim that mimesis$_2$ is "redundant." Ricoeur's response to this second accusation is to speak of the "prenarrative quality of experience"; there is a "prehistory" to stories." Ricoeur defines this quality as an "inchoate narrativity" and as "a potential story." Thus, the narration actualizes or effectuates what is tacit in temporal experience. Actualization is not redundant; it provides determination, form, universality, publicity. As Ricoeur says, "We tell stories because in the last analysis human lives need and merit being narrated. This remark takes on its full force when we refer to the necessity to save the history of the defeated and the lost. The whole history of suffering cries out for vengence and calls for narrative" (75).

62. Ricoeur, *Time and Narrative* I, 72.

Chapter 8

1. Cf. Vincent Descombes, *Modern French Philosophy*, 140.

2. Cf. Derrida, *Speech and Phenomena*, 72; also Jacques Derrida, *The Post Card from Plato to Freud and Beyond*, trans. Alan Bass (Chicago: University of Chicago Press, 1987), 123.

3. Cf. Derrida, *Limited Inc*, 48.

4. Cf. Jacques Derrida, *Limited Inc*, ed. Gerald Graff (Evanston, Ill.: Northwestern University Press, 1988), 61.

5. Cf. Derrida, *Speech and Phenomena*, 88.

6. Cf. Derrida, *The Post Card*, 67.

7. Cf. Jacques Derrida, "Psyche: Inventions of the Other," trans. Catherine Porter, in *Reading De Man Reading*, eds. Lindsay Waters and Wlad Godzick Minneapolis: University of Minnesota Press, 1989), 54–56.

8. Cf. Derrida, *Limited Inc*, 48–49.

9. Cf. Ferry and Barrault, *French Philosophy in the Sixties*, 54, where they say that Derrida thought is nothing more than Heidegger's with a different style or rhetoric.

10. Heidegger's influence can be seen in the *Introduction*'s final three pages. There, for instance, Derrida's mimics Heidegger's *Introduction to Metaphysics* by saying: "...knowing what sense is as historicity, I can clearly ask myself why there would be one history rather than nothing" (INF, 151/168).

11. Derrida never uses the word *différance* itself in the *Introduction*. He does, however, use a participial form of *différer* on 153/171. See also 138/152.

12. For other readings of Derrida's *Introduction to the Origin of Geometry* see: Rudolf Bernet, "On Derrida's 'Introduction' to Husserl's *Origin of Geometry*," in *Continental Philosophy II: Derrida and Deconstruction*, ed. Hugh J. Silverman (New York: Routledge, 1989), 139–153; John Caputo, *Radical Hermeneutics* (Bloomington, Ind.: Indiana University Press, 1987), 123–126.

13. Cf. Derrida, "'Genesis and Structure' and Phenomenology," in *Writing and Difference*, 154–68. Derrida first delivered this paper at

Cerisy-la-Salle in 1959. It was first published in 1965 in *Entretiens sur les notions de genèse et de structur*, ed. Maurice de Gandillac (Paris: Mouton, 1965), 242–268. An editor's footnote states that (242): "M. Derrida, who has revised and completed his text, has added a certain number of explicative notes and references." Then the essay was republished in *Writing and Difference*. A comparison of the 1965 and 1967 versions reveals that Derrida revised this essay again for the publication of *Writing and Difference*. Thus, because "'Genesis and Structure' and Phenomenology" predates and postdates Derrida's 1962 *Introduction to Husserl's The Origin of Geometry*, it can instruct our reading of the *Introduction*. This essay outlines a tension, indeed a unity, between genesis and structure within Husserl's entire thought.

14. I am following Derrida's translation of *Leistung* as "production"; the standard English translation, however, is "accomplishment." Cf. Derrida's footnote explaining his translation, INF, 40n27/22n3.

15. See sections 11, 14, 15.

16. The primary example of such an essence is the essence of an artwork. An artwork, by definition, is unique, singular, and yet, copies can be made. In the Appendix above Derrida discusses at length the iterability of artwork.

17. Derrida's use of the word *envoi* here in 1962 refers ahead to the "Envois" section of the 1980 *Post Card*.

18. Edmund Husserl, *Experience and Judgment*, trans. James S. Churchill and Karl Ameriks (Evanston, Ill.: Northwestern University Press, 1973 [1938]), 267.

19. This sentence states roughly the thesis of *Speech and Phenomena*. This text, which amounts to a sustained meditation on the "First Logical Investigation," attempts to question the possibility of ideal objectivity in *pure*, immediate, or noncommunicative consciousness. In other words, Derrida questions whether ideal objectivity can be constituted without mediation, specifically without the mediation of signs and language.

20. Cf. Derrida, *Speech and Phenomenon*, 10, 54, 77–82.

21. Because of the reciprocal dependence between the imperative of univocity and that of equivocity, Derrida indicates a mutual dependence between the projects of Joyce and Husserl (INF, 102–03/104–06). In *Ullyses* Joyce, according to Derrida, attempts to recollect all empirical and

cultural meanings, all equivocities, in one book; he focuses on the passive associative resonances and ignores the translatable cores. Husserl in contrast attempts to impoverish factual or empirical language down to its translatable cores in order to remember the pure structure of history. Joyce's project depends upon that of Husserl because there could be no recollection of empiricity without a structure supporting transmission; Husserl's depends upon that of Joyce because he would not be remembering the structure of *history* if no genesis had taken place. This entire discussion anticipates 1987 *Ulysse Gramophone.*

22. Derrida summarizes these preconditions on 127/136.

23. Within this word *passage,* we should hear a number of resonances (as in Ricoeur's use of it in *Time and Narrative,* III): the passage of time, the past, transition, passing something along, passage or strait, even the French negative adverb, *pas,* which itself also means step. In reference to the phrase "passage to the limit," it is also instructive to look at Derrida's discussion of Husserl final reduction in *The Origin,* INF, 119–120/127.

24. Derrida makes this transition to the discussion of the Husserlian Idea in the Kantian sense by recalling Husserl's brief analyses in *Ideas I* of inner-time consciousness (INF, 135–136/147–149).

25. Cf. Derrida, *Speech and Phenomena,* 102.

26. Cf. Derrida, "'Genesis and Structure' and Phenomenology," in *Writing and Difference,* 162.

27. Cf. Paul Ricoeur, "Kant and Husserl," in *Husserl,* 175–201.

28. We must notice that in the *Introduction* Derrida's criticism is based on the protentional phase of the living present; in *Speech and Phenomena* Derrida turns first to the retentional phase (chapter 5) and then tacitly to the protentional (chapter 7). We must also note that it is not an accident that Derrida cites Levinas's *The Theory of Intuition in Husserl's Phenomenology* (trans. André Orianne [Evanston, Ill.: Northwestern University Press, 1973]) at this point in the *Introduction,* 136n162/149n1.

29. Because of this absolute, irreducible, linguistic mediation, Derrida in a footnote can speak of phenomenology being "'overcome' or completed in an interpretative philosophy" (INF, 86n89/82n1). It is not by accident that during this very discussion of the infinite Idea's finitude Derrida cites Heidegger (INF, 138n164/151n1). In fact, at the very end

of the *Introduction* Derrida establishes a mutual dependence between ontology (in the non-Husserlian sense) and phenomenology, between, in other words, Heidegger's philosophy of finitude and Husserl's philosophy of infinite tasks (cf. INF, 150–152/167–170). This relation, however, for Derrida is not symmetrical; he lets phenomenology outstrip ontology.

30. Cf. also Derrida, "'Genesis and Structure'," 165. See also the French translation of Heidegger's *Kant and the Problem of Metaphysics* (*Kant et le problème de la métaphysique* [Paris: Gallimard, 1953]), in which de Waehlens and Biemel translate Heidegger's "*Sich-melden*" as "*s'annoncer*" on 244.

31. In this passage (and in others over the *Introduction*'s last four pages) Derrida uses *History* and *Being* somewhat synonymously. He capitalizes these words in order to indicate the inseparable unity of fact and essence within it. Historicity strictly designates the essence of history. Although capitalization of key terms is almost a fad in late fifties, early sixties French thought, Derrida uses this practice in the *Introduction*, as far as I can tell, rigorously. Whenever a term refers to what is absolute, Derrida capitalizes it. Cf. Jacques Derrida, "The Deaths of Roland Barthes," trans. Pascale-Anne Brault and Michael Nass, in *Philosophy and Non-Philosophy Since Merleau-Ponty*, ed. Hugh J. Silverman (New York: Routledge, 1988), 262.

32. Even as recently as 1967 Derrida associates *différance* with imagination; see *Of Grammatology*, 309–311. Cf. also Irene Harvey, *Derrida and the Economy of Differance*; Richard Kearney, *The Wake of the Imagination* (Minneapolis, Minn.: University of Minnesota Press, 1988), 281–296; Rodolphe Gasché, *The Tain of the Mirror*, 151–154.

33. The 1953–54 master's thesis (*Le problème de la genèse dans la philosophie de Husserl* [Paris: PUF, 1990]) clearly shows that Derrida originally conceived the notion of *différance* dialectically. In the 1990 *Avertissement* to it Derrida says the originary "contamination" of the origin (in other words the primordial unity of essence and fact) "receives then a philosophic name that I would have to renounce: the *dialectic*, an 'originary dialectic' (vii)."

34. After citing *Speech and Phenomena*, Jean-Luc Marion, for instance, says in his *Réduction et donation* (Paris: PUF, 1989) that "In principle I am confining myself to this work, which is exemplary and determinative for J. Derrida's entire later itinerary" (13n5, my translation).

35. Derrida, *Speech and Phenomena*, 65–6.

36. Derrida, *Speech and Phenomena*, 68.

37. Derrida, *Speech and Phenomena*, 67.

38. Derrida, *Speech and Phenomena*, 67–8.

39. Derrida, *Speech and Phenomena*, 69. Allison translates "*écart*" as "divergence."

40. Derrida, *Speech and Phenomena*, 82. Allison translates *le même* as "sameness."

41. Derrida, *Speech and Phenomena*, 86.

42. Derrida, *Speech and Phenomena*, 69. This is a highly qualified use of the word *dialectic*. Derrida describes the living present as a dialectic "in every sense of the term and before any speculative reappropriation."

43. Derrida, *Speech and Phenomena*, 55.

44. Derrida, *Speech and Phenomena*, 67.

45. Ricoeur, too, calls temporalization auto-affection; see TNIII, 34/54.

Chapter 9

46. Heidegger's renewed influence during this period could be inferred already from a comparison of our readings of the *Introduction* and of "White Mythology." See Part I, chapter 1.

47. Martin Heidegger, "Moira," in *Early Greek Thinking*, trans. David Farrell Krell and Frank A. Capuzzi (New York: Harper and Row, 1975), 79–101.

48. The following texts concerning Derrida's reading of Mallarmé have been consulted: Vincent Descombes, *Modern French Philosophy*, 152; Rodolphe Gasché, *The Tain of the Mirror*, 218–219; Rodolphe Gasché, "Nontotalization without Spuriousness: Hegel and Derrida on the Infinite," in *Journal of the British Society for Phenomenology*, vol. 17: 3 (October 1986), 289–307; Gregory Ulmer, *Applied Grammatology*, 176–183; Richard Kearney, *The Wake of Imagination*, 281–292; Sarah Kofman *Lectures de Derrida*, 42–46; John Llewelyn, *Derrida on the Threshold of Sense*, 114–115; Manfred Frank, *What is Neo-Structural-*

ism?, 142; Roger Laporte, "Une double stratégie," in *Ecarts,* ed. Lucette Finas (Paris: Fayard, 1977), 263; Claude Lévesque, "L'Économie générale de la lecture," in *L'étrangeté du texte* (Montreal: VLB Editeur, 1976), 117–200; David Carroll, *Paraesthetics* (New York: Methuen, 1987), 95–105.

49. The following texts on Mallarmé have been consulted: Jean-Pierre Richard, *L'Univers imaginaire de Mallarmé* (Paris: Seuil, 1961); Jacques Scherer, *Grammaire de Mallarmé* (Paris: Nizet, 1977); Judy Kravis, *The Prose of Mallarmé* (New York: Cambridge University Press, 1976); Sylviane Huot, *Le Mythe d'Herodiade chez Mallarmé* (Paris: Nizet, 1977); Wallace Fowlie, *Mallarmé* (Chicago: University of Chicago Press, 1953); Janine D. Langan, *Hegel and Mallarmé* (New York: University Press of America, 1986); Virginia A. La Charité, *The Dynamics of Space* (Lexington, Ky.: French Forum, 1987); Jean-Paul Sartre, *Mallarmé or the Poet of Suicide,* trans. Ernest Sturm, (University Park, Pa.: Penn State University Press, 1988); Gilles Deleuze, *Nietzsche and Philosophy,* trans. Hugh Tomlinson (New York: Columbia University Press, 1983); Jean Hyppolite, "Le Coup de dés de Stéphane Mallarmé and le message," in *Les etudes philosophiques,* no. 4 (1958), 463–468.

50. At the most superficial level, Derrida's interpretation of Heideggerian *aletheia* in "The Double Session" seems problematic (DIS, 192–193/219). The process sounds overly subjective; it resembles too much the creativity of genius in Kant. Perhaps this is intentional; "Economimesis," for instance, lets certain sentences in Kant resonate in a Heideggerian way. In any case, Derrida's "criticism" of Heidegger in "The Double Session" seems to aim at Heidegger's acknowledged or unacknowledged phenomenology (of the Hegelian or Husserlian sort). Even as recently as *Of Spirit* Derrida associates Heidegger's thought with phenomenology; for Derrida Heidegger does not seem to break free entirely—is this possible?—of "the epoch of Cartesian-Hegelian subjectivity." See *Of Spirit,* trans. Geoffrey Bennington and Rachel Bowlby (Chicago: University of Chicago Press, 1989), 55.

Derrida also tries to distinguish himself from Heidegger in another, perhaps more obvious, way. The later Heidegger speaks of being's fate or destiny, a history of the ways the relation between had to happen. According to Derrida in "Sending: On Representation," while Heidegger's history of being assumes nothing like a substantial identity underlying the different epochal relations, an original gathering keeps the epochs' order from being accidental and regathers history into a destination (321–322). For Heidegger according to Derrida, there is *one* history of being. (Astonishingly, Derrida makes almost the exact same comment in the *Introduction* twenty-seven years earlier [cf. INF, 149/165]). If history, however, is subject to fortune and misfortune, as the notion of *différance* implies, "we must arrange," Derrida says (in a sentence left untranslated in the English translation of *Envoi*), "to recount this history differently...in a destiny which is never certain of gathering itself up, of identifying itself, or of determining itself" ("Envoi," in *Psyche*, 142). Derrida's entire thought, therefore, could be interpreted as an attempt to "recount" Heideggerian history.

51. Miming Heidegger, Derrida also calls spacing the "mise à l'écart de l'être," the doubling of being [DIS, 216/245, 242/273, 280/312). Heidegger in *Being and Time* speaks of this doubling as the articulation of the "as." Being originary, the "as" or articulation implies that mediation precedes presence (immediacy). Derrida himself connects mimesis to the "as structure" in "The Double Session": "Everything is played out there in the paradoxes of the supplementary double: of what, being added to the simple and the one, replaces and mimes them, simultaneously resembling and different, different because—as (*en tant que*)— same as and different from what it doubles" (DIS, 191/217).

52. This entire discussion of the hymen and of the same repeats the "White Mythology" discussions of Hegelian idealization and Aristotelian time in Part I, chapter 1.

53. Cf. Gasché, *The Tain of the Mirror*, 136–142.

54. See Derrida, "Dissemination," in *Dissemination*, 306–315/ 340–351. The allusions here to Heidegger's fourfold (*Geviert*, *quadriparti*) cannot be missed. Derrida says that Heidegger's crossing out of certain words in *Über die Linie* and *Zur Seinsfrage* signifies the fourfold; the cross has four points. We should also note that the cross also functions as the multiplication sign. See "Dissemination," 354/393–94, also Derrida, *Of Spirit*, 52.

55. See Derrida, "Dissemination," in *Dissemination*, 314/349.

56. I am using atoms of air as an example because of its obvious connection to voice, to smell, and to the cave (*antre*, the homonym with *entre*). See Derrida, "Dissemination," in *Dissemination*, 314/349; also Derrida, "Economimesis," in *Diacritics*, 11.

57. Derrida, in fact, appropriates Hyppolite's phrase about Mallarmé, "the materialism of the idea," to capture all of these aspects of mim-

icry (DIS, 208/236). See Jean Hyppolite, "Le coup de dés de Stéphane Mallarmé et le message," in *Les etudes philosophique*, 1958, no. 4.

58. Richard himself notes two objections—Derrida calls these "two brief remarks"—to thematicism. First, Richard recognizes that language is differential or diacritical. Diacriticity is what Derrida calls syntax; it is the white spaces between letters and words. If every linguistic unit (signifier or signified) is context dependent, then the "whites" prevent, as Derrida stresses, "a theme from being theme, a nuclear unit of meaning, posed there before the eye, present outside of its signifier and referring only to itself" (DIS, 250/281). Richard's second objection reinforces the first. In a note (which Derrida reproduces), Richard admits that although the theme is supposed to be that which enables one to define, dominate, and classify the different occurrences of it, "it is actually the multiplicity of lateral relations that creates the *essence* of the theme" (DIS, 250/282, Richard's emphasis). If a theme exists, then Richard has no reason to mention diacritical or lateral relations; diacriticity would be only the nuclear theme's effect. Or else, if diacriticity conditions the text entirely, then Richard cannot strictly speak of themes; there only "thematic effects," as Derrida says (DIS, 250/282).

59. Cf. Lacoue-Labarthe and Nancy, *The Literary Absolute*, for the distinction between form in Schelling (or more generally in German romanticism) and figure in Hegel, 108. See also, 124.

60. Emile Benveniste, "The Notion of 'Rhythm' in its Linguistic Expression," in *Problems in General Linguistics*, trans. Mary Elizabeth Meeks (Coral Gables, Fla.: University of Miami Press, 1971), 281–288.

61. Derrida therefore interprets Mallarmé differently from Deleuze. According to Deleuze's interpretation of Mallarmé, chance and necessity are opposed; see *Nietzsche and Philosophy*, 33. According to Derrida, however, necessity and chance are not opposed; necessity is not the negation of chance, but the affirmation of it. Dissemination, as Derrida says, "*affirms* the always already divided generation of meaning" (DIS, 268/300).

62. Derrida, "My Chances/Mes Chances," in *Taking Chances*, 8–10.

63. While making almost continuous allusion to Heidegger, Derrida speaks of "The Double Session" as a note dashed off to Democritus (DIS, 279–80/312). See also, Jacques Derrida, "My Chances/Mes Chances: A Rendezvous with Some Epicurean Stereophonies," trans. Avital Ronell, in *Taking Chances: Derrida, Psychoanalysis, and Literature*,

eds. Joseph H. Smith and William Kerrigan (Baltimore, Md.: Johns Hopkins University Press, 1984), 1–32.

Conclusion

1. Paul Ricoeur's Introduction to his French translation of Husserl's *Ideas I*, *Idées directrices pour une phénoménologie*, (Paris: Gallimard, 1950), xxi. He uses the phrase *mouvement en vrille* to describe Husserl's constitutional analyses in *Ideas I* third section.

2. See Part I, chapter 1 and Part III, chapter 1.

3. Jacques Derrida, "Structure, Sign, and Play in the Discourse of the Human Sciences," in *Writing and Difference*, 289.

4. Cf. Lacoue-Labarthe and Nancy, *The Literary Absolute*, 64; see also F. Schlegel's definition of idea (*Athenaeum*, fragment 121), reproduced by Lacoue-Labarthe and Nancy: "An idea is a concept completed to the point of irony, an absolute synthesis of absolute antithesis, the continual self-engendering exchange of two thoughts in strife" (78).

5. Cf. Jean-Claude Lebenzstejn, *Zigzag* (Paris: Auber-Flammarion, 1981), 367.

BIBLIOGRAPHY ◆

Primary Texts

Books by Jacques Derrida

L'archeologie du frivole: Lire Condillac. Paris: Denoel/Gonthier, 1976. English translation by John P. Leavey, Jr. *The Archeology of the Frivolous.* Pittsburgh: Duquesne University Press, 1980.

La carte postale de Socrates à Freud et au-dela. Paris: Flammarion, 1980. English translation by Alan Bass, *The Post Card from Socrates to Freud and Beyond.* Chicago: University of Chicago Press, 1987.

La dissémination. Paris: Minuit, 1972. English translation by Barbara Johnson, *Dissemination.* Chicago: University of Chicago Press, 1981.

Du droit à la philosophie. Paris: Galilée, 1990.

L'écriture et la différence. Paris: Seuil, 1967. English translation by Alan Bass, *Writing and Difference.* Chicago: University of Chicago Press, 1978.

Eperons: Les styles de Nietzsche. Paris: Flammarion, 1978. English translation by Barbara Harlow, *Spurs: Nietzsche's Styles.* Chicago: University of Chicago Press, 1979.

De l'esprit: Heidegger et la question. Paris: Galilée, 1987. English translation by Geoffrey Bennington and Rachel Bowlby. Chicago: University of Chicago Press, 1989.

Feu la cendre. Paris: des Femmes, 1987.

French translation of and Introduction to Edmund Husserl's *L'Origine de la géométrie.* Paris: PUF, second edition, 1974 [1962]. English translation by John P. Leavey, *Edmund Husserl's Origin of Geometry: An Introduction.* Lincoln, Nebr.: University of Nebraska Press, 1989.

Glas. Paris: Galilée, 1974. English translation by John P. Leavey, Jr. and Richard Rand, *Glas.* Lincoln, Nebr.: University of Nebraska Press, 1987.

De la grammatologie. Paris: Minuit, 1967. English translation by Gayatri Spivak, *Of Grammatology*. Baltimore: Johns Hopkins University Press, 1976.

Limited Inc. English translation by Samuel Weber. Evanston, Ill.: Northwestern University Press, 1989.

L'oreille de l'autre. Montreal: VLB Editeur, 1982. English translation by Peggy Kamuf, *The Ear of the Other*. New York: Schocken Press, 1985.

Marges de la philosophie. Paris: Minuit, 1972. English translation by Alan Bass, *Margins of Philosophy*. Chicago: University of Chicago Press, 1982.

Memoires. New York: Columbia University Press, 1986.

Parages. Paris: Galilée, 1986.

Positions. Paris: Minuit, 1972. English translation by Alan Bass, *Positions*. Chicago: University of Chicago Press, 1981.

Le problème de la genèse dans la philosophie de Husserl. Paris: PUF, 1990.

Psyché: Invention de l'autre. Paris: Galilée, 1988.

Schibboleth: pour Paul Celan. Paris: Galilée, 1986.

Signsponge, tr. Richard Rand. New York: Columbia University Press, 1984.

Ulysse gramophone: Deux mots pour Joyce. Paris: Galilée, 1987.

La vérité en peinture. Paris: Flammarion, 1978. English translation by Geoff Bennington and Ian McLeod, *The Truth in Painting*. Chicago: University of Chicago Press, 1987.

La voix et le phénomène: Introduction au problème du signe dans la phénoménologie de Husserl. Paris: PUF, 1967. English translation by David B. Allison, *Speech and Phenomena and other Essays on Husserl's Theory of Signs*. Evanston: Northwestern University Press, 1973.

Articles by Jacques Derrida

"Coming into One's Own." English translation by James Hulbert, in *Psychoanalysis and the Question of the Text*, ed. Geoffrey Hartman. Baltimore: Johns Hopkins University Press, 1978, 114–148.

"Des tours de Babel." English translation by Joseph F. Graham, in *Difference in translation*, ed. Joseph F. Graham. Ithaca: Cornell University Press, 1985, 165–248.

"The Deaths of Roland Barthes," trans. Pascale-Anne Brault and Micheal Nass, in *Philosophy and NonPhilosophy since Merleau-Ponty*, ed. Hugh J. Silverman. New York: Routledge, 1988.

"Economimesis," in *Mimesis des articulations*. Paris: Aubier-Flammarion, 1975, 57–93. English translation by R. Klein, in *Diacritics*, 11, 3–25.

"Force de Loi: Le 'Fondement Mystique de l'Autorité'," in *Deconstruction and the Possibility of Justice*. New York: Cardoza Law Review (11:5–6), 1990, 919–1046.

"Fors: Les mots angles de Nicolas Abraham et Maria Torok." Preface to Nicolas Abraham and Maria Torok, *Verbier de l'homme aux loups: Cryptonomie*. Paris: Flammarion, 1976, pp. 7–73. English translation by Barbara Johnson, "Fors: The Anglish Words of Nicolas Abraham and Maria Torok." Forward to Nicolas Abraham and Maria Torok, *The Wolf Man's Magic Word: A Cryptonomie*, tr. Richard Rand. Minneapolis: University of Minnesota Press, 1986, xi–il.

"Geschlecht: sexual difference, ontological difference." In *Research in Phenomenology*, vol. XIII, 1983, 65–83.

"Geschecht II: Heidegger's Hands." English translation by John P. Leavey, Jr., in *Deconstruction and Philosophy*, ed. John Sallis. Chicago: University of Chicago Press, 1987, 161–196.

"La loi du genre/The Law of Genre." English translation by Avital Ronell, in *Glyph*, 7 (1980), 177–232.

"The Laws of Reflection: Nelson Mandela, in Admiration." English translation by Mary Ann Caws and Isabelle Lorenz, in *For Nelson Mandela*, eds. Jacques Derrida and Mustapha Tilli. New York: Seaver Books, 1987, 11–42.

"My Chances/Mes chances: A Rendevous with Some Epicurean Stereophonies." English translation by Irene Harvey and Avital Ronell, in *Taking Chances: Derrida, Psychoanalysis, and Literature*, eds. Joseph H. Smith and William Kerrigan. Baltimore: Johns Hopkins University Press, 1984, 1–32.

"No Apocalypse, Not Now (full speed ahead, seven missiles, seven missives)." English translation by Catherine Porter and Philip Lewis, in *Diacritics*, Summer, 1984, 20–32.

"Ocelle comme pas un." Preface to Jos Joliet, *L'enfant au chien-assis*. Paris: Editions Galilée, 1980.

"Of an Apocalyptic Tone Recently Adopted in Philosophy." English translation by John P. Leavey, Jr., in *Semeia* (1982), 63–95.

"The Principle of Reason: The University in the Eyes of its Pupils." English translation by Catherine Porter and Edward P. Morris, in *Diacritics*, Fall, 1983, 3–20.

"Psyche: Inventions of the Other," trans. Catherine Porter, in *Reading DeMan Reading*, eds. Lindsay Waters and Wlad Godzick. Minneapolis, Minn.: University of Minnesota Press, 1989, 25–65.

"The *Retrait* of Metaphor." English translation by Frieda Gardner, Biodun Iginla, Richard Madden and William West, in *Enclitic* (1978), 1–44.

"Scribble." Preface to William Warburton, *Essai sur les hieroglyphes des Egyptiens*. Paris: Aubier, 1977. English translation by Cary Plotkin, in *Yale French Studies*, no. 58, 116–147.

"Sending: On Representation." English translation by Peter and Mary Ann Caws, in *Social Research* vol. 49, no. 2, Summer, 1, 294–326.

"The Time of a Thesis: Punctuations." English translation by Kathleen McLaughlin, in *Philosophy in France Today*, ed. Alan Montefiore, 34–50.

"Women in the Beehive: A Seminar," in *Men in Feminism*, eds. Alice Jardin and Paul Smith. New York: Methuen, 1987, 189–203.

Books by Paul Ricoeur

À *l'école de la phénoménologie*. Paris: Vrin, 1986.

Le conflit des interpretations. Paris: Seuil, 1968. English translation by Willis Domingo, et al., ed. Don Ihde, *The Conflicts of Interpretation*. Evanston: Northwestern University Press, 1974.

De l'interpretation. Essai sur Freud. Paris: Seuil, 1965. English translation by Denis Savage, *Freud and Philosophy*. New Haven, Conn.: Yale University Press, 1970.

Du texte à l'action: Essais d'hermeneutique, II. Paris: Seuil, 1986.

Être, essence et substance chez Platon et Aristotle. Paris: Societé d'Edition d'Enseignement Superieur, 1982.

Essays on Biblical Interpretation. Philadelphia: Fortress Press, 1980.

French translation, with footnotes, of Edmund Husserl's *Idees directrices pour une phénoménologie*. Paris: Gallimard, 1950.

Gabriel Marcel et Karl Jaspers: Philosophie du mystere et philosophie du paradoxe. Paris: Temps present, 1947.

Hermeneutics and the Human Sciences, tr. John B. Thompson. New York: Cambridge University Press, 1981.

Histoire et vérité. Paris: Seuil, 1955. English translation by Charles A. Kelbey, *History and Truth*. Evanston: Northwestern University Press, 1965.

Husserl: An Analysis of his Phenomenology, trs. E. G. Ballard and L. E. Embree. Evanston: Northwestern University Press, 1967.

Interpretation Theory: Discourse and the Surplus of Meaning. Fort Worth: Texas Christian University Press, 1976.

Karl Jaspers et la philosophie de l'existence (with Mikel Dufrenne). Paris: Seuil, 1947.

Lectures on Ideology and Utopia, ed. George H. Taylor. New York: Columbia University Press, 1986.

Main Trends in Philosophy. New York: Holmes and Meier, 1979.

La métaphore vive. Paris: Seuil, 1975. English translation by Robert Czerny with Kathleen McLaughlin and John Costello, SJ, *The Rule of Metaphor*. Toronto: University of Toronto Press, 1977.

Philosophie de la volonté: Le volontaire et l'involontaire, Tome I. Paris: Aubier, 1950. English translation by Erazim Kohak, *Freedom and Nature*. Evanston: Northwestern University Press, 1966.

Philosophie de la volonté. Finitude et culpabilité: L'homme faillible, Tome II. Paris: Aubier, 1960. English translation by Charles Kelbey, *Fallible Man*. Chicago: Henry Regnery, 1965.

Philosophie de la volonté. Finitude et culpabilité: La symbolisme du mal (Tome III). Paris: Aubier, 1960. English translation by Emerson Buchanan, *The Symbolism of Evil*. New York: Harper and Row, 1967.

The Philosophy of Paul Ricoeur, eds. Charles Reagan and David Stewart. Boston: Beacon Press, 1978.

Political and Social Essays, eds. David Stewart and Robert Bien. Athens, Ohio: Ohio University Press, 1974.

The Religious Significance of Atheism. New York: Columbia University Press, 1969.

La sémantique de l'action. Paris: Éditions du Centre National de la Recherche Scientifique, 1977.

Soi-même comme un autre. Paris: Seuil, 1990.

Temps et récit, Tome I. Paris: Seuil, 1983. English translation by Kathleen McLaughlin and David Pellauer, *Time and Narrative*, vol. I. Chicago: University of Chicago Press, 1984.

Temps et récit, Tome II. Paris: Seuil, 1984. English translation by Kathleen McLaughlin and David Pellauer, *Time and Narrative*, vol. II. Chicago: University of Chicago Press, 1985.

Temps et récit, Tome III. Paris: Seuil, 1985. English translation by Kathleen Blamey and David Pellauer, *Time and Narrative*, vol. III. Chicago: University of Chicago Press, 1988.

Articles by Paul Ricoeur

"Biblical Hermeneutics," in *Semeia*, 4 (1975), 29–148.

"The Function of Fiction in Shaping Reality," in *Man and World*, 12 (1979), 123–41.

"The Fragility of Political Language," in *Philosophy Today* (Spring, 1987), 35–44.

"Hegel and Husserl on Intersubjectivity," in *Reason, Action, and Experience: Essays in Honor of Raymond Klibansky*, ed. Helmut Kohlenberger. Hamburg: Felix Meiner, 1979, 13–29.

"Hermeneutics and the Idea of Revelation," in *Protocol* for the Center for Hermeneutical Studies in Hellenistic and Modern Culture, Berkeley, 1977.

"History and Hermeneutics," in *Journal of Philosophy*, 73 (1976), 683–94.

"Hope and the Structure of Philosophical Systems," in Proceedings of the American Catholic Philosophic Association, vol. 44, 1970.

"Husserl and Wittgenstein on Language," in *Phenomenology and Existentialism*, eds. E. N. Lee and M. Mandelbaum. Baltimore: Johns Hopkins University Press, 1967.

"Ideology and Utopia as Cultural Imagination," in *Being Human in a Technological Age*, eds. Donald M. Borchert and David Stewart (Athens, Ohio: Ohio University Press, 1979), 107–125.

"Imagination in Discourse and in Action," in *Analecta Husserliana*, vol. 7, ed. Anna-Teresa Tymieniecka. Dordrecht: D. Reidel, 1978, 3–22.

"Irrationality and the Plurality of Philosophical Systems," in *Dialectica*, vol. 39 (1985), 297–319.

"Language and Image in Psychoanalysis," in *Psychiatry and the Humanities*, vol. 3, ed. Joseph H. Smith. New Haven: Yale University Press, 1978, 293–324.

"La raison pratique," in *Rationality Today/La rationalité aujourd'hui*, ed. T.F. Gereats (Ottowa: University of Otowa Press, 1979).

"The Metaphorical Process as Cognition, Imagination, and Feeling," in *Philosophical Perspectives on Metaphor*, ed. Mark Johnson. Minneapolis: University of Minnesota Press, 1981, 220–47.

"My Relation to the History of Philosophy," in *The Iliff Review* (Fall, 1978), 5–12.

"On Interpretation." English translation by Kathleen McLaughlin, in *Philosophy in France Today*, ed. Alan Montefiore, 175–197.

"Phenomenology," in *Southwestern Journal of Philosophy*, Fall 1974, trs. Daniel J. Herman and Donald V. Morano, 149–168.

"Phenomenology of Freedom," in *Phenomenology and Philosophical*

Understanding, ed. Edo Pivcevic. New York: Cambridge University Press, 1975, 173–94.

"Philosophie et langage," in *Revue philosophique de la France et de l'Etranger*, 4 (1978), 449–63.

"The Power of Speech: Science and Poetry," in *Philosophy Today*, vol. 29 (1985), 59–70.

"The Problem of the Foundation of Moral Philosophy," in *Philosophy Today* (Fall, 1978).

"Psychoanalysis and the Work of Art," in *Psychiatry and the Humanities*, vol. 1, ed. Joseph H. Smith. New Haven: Yale University Press, 1976, 3–33.

"Rhétorique—Poétique—Herméneutique," in *De la metaphysique à la rhetorique*, ed. Michel Meyer (Brussel: Editions de l'Université de Bruxelles, 1986), 143–55.

"Sartre and Ryle on the Imagination," in *The Philosophy of Jean-Paul Sartre*, ed. Paul Arthur Schilpp (LaSalle, Ill.: Open Court, 1981), 167–178.

"Schleiermacher's Hermeneutics," in *Monist*, 60 (1977), 181–97.

"The Text as Dynamic Identity," in *The Identity of the Literary Text*, eds. Mario J. Valdes and Owen Miller (Toronto: University of Toronto Press, 1985), 175–86.

"What is Dialectical?" in *Freedom and Morality*, ed. John Bricke (Lawrence, Kans.: University of Kansas Press, 1976), 173–89.

Secondary Sources

Albano, Peter Joseph. *Freedom, Truth and Hope: The Relationship of Philosophy and Religion in the Thought of Paul Ricoeur*. Lanham, Md.: University Press of America, 1987.

Allen, Jeffner, and Young, Iris Marion, eds. *The Thinking Muse: Feminism and Modern French Philosophy*. Bloomington, Ind.: Indiana University Press, 1989.

Allison, David B. *Derrida's Critique of Husserl: The Philosophy of Presence*. Diss. Pennsylvania State University, 1974.

———. "Derrida and Wittgenstein: Playing the Game," in *Research in Phenomenology*, vol. 8, 93–109.

Arac, Jonathan, Godzick, Wlad, and Martin, Wallace, eds. *The Yale Critics*. Minneapolis: University of Minnesota Press, 1983.

Bloom, Harold, et al. *Deconstruction and Criticism*. New York: Continuum, 1979.

Bourgeois, Patrick. *Ricoeur's Hermeneutical Phenomenology*. Diss. Duquesne University, 1970.

———. *Extension of Ricoeur's Hermeneutics*. The Hague: Nijhoff, 1975.

———. *The Religious Within Experience and Existence*. Pittsburgh, Pa.: Duquesne University Press, 1990.

Bourgeois, Patrick, and Schalow, Frank. *Traces of Understanding: A Profile of Heidegger's and Ricoeur's Hermeneutics*. Atlanta, Ga.: Rodopi, 1990.

Brusiloff, Paul David, ed. *Deconstruction and the Possibility of Justice*. New York: Cardoza Law Review (11: 5–6), 1990.

Bubner, Rudiger, *Essays in Hermeneutics and Critical Theory*. New York; Columbia University Press, 1988.

John Caputo. *Radical Hermeneutics*. Bloomington: Indiana University Press, 1987.

Carroll, David. *Paraesthetics*. New York: Methuen, 1987.

———, ed. *The States of "Theory."* New York: Columbia University Press, 1990.

Clément, Catherine, ed. *Derrida*, special issue of *L'arc*, 54. Paris: Nouveau Quartier Latin, 1973.

Culler, Jonathan. *The Pursuit of Signs*. Ithaca: Cornell University Press, 1981.

———. *On Deconstruction*. Ithaca: Cornell University Press, 1983.

DeGreef, J. "De la métaphore," in *Cahiers de litterature et de linguistiquée*, nos. 3–4. Kinshassa, Zaire: Faculté des lettre de l'Université National, 1971, 45–50.

Deleuze, Gilles. *Différence et répétition*. Paris: PUF, 1968.

De Man, Paul. *Allegories of Reading*. New Haven: Yale University Press, 1979.

———. *Blindness and Insight*. Minneapolis: University of Minnesota Press, 1983.

———. *The Resistance to Theory*. Minneapolis: University of Minnesota Press, 1986.

———. *The Rhetoric of Romanticism*. New York: Columbia University Press, 1984.

Descombes, Vincent. *Modern French Philosophy*, trs. L. Scott-Fox and J. M. Harding. New York: Cambridge University Press, 1980

Evans, Fred. "Language and Political Agency: Derrida, Marx and Bakhtin," in *The Southern Journal of Philosophy*, vol. XXVIII, no. 4, 505–524.

Evans, J. Claude. *Strategies of Deconstruction: Derrida and the Myth of Voice*. Minneapolis, Minn.: University of Minnesota Press, 1991.

Ferry, Luc, and Renault, Alain. *French Philosophy in the Sixties*, trans. Mary Schnackenberg Cattani. Amherst, Mass.: University of Massachusetts Press, 1990.

Finas, Lucette, ed. *Écarts*. Paris: Fayard, 1977.

Frank, Manfred. "Die Aufhebung der Anschauung im Spiel der Metapher," in *Neue Hefte für Philosophie*, 18/19, 1980.

———. "Schelling's Critique of Hegel and the Beginnings of Marxian Dialectics, trans. Joseph Lawrence, in *Idealistic Studies*, 19:251–268.

———. *What is Neo-Structuralism?* Minneapolis, Minn.: University of Minnesota Press, 1989.

Gadamer, Hans-Georg. "The Hermeneutics of Suspicion," in *Hermeneutics: Questions and Prospects*, eds. Gary Madison and Alan Sica. Amherst, Mass.: University of Massachusetts Press, 1984, 54–65.

———. *Philosophical Hermeneutics*, trans. David E. Linge. Berkeley, Calif.: University of California Press, 1977.

———. *Reason in the Age of Science*, tr. Frederick G. Lawrence. Cambridge: The MIT Press, 1981 (1976).

———. *The Relevance of the Beautiful*, ed. Robert Bernasconi. New York: Cambridge University Press, 1986.

———. *Truth and Method*, second revised edition, translation revised by Joel Weinsheimer and Donald G. Marshall. New York: Continuum, 1989.

Gandillac, Maurice, ed. *Entretiens sur les notions de genèse et de structur*. Paris: Mouton, 1965.

Gasché, Rodolphe. "Deconstruction as Criticism," in *Glyph* 6, 177–215.

———. "Nontotalization without Spuriousness: Hegel and Derrida on the Infinite," in *Journal of the Bristish Society for Phenomenology*, 17: 3 (October 1986), 289–307.

———. *The Tain of the Mirror*. Cambridge: Harvard University Press, 1986.

Gerhart, Mary. *The Question of Belief in Literary Criticism: An Introduction to the Hermeneutical Theory of Paul Ricoeur*. Stuttgart: Akademischer Verlag, 1979.

Gisel, Pierre. "Paul Ricoeur: Discourse between Speech and Language," in *Philosophy Today*, supplement to vol. 4: 4 (Winter 1977).

Graham, Joseph F., ed. *Difference in translation*. Ithaca, N.Y.: Cornell University Press, 1985.

Greich, Jean. *Herméneutique et grammatologie*. Paris: Editions du CNRS, 1977.

Hartman, Geoffrey H., ed. *Midrash and Literature*. New Haven, Conn.: Yale University Press, 1986.

Harvey, Irene. *Derrida and the Economy of Differance*. Bloomington, Ind.: Indiana University Press, 1987.

———. "Metaphorics and Metaphysics," in *Journal of the British Society for Phenomenology*, 17: 3 (October 1986), 308–330.

Hopkins, Burt. "Derrida's Reading of Husserl in *Speech and Phenomena*: Ontologism and the Metaphysics of Presence," in *Husserl Studies*, vol. 2, 193–214.

Ihde, Don. *Hermeneutic Phenomenology: The Philosophy of Paul Ricoeur*. Evanston, Ill.: Northwestern University Press, 1971.

Jardin, Alice, and Smith, Paul, eds. *Men in Feminism*. New York: Methuen, 1987.

Johnson, Galen, and Smith, Michael B., eds. *Ontology and Alterity in Merleau-Ponty*. Evanston, Ill.: Northwestern University Press, 1990.

Johnson, Mark, ed. *Philosophical Perspectives on Metaphor*. Minneapolis, Minn.: University of Minnesota Press, 1981.

Kearney, Richard. *The Wake of Imagination*. Minneapolis, Minn.: University of Minnesota Press, 1988.

Kearney, Richard, ed. *Dialogues with Contemporary Continental Thinkers*. Dover, N.H.: Manchester University Press, 1984.

Kemp, T. Peter, and Rasmussen, David, eds. *The Narrative Path: The Later Work of Paul Ricoeur*, special issue of *Philosophy and Social Criticism*, 14:2.

Klemm, David E. *The Hermeneutical Theory of Paul Ricoeur*. Lewisburg, Pa.: Bucknell University Press, 1983.

Kofman, Sarah. "The Economy of Respect: Kant and Respect for Women," trans. Nicola Fisher, in *Social Research*, 49, 383–404.

———. *Lectures de Derrida*. Paris: Galilée, 1984.

———. *Les respect des femmes*. Paris: Galilée, 1982.

Lacoue-Labarthe, Philippe. *Typography*, ed. Christopher Fynsk. Cambridge, Mass.: Harvard University Press, 1989.

Laruelle, Francois. *Les philosophies de la différence*. Paris: PUF, 1986.

Lebensztejn, Jean-Claude. *Zigzag*. Paris: Auber-Flammarion, 1981.

Lévesque, Claude. *L'étrangeté du texte*. Montreal: VLB, 1976.

Levey, John P., Jr. *Glassary*. Lincoln, Nebr.: University of Nebraska Press, 1988.

LLewelyn, John. *Derrida on the Threshold of Sense*. New York: Saint Martin, 1985.

Lyotard, Jean-Francois. *The Differend: Phrases in Dispute*, trans. George van der Abeele. Minneapolis, Minn.: University of Minnesota Press, 1988.

————. *La Faculté de juger*. Paris: Minuit, 1985.

Madison, Gary. *Hermeneutics of Postmodernity*. Bloomington, Ind.: Indiana University Press, 1988.

————, ed. *Sens et existence, en hommage à Paul Ricoeur*. Paris: Seuil, 1975.

Major, Rene, ed. *Affranchissementdu tranfert et de la lettre*.   P a r i s : Confrontation, 1982.

Malabou, Catherine, ed. *Revue philosophique de la France et de l'étranger: Derrida*. Paris: PUF, 1990.

Megill, Allan. *Prophets of Extremity*. Berkeley: University of California Press, 1985.

Marion, Jean-Luc. *Réduction et donation: Recherches sur Husserl, Heidegger et la phénoménologie*. Paris: PUF, 1989.

Mortley, Raoul. *French Philosophers in Conversation*. New York: Routledge, 1991.

Muller, John P., and Richardson, William J. *The Purloined Poe: Lacan, Derrida, and Psychoanalytic Reading*. Baltimore, Md.: Johns Hopkins University Press, 1988.

Nancy, Jean-Luc. *Le partage des voix*. Paris: Galilée, 1982.

Nancy, Jean-Luc, and Lacoue-Labarthe, Philippe, eds. *Les fins de l'homme—Colloque de Cérisy*. Paris: Galilée, 1981.

Norris, Christopher. *The Deconstructive Turn*. New York: Metheun, 1984.

————. *The Contest of the Faculties*. New York: Metheun, 1986.

————. *Derrida*.

Palmer, Richard. *Hermeneutics*. Evanston, Ill.: Northwestern University Press, 1975.

Palmer, Richard, and Michelfelder, Diane. *Dialogue and Deconstruction*. Albany, N.Y.: State University of New York Press, 1989.

Phelps, Louise Wetherbee, ed. *Ricoeur and Rhetoric*, special issue of *Pre/Text*, Fall/Winter, 1983.

Philbert, Michel. *Paul Ricoeur où la liberté selon l'espérance.* Paris: Seghers, 1971.

Protevi, John. "'A Certain Outside': The Establishment of Exteriority in General in Derida's *Speech and Phenomena.*" Unpublished manuscript.

Rapaport, Herman. *Heidegger and Derrida.* Lincoln, Nebr.: University of Nebraska Press, 1989.

Rasmussen, David. *Mythic-Symbolic Language and Philosophical Hermeneutics.* The Hague: Nijhoff, 1971.

Reagen, Charles E., ed. *Studies in the Philosophy of Paul Ricoeur.* Athens, Ohio: Ohio University Press, 1979.

Rotman, Brian. *Signifying Nothing: The Semiotics of Zero.* New York: St. Martin's Press, 1987.

Rorty, Richard. *Consequences of Pragmatism.* Minneapolis: University of Minnesota Press, 1982.

Rosen, Stanley. *Hermeneutics as Politics.* New York: Oxford University Press, 1987.

Ryan, Michael. *Marxism and Deconstruction.* Baltimore: Johns Hopkins University Press, 1982.

Sacks, Sheldon, ed. *On Metaphor.* Chicago: University of Chicago Press, 1979.

Sallis, John, ed. *Deconstruction and Philosophy.* Chicago: University of Chicago Press, 1987.

———. *Delimitations.* Bloomington, Ind.: Indiana University Press, 1986.

Salusinszky, Imre. *Criticism in Society.* New York: Metheun, 1987.

Searle, John. "Reiterating the Differences: A Reply to Jacques Derrida." *Glyph* I, 1977, 198–209.

Silverman, Hugh J. *Inscriptions.* New York: Routledge and Kegan Paul, 1987.

———, ed. *Derrida and Deconstruction: Continental Philosophy,* II, New York: Routledge and Kegan Paul, 1989.

———. *Philosophy and Non-Philosophy since Merleau-Ponty.* New York: Routledge, 1988.

———. "Writing (on Deconstruction) on the Edge of Metaphysics," in *Research in Phenomenology,* vol. XIII, 97–112.

Silverman, Hugh J. and Ihde, Don, eds. *Hermeneutics and Deconstruction.* Albany, N.Y.: State University of New York Press, 1986.

Smith, Joseph H., and Kerrigan, William, eds. *Taking Chances: Derrida, Psychoanalysis, and Literature*. Baltimore: Johns Hopkins University Press, 1984.

Staten, Henry. *Wittgenstein and Derrida*. Lincoln: University of Nebraska Press, 1985.

Surber, Jere Paul, ed. *Paul Ricoeur's Philosophy*, special issue of *The Iliff Review* (Fall, 1978).

Taminiaux, Jacques. *Dialectic and Difference*, eds. Robert Crease and James T. Decker. Atlantic Highlands, N.J.: Humanities Press, 1985.

————, ed. *Paul Ricoeur: Temporalité et Narrativité*, special issue of *Études phénoménologiques*, vol. VI, no. 11 (1990).

Thompson, John B. *Critical Hermeneutics: A Study in the Thought of Paul Ricoeur and Jürgen Habermas*. New York: Cambridge University Press, 1981.

Ulmer, Gregory. *Applied Grammatology*. Baltimore: Johns Hopkins University Press, 1985.

Valdes, Mario J., and Miller, Owen, eds. *The Identity of the Literary Text*. Toronto: University of Toronto Press, 1985.

Van Leeuwen, T. M. *The Surplus of Meaning: Ontology and Eschatology in the Philosophy of Paul Ricoeur*. Amsterdam: Rodopi, 1981.

Wachterhauser, Brice R., ed. *Hermeneutics and Modern Philosophy*. Albany, N.Y.: State University of New York Press, 1986.

Wallulis, Jerald. *The Hermeneutics of Life History*. Evanston, Ill.: Northwestern University Press, 1990.

White, Alan. "Reconstructing Husserl," in *Husserl Studies*, vol. 4, 45–62.

Wood, David. *The Deconstruction of Time*. Atlantic Highlands, N.J.: Humanities Press, 1989.

Wood, David, and Bernasconi, Robert, eds. *Derrida and Différance*. Evanston, Ill.: Northwestern University Press, 1988.

INDEX